MIDNIGHT MATINEES

JAY SCOTT
MIDNIGHT MATINEES

TORONTO
OXFORD UNIVERSITY PRESS
1985

For
Mary Etta
Mary Leta
Mary Beth

CANADIAN CATALOGUING IN PUBLICATION DATA

Scott, Jay.

Midnight matinees

Includes reviews previously published in the Globe and Mail.

Includes index.

ISBN 0-19-540504-8

1. Moving-pictures – Addresses, essays, lectures.   2. Moving pictures – Reviews.
I. Title.   II. The Globe and Mail.

PN1995.S37 1985   791.43   C85-099341-5

OXFORD is a trademark of Oxford University Press

1 2 3 4 — 8 7 6 5

Printed in Canada by

Webcom Limited

Contents

Acknowledgments

David Overbey, for more than he knows; Linda Beath and Bart Testa, gurus extraordinaires; Karen York and Ray Mason at *The Globe and Mail* for making it easy, Ed O'Dacre, Les Buhasz, Cameron Smith, and Norman Webster for permitting it to be; in Albuquerque: Muriel Chenburg, Olivia Carabajal, Maureen O. Bunch, Howard Mensch, Charles Andrews, Frankie McCarty, Cather MacCallum, Logan Houston, John Nichols, Bert Manzari, Liska Pepper; points east: Helga Stephenson, Peter J. Dawes, Jamie Portman, Wayne Clarkson, Ann Mackenzie, Hannah Fisher, Gale Garnett, Rick Gallagher, Joan and Dusty Cohl, Karen Jaehne, Robert J. Mottershead, Gerald Peary; Sally Livingston; Richard Teleky, who made editing art; Gene Michael Corboy, who made so much possible.

Introduction

Once upon a time when movies mattered—when they *really* mattered—it was always midnight, yet every screening was a matinee. The lights might dim when it was already dark outside or they might go down while the sun was still up, and it made not an iota of difference: the witching hour instantly and magically arrived, everything was possible, and anything could (and usually did) happen. People who were serious about or just addicted to movies tried to be present on opening day; people who were serious about or just addicted to movies were willing victims of pumpkin fever, afraid that if they hadn't settled snugly into their theater seats at the first possible opportunity the fairy tale might pass them by; people who were serious about or just addicted to movies bought their tickets and popcorn and nodded happily to each other, enchanted members in good standing of the Cinderella community. True believers are not extinct nowadays, but their crystalline cult is a mere shard of its former slipper. At a time when movies *don't* really matter—not in the sense of being the pre-eminent purveyor of popular culture, a role usurped by television, the thing Renata Adler has christened "an appliance through which reviewable material is sometimes played"—the community has diminished to the size of a Cub Scout pack; indeed, at a time when "community" itself is little more than a nostalgic concept evoking the homespun homilies of Andy Griffith's Mayberry, one of the few venues available to the matinee communards of old is the midnight movie, the cult film endlessly repeated until everyone knows exactly what Harold is going to do to Maude, exactly what kind of havoc Rocky Horror will wreak, exactly what forces will drive Alan Bates bare-bottomed onto the throne of the *King of Hearts*.

Those are midnight matinees: joyful movie experiences that replicate for a moment what movies used to be, the most significant communal entertainments on earth and the most fun to be had short of being had. Sadly, even the cultists have been chilled by the slow freeze of the cowardly new world of the video cassette. "How many times can you show *King of Hearts*?" a man who ran a revival house wondered rhetorically and despairingly not long ago. "I tell you: until they buy the damned thing. Repertory cinemas are dying. It's all going into video." The phenomenon is far from peculiar to cult or even so-called classic films: every-thing is leaving the theater and going into video. Video is unquestionably a marketing marvel and a technological revolution, but it so far repre-sents a process of esthetic devolution, a cause for strongly voiced (if largely impotent) alarm among purists who know the smoldering beaut-ies of Philip Borsos's *The Grey Fox* will become inky smudges on the small screen, who know the masterly compositions of Francesco Rosi's *Carmen* will be cropped to dusty motes in the wee iris of the square eye, who know the majesty of Carroll Ballard's *The Black Stallion* reduced and televised will become Shetland pony-sized. Some people argue that if a movie works in the theater, it will work on TV. Sometimes yes: *Testa-ment* does. Sometimes no: *Nashville* doesn't. And anyway: you do get an idea of the Mona Lisa when the lady is printed on a bath towel, but what kind of idea is that? On the other hand, who would order struggling par-ents with three kids to risk an expensive evening at the moving picture show when chances are about even that the picture in question will have been designed from inception to show up on what Judy Garland called ''the hell where all little movies go when they're bad''—television? Bet-ter by far to rent *Trading Places* for five bucks and save fifty. And that's the real devastation accomplished by video: because films can be sold to so many markets (first theaters, then pay TV, then free TV, then video stores—and not necessarily in that order), there are films that make back their costs before they ever leave the editing room. The opinions of movie-goers are thus rendered irrelevant; the audience is an abstraction to which heed need not be paid; and the movies themselves are the unfettered fan-tasies of whatever the producers presume people will buy. Presumption is the operative word: because producers have scant stake in the outcome —their salaries have already been paid, off the top—there is no im-perative for them to attempt to imagine creatively what might strengthen the art or the appeal of movies. The technology of television destroyed the hegemony of film in the fifties; video cassettes weakened the invalid in the seventies; and the ineptitude, cowardice, and greed of the Holly-wood studios in the face of the video devolution have nearly delivered the last rites in the eighties.

But not quite. As the material in Part Two—reviews published in *The Globe and Mail* between 1978 and 1985—argues by implication, the ail-ing art form is a surprisingly imaginative invalid. The barrier between ''art films'' and ''entertainment'' has never been higher, but there are occasional movies (*Diva*, for example) that transcend the categories, that do become midnight matinees, cheery artifacts with something for nearly everyone; and there are art films that may not be for everyone but that enrich the hearts and minds and eyes of those who do respond to them so thoroughly that their influence extends beyond their box office; and there are frowsy Hollywood products designed solely to be hits that against all odds transmute commerce into art. The reviews have been picked to document the spectrum—the good, the bad, the abominable.

Part One consists of several behind-the-scenes articles, a couple of informal histories (one of teen movies, the other of Canadian films), and a rather weird seven-year journal of the rather weird Cannes Film Festival; this section of the book is new in concept if not entirely in content. The single article to be reprinted substantially unchanged is the first half of the history of the movie boom in Canada, "The Burnout Factory," which appeared in *American Film*. Because present-tense immediacy best gets across the craziness of those years, I have not altered it, but I have expanded it considerably by way of a sequel that retains the approach. Two other chapters, "The Death Factory" and "The Teen Factory," were commissioned by *American Film*, but they are published here in vastly revised form. "The Death Factory" is in fact my original draft on the making of *Mishima*; the *American Film* version was reorganized and shortened to reflect the magazine's understandable lack of interest in the novelist himself. "The Teen Factory" has been rewritten—updated and augmented—to take into account recent developments on the cinematic teen scene. The summary of the career of Rainer Werner Fassbinder was dictated by his prolific output and by the timing of his death: his breakthrough into the consciousness of the mass media in North America took place in 1978 and 1979, and will no doubt continue to the end of the eighties with posthumous releases of films made for German television. ("Rainer," ran a Cannes Film Festival joke that Fassbinder would have appreciated, "is the only filmmaker so dedicated the movies keep coming from beyond the grave.") The remaining chapters began as pieces in the *Globe*, but in every case I have returned to my notes and memories, not because I wanted to disown the *Globe* articles but because newspapers and magazines impose constraints that demand the drastic compression of reality as the writer perceives it. Abridgment is the raison d'être of newspaper reporting, even at the *Globe*, a newspaper that allows its writers more freedom than most reporters believe possible (colleagues at the *London*, *New York*, and *Los Angeles Times* are envious); however, even the *Globe's* brand of liberally extended abridgment is not always able to encompass everything one might wish. An example: no newspaper and few magazines would countenance the printing of a meandering monologue from Maureen Stapleton on her love of Trivial Pursuit, but when Stapleton discusses the game, she reveals more about herself and about her profession than she does when she discusses either of those things directly. Allowing an interview subject to construct an impression by indirection requires time and space, and both are in short supply in periodicals. So after years of swearing to myself I would never permit a book of reprints, I've partly reneged on the oath, but only partly, in that Part One is not so much resurrected as reincarnated: while the soul remains the same, the body has been transformed. I certainly don't mean to argue that the popular journalism to be found herein is in any way immortal, but toiling in the Dream Factories has been a way to redeem—and in some cases to expose for the first time—material that, properly reconstituted, may deserve to live longer than a single sunrise.

The Death Factory:
Paul Schrader's Tokyo

"I have never seen such a strange factory. In it all the techniques of modern science and management, together with the exact and rational thinking of many superior brains, were dedicated to a single end—Death."
—Yukio Mishima, *Confessions of a Mask*

An enormous Japanese lesbian in a red and white rugby shirt is cheerfully belting out "Unchained Melody" in a voice that arches over the falsetto of Gene Pitney and dives under the rumbling basso of Sarah Vaughan. Arranged around her on brown corduroy banquettes in a room smaller than the washrooms at Radio City are an assortment of Japanese, Korean, and Taiwanese businessmen, severe black-suited figures offset by the open-necked sportiness of three or four Occidentals. One of them, demure in a white shirt and black slacks, is a round-faced American filmmaker, Paul Schrader, director of *Hardcore*, *Cat People*, *Blue Collar* and *American Gigolo*. He is well known here at the New Monte, a "cozy house," as its matchbooks call it, in the Asakasa district of Tokyo. In the summer of 1983 he introduced the joint to composer Philip Glass, hired by Schrader to score *Mishima*, a cinematic biography of the astoundingly prolific (one hundred volumes) novelist, essayist, playwright, and actor Yukio Mishima. Glass was intitially repelled but then entranced by the new Monte women, performers and conversationalists who leave their places next to the bar's customers—each woman in the place is an employee; each man beside her is her employer—to take the microphone and sing everything from brassy Yankee show tunes like "Mame!" to the teary laments of the genre known as *enka*, the indigenous pop music of Japan. At the moment, Schrader is drinking beer. Trying not to think. Each time he puts down his glass, the New Monte woman sitting next to him refills it. When he shows no interest in talking to her, she converses quietly with a colleague. "They're here for the patrons," Schrader mumbles. "Don't worry about not talking to them if you don't want to. The minute your ass hit the corduroy you spent $100." Glum silence. A hand is placed on his shoulder and he looks up: his older brother, Leonard, has arrived. For most of the afternoon and evening, the beefy and boyish Leonard has been closeted in a meeting with *Mishima*'s co-producers, Tom Luddy of San Francisco (the special-projects director for Francis Coppola's Zoetrope Studios and director of the Telluride Film Festival), and Mataichiro Yamamoto, an independent Tokyo entrepreneur. "We're five days behind schedule," Paul Schrader had explained that morning. "If I can't get those five days, I cut the scenes I planned for the last week. The gay stuff and the politics. Without them, the movie suffers." He joins Leonard for a hurried conference. "We sacrifice all around," he reports when he returns, ordering another Kirin. "I've just given up my reimbursements." But he's smiling: the "gay stuff," the politics, will be shot.

The next morning—June 14, 1984—Luddy will send a Telex to Zoetrope: "To continue here until June 26. Basically everyone working for free after June 21." Affixed to the wall near the Telex in the *Mishima* offices at Toho Studios are two other messages, a thank-you note from Mrs. Paul Schrader, the actress Mary Beth Hurt, for having been shown a good time on her visit to Tokyo, and a telegram from one of *Mishima*'s two American executive producers. "Wishing you the best on your first day of shooting," it says. "May The Force be with you. Love, George Lucas." The transmission is dated four months earlier.

That was in March, when it was apparent to the Schraders their movie was about to fall apart—the two major Japanese corporate investors, Toho-Towa Distribution and Fuji Television, were threatening to pull out—and they decided their sole chance to save it was to commence filming ahead of schedule; they gambled, shrewdly as it turned out, that it would be more difficult to sink a ship that had set sail than to blow it up in dry dock. In addition to the financial shortfalls that prompted them to seek the help of Lucas and the other American executive producer, Francis Coppola, there was chronic combat with Yoko Hiraoka, the writer's widow, who was not averse to calling reporters to denounce the project she and Mishima's hand-picked literary executor, Jun Shiragi, had reluctantly approved in an agreement hammered out over four years of negotiations—a monumental battle of wills that included an eighteen-month period when discussions were held daily, usually with Leonard (an ex-college professor and ex-Japanese resident married to a Japanese woman), Luddy, and George Hayam, Zoetrope's lawyer.

"No one who knows Japan and Mishima can believe we got an agreement," Leonard crows over coffee in his office at Toho. Few who knew the United States and Paul Schrader could believe it, either. What equipped

Paul, to all appearances a homophobic ex-Calvinist from the Midwest —responsible for the voyeuristic puritanism of *Hardcore*, the gay-bashing of *American Gigolo*, the misogynist schlock of *Cat People*—to deal with Mishima? What equipped him to cope with Japan? The Schraders had collaborated on one ostensibly Japanese film, *The Yakuza*, with Robert Mitchum (Robert Towne and Paul wrote the script from a story by Leonard) and that picture had contained even more risibility than customary in Schrader's films, where what would be sublime is frequently ridiculous. Heads shook in two cultures. The gay press in the United States cried foul while the Japanese press was virtually silent, which amounted to the same thing.

If the Schraders seemed fabulously inappropriate Mishima storytellers, by the time Mrs. Mishima was through with them it looked as if there would be no story to tell. Mishima died by committing public *seppuku* (hara-kiri) at the age of forty-five and was beheaded by a twenty-five-year-old man many people think was his lover; he posed for a series of homoerotic photos published under the title *Ordeal By Roses*; he was well known in certain New York homosexual circles; he was not unknown in those same circles in Tokyo—nevertheless, Mrs. Mishima extracted from Schrader an extraordinary and debilitating list of promises that forbade him to depict a great deal of that. For many years the widow has intransigently protected her version of her husband's image; she has, for example, been successful, so far as any one knows, in her campaign to destroy every print of *Patriotism*, a film adapted and directed by Mishima from his 1961 short story, a film in which he lovingly records himself committing a gruesomely staged *seppuku* as part of a *shinju*, a love suicide.

Under the terms of their understanding with Mrs. Mishima, the Schraders would not try to use some material from Mishima's most famous (but homosexual) novel, the autobiographical *Confessions of a Mask* (1949). (The rights to the book are actually controlled by Mishima's mother.) They would be able to use no material from the less fine but autobiographically important (and also homosexual) novel *Forbidden Colors* (1951). They would not be allowed to allude to Mishima's "other life." Period. (When Paul met Mrs. Mishima, she commented, "You know, some people say my husband was homosexual . . ." Dumbfounded, he let the statement trail off into the air; she had said the same thing, with the same ingenuousness, to John Nathan, author of one of two English biographies of Mishima, years before. She cooperated with Nathan but then bought up the few copies of the book that entered Japan and was instrumental in keeping the other English biography, by Henry Scott-Stokes, out of the country entirely.) Neither would the Schraders be permitted to include on-screen representations of the surviving family—not the wife, not the twenty-two-year-old son, not the twenty-five-year-old daughter. They would not be allowed to stage in any detail, gruesome or otherwise, the supreme climax of Mishima's life, the moment following events on Nov. 25, 1970, when Mishima and several boys in his right-wing Shield Society, theoretically dedicated to restoring respect for the divinity of the Emperor, had taken over the office of a general at the Eastern Army Headquarters in Tokyo. The takeover was Mishima's excuse to harangue the troops below, fail in his efforts to incite them to rebellion (the failure was evidently part of the plan), and re-enter the office. Once inside, with his cohorts and the captive general looking on, Japan's most famous novelist knelt on the floor, undid his trousers, sliced open his abdomen and groaned as his intestines spilled across his samurai *fundoshi* (loincloth). "In feudal times we believed sincerity resided in our entrails, and if we needed to show our sincerity, we had to cut our bellies and take out our *visible* sincerity," he had written. How could Paul, unable to depict this scene, unable to depict the homosexuality that fed the narcissism that fed the romantic nihilism of Mishima's world view —"Man gives his seed to woman. Then commences his long, long, non-descript journey toward nihilism," he wrote in 1966—make the movie at all?

In two ways, he decided. One, by waiting until the last week in Japan to film several short scenes not in the script, and, two, by legally skirting the widow's demands—he worked into the script revelatory material from three non-proscribed novels, *The Temple of the Golden Pavilion* (1956), *Runaway Horses* (1968), and the as-yet-untranslated *Kyoko's House* (1959). He also inserted incidents from the forbidden novels, but only if he could prove they were autobiographical. In terms of Mishima's life and art, one was mandatory: the narrator of *Confessions*, an adolescent Mishima, masturbates while viewing a reproduction of Guido Reni's painting of an arrow-pierced, ecstatic St. Sebastian ("That day, the instant I looked upon the picture, my entire being trembled with some pagan joy"). Schrader was able to get away with the indispensable vignette—the most indelible image of Mishima on record is his photographic re-creation of the painting with himself as the saint—because he was able to obtain approval from Shiragi, who felt the incident was autobiographical. (Mrs. Mishima angrily informed the filmmakers that when her son read the script the scene raised questions about his father he had not thought to ask.) Another incident, filmed during the crew's final week in Japan—Mishima dances with a male in a Tokyo gay bar—was approved because there was on file an affidavit claiming autobiographical truth from

Mishima's close friend, the renowned transvestite "actress" Miwa, who also told the Schraders he did not believe the "soldier" who beheaded Mishima was his lover, as Scott-Stokes categorically concluded (with as little direct evidence) in his biography. The Miwa account, true or not, was received with gratitude: one more thing not to have to feel guilty about not including.

Schrader rationalizes his atypically discreet handling of the death by observing that he leaves Mishima "when he lost control of his life," the second the dagger entered the body. The movie begins in Mishima's kitschy Victorian-style mansion on his last day. (Ken Ogata, star of *The Ballad of Narayama*, winner of the 1983 Cannes Film Festival Palme d'Or, is an unexpectedly macho but otherwise convincing Mishima; Schrader cast him when "more androgynous" performers, closer to Mishima in type, failed to persuade him they could handle the role.) The writer dons a garish turquoise silk dressing gown, a garment that for Ogata turned out to be the key to the flamboyance and intentional artificiality of the character, in that most Japanese men, regardless of wealth, prefer a simple cotton *yukata*. Almost immediately, Mishima's superficially mundane morning is disrupted by flashbacks in black and white to his childhood, characterized by fetid relationships with an invalid grandmother and a suffocating mother. In due course Schrader introduces the first of the highly theatrical sequences taken from the novels, sequences designed by Eiko Ishioka, whose high-tech advertising concepts for the Parco shopping centers in Tokyo have been collected in the mammoth book published in North America under the title *Eiko by Eiko*. (There are forty-three sets in Mishima, twenty-three naturalistic and designed by Take Naka, the other twenty stylized by Ishioka; the average for most movies is fifteen.)

The script itself is polyphonic in structure—a fugue—united by the theme of the last day. Beauty, the first quarter, encompasses Mishima's childhood and a sequence from one of his few undisputed masterpieces, *The Temple of the Golden Pavilion*, in which a stuttering monk (Yasosuke Bando) serving at a fifteenth-century Zen temple in Kyoto destroys the structure because he believes its perfection mocks his life; he believes the only thing more beautiful than beauty is its dissolution—its sudden, radiant dissolution. "How can I reach out and touch life with one hand, when I've got eternity on the other?" he asks. "That's the power of beauty's eternity. It poisons us. It blocks out our lives." It is no accident that in World War II Mishima worked in a kamikaze factory ("dedicated to a monstrous nothingness") and came to think of himself as "beauty's kamikaze": his life was a kamikaze projectile, and Schrader has designed the movie as a simulacrum, as an aerodynamic voyage into nothingness. *The Golden Pavilion* sequences, shot by cinematographer John Bailey to emphasize gold and green, establish Mishima's death's-head esthetic, full of fear and loving for the ideal.

In the second part, Art, *Confessions of a Mask* is published, Mishima becomes a lionized writer, and scenes from *Kyoko's House* are dramatized with Japanese pop star Kenji Sawada in the role of the novel's narcissistic actor hero, Osamu. (For Japanese audiences, this section of the film is a hall of mirrors, in that Sawada—nicknamed "the Japanese David Bowie," but closer conceptually to Bryan Ferry—once did a photo book on Narcissus with Ishioka; he is so popular he was asked by a member of the *Mishima* crew to autograph a car with a can of permanent gold paint.) Mishima transformed his pale, sickly body by working out with weights, and Osamu, too, visits a gym and builds himself up, so his body will be perfect when sweetly tortured in sadomasochistic sex by his mistress—so his body will be gorgeous when he dies with his woman in an orgiastic *shinju*. In love with himself but condemned to asking "Do I really exist or not?", Osamu is less an alter ego for Mishima than a harbinger of his future; it is Osamu for whom art is finally not enough, for whom it becomes "the shadow of a shadow." The color scheme utilized by Bailey is reminiscent here of his work for Schrader on *American Gigolo*: creamy pinks and soft grays.

Action, Part Three, contains a Mishima voice-over: "The average age for man in the Bronze Age was eighteen, in the Roman era twenty-one. Heaven must have been beautiful then. Today it must look dreadful." By now Mishima is a cultural institution, but he is no less attracted to death and while rehearsing a play is obsessed by blood—"It must glisten!" he orders. The Mishima novel dramatized this time, in shades of black and red, is *Runaway Horses*, the second volume in The Sea of Fertility tetralogy, the final instalment of which, *The Decay of the Angel,* he left for his publisher on the morning of his death. The hero of *Runaway Horses* is Isao, a terrorist who commits *seppuku* in the early thirties after stabbing an aged businessman to death as part of an abortive right-wing revolution. Again, Mishima is rehearsing his demise. The last sentence of *Runaway Horses*, a description of Isao's experience of *seppuku*, is the final speech of Schrader's movie (in Part Four): "The instant the blade tore open his flesh, the bright disk of the sun soared up behind his eyelids and exploded."

In Part Four, The Harmony of Pen and Sword, Mishima becomes his own work of art—thought and action are united, the *seppuku* is carried out. "Among my incurable convictions," he argued, "is the belief that the old are eternally ugly, the young eternally beautiful. . . . The longer people live, the worse they become.'' The thought of losing to decay the body he had worked so hard to achieve was repulsive to him. Because he has become his own fiction, no novel is dramatized in Part Four; life and art are one. Schrader ends the movie with a series of celluloid shards from Mishima's life and work, but the final image of the man himself is a close-up of the face, turned by pain into the visage of a gargoyle, a mask confessing agony. As the knife enters the abdominal wall off-screen, the lens zooms in and the camera dollies back in the same perceptually disorienting movement that forced the spectator to share the nausea of looking down the bell tower in Alfred Hitchcock's *Vertigo*. The sun that soars up behing Isao's eyelids as the blade punctures his flesh (the first and final shots in the movie are of suns rising and setting) is the last sight the viewer sees. This can be said of Schrader's *Mishima*: it is innovative, it is beautiful, it is respectful of the man whose story it tells, and it is true to one defensible interpretation of it.

That version, The Schrader Version, is naturally non-definitive (the only definitive biography of this most protean of artists is likely to remain the one he buried in his books) and it has changed over time. ''It's not the same movie it would have been five years ago, when we first began talking about it,'' Luddy remarks one day while hanging from a subway strap on the way to Toho Studios. ''That was in Paul's *Cat People* period. I supported him and I liked *Cat People*, but I thought he was going to die. Literally. He was really fucked up.'' (Later, in the office at Toho, Schrader casts a quick and contemptuous glance at *Wired*, the John Belushi book by Bob Woodward. ''I wouldn't talk to Woodward,'' he snorts. ''He didn't want to give the story a sociological dimension and it was too early to do an Edie Sedgewick and make it a portrait of an era. I couldn't figure out what he wanted except exploitation. When I knew John''— he laughs grimly—''he was a nose on wheels.'') Shiragi remembers Schrader's earliest vision of *Mishima*, too. ''The first script we were given years ago was very bloody and sexual. It was totally unacceptable.''

''Paul,'' Luddy reiterates, ''was on a real death trip. The reasons he was interested in Mishima were all too obvious, maybe. But because of what's happened to him, his marriage to Mary Beth Hurt, the birth of his child and everything else, he's changed a lot. He's never going to be anyone's choir boy, but . . .''

But Schrader now feels he is able to understand Mishima without aping him and even believes the constraints pressed on him by the widow have been profitable. When Mishima was alive, much of his life was lived in the dark, and much of what he found there was communicated in code; Schrader has been forced to adopt some of Mishima's own methods. There are other, less salutary parallels. When Mishima was alive, there were Japanese critics so disgusted by his irrational, posturing politics and his sadomasochism (in *Confessions*, the narrator fantasizes cooking and eating a man to whom he is sexually attracted) they dismissed him as a literary masturbator, despite their admiration for the style with which he spilled his seed. Similar attacks have been levelled at Schrader, whose oeuvre is as dankly obsessive as any of Mishima's books.

Other directors—Elia Kazan, Roman Polanski, Nicolas Roeg, Bob Rafelson—expressed interest in solving the seemingly insoluble complexities of this sobering life but received a cold shoulder from Shiragi and Mrs. Mishima. Why did the pair warm to the Schraders? The answer has to do with connections and perseverance. "I never thought it would get this far," Shiragi, a Korean in his fifties, a man with his own literary career, confides one morning in flawless English. "His life story alone is not that interesting. Malraux, for instance, had a much more dramatic life. It was lucky that I conceived the structure of the script." This raises protests from Luddy and the Schraders, albeit muffled—they need Shiragi, whose intelligence they respect but whose script, they maintain, was an unwieldy tome impervious to improvement. (Both sides dub it "the reference script.") Shiragi is in any event a man of divided loyalties, and because his responsibilities to the widow and to Mishima are not always identical, a conversation with him is a study in suggestion. Many of Mrs. Mishima's objections to the script cannot, he says in measured tones, "be understood rationally. There is lately no justification for much of what is said. It's a legal question now, really. I don't think one can accuse the widow easily: her actions must be taken with a certain amount of sympathy."

And empathy. There were unpleasant moments when her worst fears came true. In August 1983, a Japanese publication held a contest to find "the most beautiful boy in Japan" concurrent with the opening of Coppola's *The Outsiders*; the winner, said the come-on, would be cast in *Mishima*. Coppola had no connection with the contest, but it took a great deal of effort to reassure Mrs. Mishima that she was dealing with responsible people. It did not cross her mind, however, that anything was amiss when she later received a piddling $800 on the day a check for $100,000 was due from Zoetrope for the rights to her husband's life—Zoetrope was then in a fiscal pit and Luddy could scrape together no more money. Mrs. Mishima said nothing and patiently monitored the instalments as they dribbled in.

Shiragi is philosophical about the widow's trials. "What she must go through is, I suppose, the sacrifice for having had such a great husband." Lest he sound more callous than he is, it should be pointed out that Mishima's marriage was arranged, not romantic; it was not, nor did either party ever need to pretend that it was, a mating of passion. Homosexuality is tolerated in Japan so long as it remains private, a not especially discriminatory state of affairs in that all activities of a romantic and/or sexual nature are expected to remain private. And all men, homosexual or not, are expected to have families, as are all women who do not become geisha or nuns. What scandalized Japanese society was not Mishima's homosexuality per se but his insistence on publicizing it. It should also be noted that as the film was being planned, Mishima's daughter was nearing the age at which most Japanese women marry: from her perspective as a member of an almost pathologically image-conscious people, the timing of a dramatization of dad's indelicate but by now nearly forgotten condition could not have been less fortunate. It could, in fact, have been disastrous, as she and her mother let the filmmakers know one tempestuous evening when they tearfully begged Schraders not to endanger the daughter's future. Mrs. Mishima's apparent refusal to face the facts of her husband's life and her desire to disguise the reality of his death may seem pathetic or unrealistic, but they are neither—not totally, not even mostly. Not in Japan. Mrs. Mishima has proved to be, in the words of biographer Scott-Stokes, "a samurai widow," not unlike in strength and business acumen and survival instinct that other Yoko, the one named Ono.

Shiragi and Paul Schrader concur that Mishima "was not a politically sensitive man" and the only sector of Japanese society apt to disagree is the right wing. Mishima may be a god to the extreme right wing (Schrader: "In modern Japan, the left is a wing and the right is the house") but Shiragi reports that to the day of his death Mishima could not abide the extremists. (Both biographers and the vast majority of Western insiders agree that Mishima's *seppuku* was inspired by Eros and Thanatos, not politics; the Japanese interpretation remains a mystery.) "He said in my presence the extremists were scum," Shiragi recalls. "What he hated was that everything was becoming subordinate to money, and much of what he was afraid would happen to Japan has come about. So he tried, romantically and nostalgically, to be a samurai. This was of course futile, because he had not even fought in a single war, as had, for example, D'Annunzio, whom he admired. He was full of contradictions. When I first met him in the fifties it was with Truman Capote and Tennessee Williams. I translated. Williams said to me, 'He's one of the greatest writers living today.' That astonished me. But I do think he became a great writer. I think the film could perhaps be a very good film—it is a satisfactory script. To be frank with you, I was not impressed with Schrader as a director. I thought *Blue Collar* the best of his movies, minor but fine, and of course I liked his script for *Taxi Driver*, but what finally convinced me and the widow was Coppola. The man who made *The Conversation* is an artist. He understood I was interested in exporting art, not just automobiles and computers, and I felt *Mishima* was the ideal product.''

Trapped in a cul-de-sac, the Schraders had asked Coppola to intercede with the widow. The *Godfather* Saga strikes a strong chord in a society noted for synchronicity—Al Pacino's being forced for the good of the family to leave behind his individualistic dreams has deep meaning in Japan. As a result, Coppola has become a media star and has even made TV spots for Suntory whiskey with Akira Kurosawa, an interlude of commercialism that is viewed affectionately in Tokyo as a kind of trash of the titans: it seems fitting that the giant of the East should meet the master of the west, and that both should profit. Not only did Coppola "charm" (Luddy's word) Mrs. Mishima, but his involvement was sufficient to allow the Japanese producer, Yamamoto, to raise promises of $2.1–2.4 million. It was Lucas, on the other hand, who was able to raise the remainder of the $5-million budget from Warner Brothers on a negative pick-up distribution deal in March 1984, when Zoetrope all but collapsed.

Coppola, Yamamoto, et al., had conducted an amiable press conference at the Imperial Hotel in June 1983 to announce the deal. When Coppola was asked what one question he would put to Mishima if the ghost should suddenly appear, "I'd ask him to star in the movie," he quipped. "I have a copy of *Ordeal by Roses*, that incredible artifact," he revealed a year later, while looping *The Cotton Club*. "I was a fan of Mishima and what he did with his life—of how that affects questions of art and artists. Mishima was my little pet interest for a long time. I wanted to film *Spring Snow*, that beautiful book, the first of the tetralogy, and Zoetrope bought the rights to all four books. Quite from somewhere else appeared Paul Schrader when we were setting up Zoetrope. We wanted to get involved in diverse and crazy things, so when it came time, I did my own good part for him. I'd always liked him, because his movies had personality. They were always decadent and overblown, but that's what I do, too. I thought *American Gigolo* was a good movie and I thought Paul was an intelligent guy. Then George Lucas came along when he was needed and all he had to do was snap his fingers. Warner Brothers just wanted to get in his good graces."

Back in Tokyo, Schrader turns on a video machine in his office and plunks in a cassette of a mesmerizing time-capsule his researchers have unearthed: a "Small World" television show circa 1959, with Edward R. Murrow as the host and three guests: the British critic Dilys Powell (in London), Tennessee Williams (in New York), Yukio Mishima (in Tokyo). Williams, a bit inebriated, says coyly of Mishima, "We met in New York in a rather unfashionable district and in a rather Bohemian quarter, but we had a marvelous time." As the conversation continues, across the miles and, on this day in Tokyo, across the years, a conflict shapes up between forces of "health," represented by Miss Powell, who comes to the telecast, as Edward Seidensticker once wrote of Edith Sitwell, "all tinklingly tea-table British," and the forces of what for Williams is a knock-out combination, "brutality and elegance," incarnated by two unapologetic devotees of very different kinds of decadence. When Williams congratulates Mishima on his screen adaptation of *The Temple of the Golden Pavilion*, Miss Powell says she found the film difficult to understand. "Miss Powell," Williams smirks, "you have to be a decadent Southerner to understand Japanese cinema." Mishima in turn congratulates Williams on *Suddenly, Last Summer*, "the most representative mixture of brutality and elegance." Miss Powell is perturbed. "I do think violence is getting an appalling hold on art," she sniffs, and directs an accusation at the two bemused men: "I think under cover of denigrating violence you are exalting it." Williams grins and says, "You have a possible point, darling, providing we're all masochists." Everyone laughs: how silly. Schrader nods—knowingly, ironically—and excuses himself to return to the set of his movie, to his tribute to the man whose mother said at his wake, "You should have bought red roses for a celebration. This is the first time in his life [he] did something he always wanted to do. Be happy for him."

June 1984

The Auteur Factory:
Bob Swaim's Paris

June 1982:
The ride to Puteaux, an Arab slum on the outskirts of Paris, is brief:
the city is compact and the transit system is excellent. The route takes
me through Neuilly, site of the American Hospital, where the rich and
famous of every nationality come to die (Aristotle Onassis was one of
them), and on to industrial centers where factories manufacture the
"authentic" North African gewgaws (kaftans, bracelets, statues of
elephants) hawked relentlessly by poor blacks to tourists in every part of
France. The physical ride to Puteaux doesn't take long. The spiritual
journey takes forever.

Sunset, or shortly before. A film crew has gathered in an Arab-operated
Italian pizzeria next to a raised highway that runs blithely past the entrance to Puteaux. Dinner time for the movie people, and the talk at the
tables runs to the location, which intrigues the French—the portals of
Puteaux open on a world of childhood starvation, teenage drug addiction, and the pathological abuse (at least by non-Arab standards) of adult
females by their impoverished mates, a sordid reality that both attracts
and repels the crew. A furious argument is raging between an American
extra, Bonnie Bruman, who works at the Paris-based, English-language
magazine, *Passion*, and another American extra, a woman new to the
city. "Arab men," Bruman warns her friend, who has admitted to a strong
fascination with the dark eyes and silky hair and arrogant attitudes everywhere in Puteaux, "are sexist pigs, so be careful. I'm sorry, I'm not
racist, but when you've lived in Paris as long as I have, and have had to
put up with what I've had to put up with, you'll see what I mean. They
treat their own women bad enough. God knows what they'd do to you."
The friend agrees to be cautious and orders another liter of *vin ordinaire*
for the table. To ensure that the cast and crew are served on time—the
plan is to shoot until 4:00 A.M., until sunrise—the entire restaurant has
been rented for the evening. An expenditure of this sort means little to a
movie with a budget of $3 million, a budget that in terms of quotidian
French production is astronomical: *Diva* was made for about half that.

When the company finishes eating and the restaurant is deserted, a few local Arabs attempt to enter. They are pushed, rudely and literally, back into the street; the owners have more than made their money for the night, and they're keeping the doors open solely to serve the select few in the crew with the time to cool their heels. A policeman who has been eating unobtrusively by himself in the corner materializes when an Arab is particularly obstreperous and stands silently next to one of the restaurant's owners, a woman who rather jauntily orders the quickly gathering crowd to disperse. She is wearing a black leather motorcycle jacket, two thick swaths of eyeliner the color and sheen of the jacket, and a delicate Arab anklet that accents her murderous black stilettos like fur accents fangs. Because the film on the docket tonight is about Arabs and cops and hookers, a lot of people assumed the cop and the leather lady were in costume for their parts. Not so. What they are in costume for is life.

They are not in the film, but they are: when the cameras begin rolling down the winding street, the scene recorded will be their scene. The movie is entitled *La Balance*, which can be translated variously as *Snitch* or *Squealer* or *Fink*. (Because the director is an American expatriate, the title of the English version is discussed before there is a foot of film in the can. Everybody hates *Snitch* and *Squealer* and *Fink*. "Too bad," somebody says, "that *The Informer*'s already been taken." "Yeah," somebody else replies, "it is. But we wouldn't dare.") Much of *La Balance* take place in Belleville, the most famous—infamous—of Paris's Arab slums. But Belleville is in Paris itself, rather than in the environs like Puteaux; conditions in the latter are thought by authorities to be more amenable to control than conditions in the former, where so much of Paris's major criminal activity occurs. All of *La Balance* is concerned with the police, and specifically with one branch of the police, a quasi-legal, Serpico-like undercover agency that employs an extensive network of informers, many of whom are blackmailed by their ostensible "employers."

Bob Swaim, the American director, has lived in Paris for seventeen years, long enough to feel comfortable with devoting several years of research to a script he has written in French, his second language. "The French *policier* has not changed in years," he observes the day before the Puteaux shoot at the home of Paris film critic David Overbey, who will play an assassin in the movie. "But the police have changed. I spent six months with them, and it's no longer Lino Ventura in a three-piece suit. These guys have long hair, they read the Communist newspaper *Libération* or the intellectual left-wing newspaper *Le Matin*, and they listen to rock music on headphones. Many of them were students during the '68 riots. I asked one why he became a cop and he said, 'The economy.'

Without a degree in France there is very little opportunity. Another told me, 'It's fun. We keep our own hours.' They 'hang out,' that's how they work. There is an anarchist thing about them; they're outsiders among the rest of police, non-conformists in this incredibly tightly structured society that is France. Their entire system is based on informants, at least ninety-nine percent. They work at the very limits of what is legal and sometimes they go beyond that; there's a lot of entrapment. On the other hand, they are very funny people living in a very violent world. It's like Robert Altman's *M*A*S*H*. That mixture of extreme violence and humor was fascinating to me.''

Entrée was gained to this special world in part because Swaim found an unexpected fan—the thirty-two-year-old commissioner in charge of the undercover cops had seen and admired Swaim's first film, *La Nuit de St. Germain des Prés*, released in 1977 and screened to respectable acclaim at film festivals around the world. *La Nuit de St. Germain des Prés* is a film noir derived from a detective novel by Léo Malet; the hero, Nestor Burma, private eye, is a denizen of the St. Germain des Prés section of Paris in 1951, the year Albert Camus finished *The Stranger* at a nearby sidewalk café, the year Juliette Greco was singing all dressed in black at the Rose Rouge, and the year Boris Vian was playing trumpet at the Club St. Germain. It was his first feature, but not his first film: when Swaim came to France in 1965, he had graduated with a degree in anthropology from the University of California and had expected to complete his doctorate in Paris under Claude Lévi-Strauss. Because he had grown up in southern California and because his parents had been in show business, he had never connected ''glamor or excitement with the movies.'' He began attending films at the Cinémathèque because ''they were cheap'' and discovered a whole new world in the movies of his own country, movies he had always dismissed—the French response to American film altered his outlook and he switched his course of study from anthropology to film at the École Nationale de la Photographie. During the next decade, he made more than fifty short films, primarily of the industrial variety. After *La Nuit de St. Germain des Prés* was released and resulted in no further offers of work, he went back to industrial films and commercials to support his family. But he was counting on something to get him out, and that something was the *La Balance* script. It had become legend long before Swaim was ready to find a producer—like most big cities, Paris is a small town, and every actress in France knew there was a great role in the film's hooker, just as every actor knew the guy who got to play the pimp had a good chance of copping a César, the French Oscar. Swaim went with Nathalie Baye, his first choice, and he hired one of her ex-lovers, Philippe Léotard, for the pimp. A gamble. "This is their first meeting, I think, after their estrangement. They haven't acted together yet," Swaim says at Overbey's. "It can be great or it can be a disaster. It's a big, big risk, because their relationship was very volatile, but this project is nothing without risk."

Out in Puteaux, risk is palpable. A block of the Arab quarter has been cosmetically dressed with a blinking neon HOTEL sign and a modest collection of similar commercial appurtenances to give the mainly residential side-street the look of a more important *rue*. The environment is otherwise unchanged; many of the people in the background, in and out of camera range, belong there. The street is blockaded on three sides, but residents wander through the blockades anyway, some absent-mindedly, some drunkenly, some aggressively. A man whose face has been turned into the texture of fresh hamburger by a fight staggers across the street, lurches into camera range, lurches out into the night. Bonnie Bruman, outfitted as a hooker in a white leather miniskirt and a tight white satin tank-top, is being buried in a landslide of verbal abuse from a trio of Arab men objecting to the way she's rubbing up against the actor playing her trick. The men sneering at her as a *salope* (slut) are from Puteaux, they're in the film, and they've been carefully arranged on kitchen chairs in front of a bar by an assistant director. They have not been directed to harass "the whore": unable or unwilling to separate reality from fantasy, they are objecting in the nastiest language possible to behavior that contravenes the indigenous macho Moslem code. Bruman is in acute distress but is trying to hide it. "There's nothing to do but hope they get the shot before they lose control of the set," she says shakily. The shot in question will open *La Balance*: it's a long take down the center of the street, as the "colorful" inhabitants come and go, not talking of Michelangelo. Swaim calls it "my one Hollywood sequence, the big crowd scene." Bruman continues to hide her distress for seven more takes. By now the men are pitching things at her and inserting their fingers into their mouths and moving them back and forth. When Swaim cheerfully announces, "It's a wrap," and walks down the street to congratulate all concerned, Bruman ducks into the restaurant and emerges in a modest, knee-length gray coat. Joining her similarly distraught girlfriend, for whom Arab exoticism has lost its allure, she heads without comment for the highway. The taxi fare back to the Champs Elysées is less than five dollars.

October 1982:
La Balance opens in Paris. The reviews are good and the lines circle the

block. Swaim has blended the crisp violence of Clint Eastwood's *Dirty Harry* with the moral uncertainties of French *policiers* and the lurid low-life romanticism so many Americans find in Paris (or want to find). The film is a triple-threat combo, an explosive mixture that makes for fast, entertaining melodrama, and Swaim's dexterity with the camera makes everything old seem new again. Almost.

By European standards the picture, outfitted with a bluesy, acidic Algerian-influenced score and a title tune belted out by Eléonore Lytton, the Gallic Janis Joplin, whistles by like a bullet, but Swaim takes his time in unexpected ways. The two stars—Baye's whore is named Nicole, Léotard's pimp is known as Dédé—don't enter for half an hour; the leisurely first movement of the movie is given over to an intricate exploration of the undercover squad. The cops are, as Swaim promised, a different species from the thickly accented *gendarmes* so helpful in American musicals and so inept in American comedies. They are indeed hip, fast-talking kids, the rock 'n' roll arm of law enforcement, and their finger-snapping repartee does brand them as dramatic descendants of the surgeons in *M*A*S*H*—punchlines under pressure—instead of the stolid, sadistic burghers of the Los Angeles Police Department according to Joseph Wambaugh. *La Balance* is sympathetic to the dilemmas faced by its quasi-countercultural cops (they are the people they warned themselves against, back in '68) but it does not always approve of their tactics—a fine but important line the movie treads with the misleading effortlessness of an accomplished tightrope walker. To balance *La Balance* Swaim relies on the considerable charms of Baye and Léotard, and they arrive just as the film is in danger of becoming a doting billet-doux to the boys in blue.

Nicole is a thoughtful, resourceful, and efficient hooker (too much of all that, maybe) going about her lucrative business when she is leaned on by the cops. They want her to persuade her pimp and lover Dédé to snitch on the activities of a drug smuggler, Massina (Maurice Ronet, arguably the best-known face with the least-known name in all French cinema), but Nicole has her own fiercely defended code of honor, and she refuses. "I'm a whore, but not a tramp," she snaps. The cops pay no attention and proceed vigorously—viciously—to blackmail both pimp and prostitute. The bulk of the picture contrasts the single-minded and sometimes disastrously incompetent undercover investigation with the effect that collaborating has on the lives of the two petty criminals. Swaim is heavy-handed in his desire to get the audience to care about the pair (does the sloe-eyed pimp have to sniff roses?) and the irony is that he need not have worried—cast against type, the squeaky-clean Baye is a kinky rev-

elation in skin-caressing sleaze, and Léotard, equipped with that photogenic battered-bulldog face, could be half the actor he is and still steal
the audience's heart. But this is a quibble. The months of research with
the rock-on cops have resulted in a picture that gleefully turns the esthetic screws, a smart, slick neon tour through the tough new Paris of
Big Macs, cocaine, and couscous.

February 26, 1983:
La Balance wins the César award for best picture; Nathalie Baye is named
best actress and Philippe Léotard best actor. The award for best director
goes to Andrzej Wajda for *Danton* but Swaim, astonished that *La Balance*
has won so much, hardly notices. At the box-office, the movie is a spectacularly solid number two. *E.T.* is number one.

May 9, 1983:
The sun is rising above the palm trees. At the Gallia Montfleury, an apartment complex in the hills overlooking Cannes, Linda Beath—who has
formed a major North American art-film distribution company based in
New York, Spectrafilm, and has purchased the North American rights to
La Balance—is awaiting the arrival of the babysitter who will watch her
two-year-old son, Simon, while she meets Bob Swaim and her company's
publicist, Renée Furst, to discuss strategy. Simon is wondering how to
get Mummy's attention so he can show her his new truck. Mummy is
wondering how to make Bob Swaim a star.

Over at the Majestic Hotel, in Furst's more-than-majestic suite rented
for the duration of the Cannes Film Festival, a breakfast of flaky crois-
sants and tiny cups of ebony coffee is being ordered. Responsible for the
promotion of *Napoleon* and *Apocalypse Now* ("I love Francis Coppola,"
she says), Furst is an expansive and motherly woman of sharp, calculating intelligence. She is also an unabashed groupie—"I'm mostly interested in directors, and I love American independent directors. I love
discovering directors. I'm not so interested in actors." She has photographs of herself with François Truffaut, with Wajda, with just about
every other European director of note. She has pushed art films tirelessly
in New York: her career extends back to *La Dolce Vita* and a little beyond.
She likes to remember that although the French New Wave began in
1959, the movies did not arrive in New York until 1960, and in that year
Shoot the Piano Player, *Last Year at Marienbad*, *Peeping Tom*, *La Dolce
Vita*, and several others altered the face of film. "I like to say I came out
with Godard and Truffaut and all the rest. It was a vintage year." Furst
wanted to work in movies "from birth" but it was not until she went

free-lance with Volker Schlöndorff's first film, *Young Törless*, that she hit on a formula that made her happy: she could work from home (which made her husband happy) and she could represent only the movies she liked.

(In the eighties, she represented Pia Zadora's *Butterfly*. Did she like it? "I still think with the right property she'd be wonderful. I've never known anyone to work as hard as Pia. I think she's real talented. Now don't laugh, but I thought she looked more like Sophie than Meryl Streep, though I know she couldn't carry such a heavy picture yet. By the way, do you know that Bonnie Bruman is no longer in Paris? She's working for Pia.")

Linda Beath came to New York from Toronto, where she headed New Cinema, Canada's most respected art-film distribution company, by way of a short stint as director of United Artists Classics Canada Ltd. The parent company, UA Classics, had been in desultory existence for four years when Nathaniel Kwit hired Tom Bernard in 1980. The original idea had been to keep UA pictures in circulation, but Kwit and Bernard saw other possibilities and moved rapidly to make them reality; for a time, UA Classics had so many films playing simultaneously in New York (the catalogue included *Lola*, *Le Beau Mariage*, *Veronika Voss*, *Hair*, and *Chilly Scenes of Winter*) the company bought its own block advertisements in the *New York Times*. UA Classics' unprecedented success led almost everyone else to enter the art-film field, Columbia through a company called Triumph, and Twentieth Century-Fox and Universal through their own "classics" divisions. Bidding on the most popular pictures, which meant pictures the distributors prayed would be popular, shot through the roof: the North American rights for *Montenegro* went for $375,000; Roger Corman invested $400,000 in *Fitzcarraldo* in exchange for an agreement to distribute; *Yol* was sold to Triumph for close to $300,000. Heretofore, $100,000 to $150,000 had been standard.

Strange things happened between 1980, when the boom began, and 1984, when most of the classics divisions were dismantled, victims of their own fiscal irresponsibility in the face of audience indifference:

✪ When *Gregory's Girl* was first shown at Cannes, immediately prior to the boom, no one wanted it. The accepted wisdom was that it was "cute" but that the thick Scottish accents precluded North American distribution. Bill Forsyth, the writer and director, remembered how all that changed, how he became a household word with the Yanks: "Mr. Sam Goldwyn, who had his own classics company, went along and saw it one night in London, where it had been running for months. He liked it. He asked me to redub the movie with softer accents and I was perfectly happy to do it." It made a tidy mint.

✡ The French thriller *Diva* was turned down twice by every art-film distributor in New York. Screened in advance for the press at Toronto's Festival of Festivals, its first North American showing, it received rave reviews that ensured full houses and repeat screenings—audiences went mad for the movie, and UA Classics hastily reconsidered.

✡ No contract was signed to distribute Yilmaz Guney's *Yol*, though it won the top prize at Cannes in May of 1982, until September of the same year; the company selling the movie, Cactus Films of Switzerland, was holding out for an enviable deal and got it. But *Yol* premiered at the New York Film Festival in the midst of dozens of other movies and the reaction was tepid; only the critics who had seen it on opening day at Cannes, months earlier (Jack Kroll of *Newsweek*, Richard Corliss of *Time*) were enthusiastic.

✡ The Italians demanded huge advances for *Identification of a Woman*, based on the reputation of its masterly septuagenarian director, Michelangelo Antonioni. When they didn't get what they wanted at Cannes, they decided not to dicker; they decided to wait until the New York Film Festival, confident the reviews would drive the price even higher. The critics slaughtered the picture. Three years later it has yet to achieve wide distribution.

Much of this is past history when Beath enters Furst's suite at the Majestic and bites into her first croissant of the day. *La Balance* has been a big hit in France—it is being screened in Cannes for potential buyers, not as an official entrant in the festival—but both Furst and Beath know the French reaction means exactly nothing in North America. Nor does the César guarantee the sale of a single seat on Times Square. Furst has not in fact seen the film, but she has agreed to act as in-house publicist for Beath's company at Cannes and she's sure she will like it; all her friends tell her she will. The print at Cannes is being shown in French, *sans* English subtitles. "I'll wait until I can see it with the subtitles," she says. "We'll make the New York critics wait, too. Some of them have a smattering of French, but not enough. We'll let them know we'll screen it for them in New York." Bob Swaim arrives. Kisses all around. Beath asks how he's bearing up. (She already knows some of the answer: good, but not great. The day before, she had lunch on the beach with Swaim's friend David Overbey, the assassin in *La Balance*. "You have to understand success has been a mixed blessing for Bob," he warns her. "The night before the Césars everyone was congratulating him because no one thought he would win. After the awards, no one spoke to him. *France Soir*, the popular newspaper, did a picture spread on the Césars. No picture of Swaim. In France they hate success, especially if the successful person is not French.'') Swaim answers slowly; his attitude is melancholy. ''Six months ago, people looked through me. Now, all of a sudden, they see me and ask me to lunch. Almost twenty years I lived in France and never had a Christmas card. This year, I had over two hundred. In the past few months I've had lunch with every producer in France. I don't know if I'll work for any of them, but I've waited fifteen years to meet these people, so I went to lunch. The movie was very popular with working people in France, which makes me happy, but the movie people were only behind me when I had been struggling and it looked like I might have a little moment of glory. That was all right with them. When *La Balance* started to make so much money, the jealousy and resentment began. By the time of the Césars, I was being publicly attacked.''

Beath and Furst are silent. Spoons stir coffee. Then Beath says the New York Film Festival has asked for *La Balance* and she's worried. ''They'll screen it in the middle, when the critics are tired. They killed *Yol* that way last year.'' Furst nods. ''But Linda,'' she points out, ''we can screen it for them in August, before they get tired.''

Swaim asks who is likely to interview him from the *New York Times*. ''I had lunch with Vincent Canby once,'' he says, ''but I don't know if he'd remember.'' Furst grimaces. ''At the *Times*, you have to go through channels. Canby is very remote, never talks to filmmakers. But I'll certainly call and invite him to the screening. By the way''—she turns to Beath—'Entertainment Tonight' is coming to the party where you are announcing Spectra and its acquisitions, but they may bring someone interviewable, some star, out with them.'' Back to Swaim. ''We need to talk about stars. We can bring you to New York, and you'll do a lot of interviews . . .''

''Won't he be a *good* interview?'' Beath asks rhetorically.

''Terrific, but directors are only good for some things and not for others. 'Good Morning America' and 'The Today Show' will not have directors, unless they're Francis, maybe. We're crossing an ocean, and a European director—you're American, Bob, but this is a European film—is not easy to do. We have to have one of the stars.''

Silence.

''Philippe Léotard is brilliant in the film,'' Beath mumbles, ''but he's difficult.'' Swaim agrees. ''But we can try him, if you want, Renée.'' Furst does not want. ''How difficult?'' she asks. ''Very''—from Swaim and Beath. ''I've never had trouble with any star, even with the ones, like Gary Busey, who are supposed to be trouble, and maybe that's because I headed it off,'' Furst conjectures. ''So maybe we should leave Mr. Léotard in France.''

Beath: "I had Kenneth Anger in Toronto once, for a retrospective of *Scorpio Rising* and all the rest. He found a two-thousand-page edition of the works of the magician Alistair Crowley and went into a room in my house and wouldn't come out for seven days. He asked me to put food out in the morning and at night, and I did. I never saw him. At the end of the seven days, he came out and said the ceiling had fallen in. Somehow, it had. Now what would you have done to head that off, Renée?"

Furst shrugs. "I wouldn't have put the food out."

Laughter all around.

Furst: "So. No Philippe Léotard. What about Nathalie Baye?"

Long silence.

Swaim: "She's pregnant with Johnny Hallyday's baby. She's not anxious to work; she's in Nashville where he's making a record, and she's not too nice about the film. I've called her 'tears and twinkles' and she knows about that. It bothered her that when she played a whore for the first time, something she hadn't been doing, she got this tremendous acclaim. But *La Balance* has made her the number-one star in France."

Beath: "Spectra is releasing another of her movies, *I Married A Shadow*."

Furst: "Then, we *have* to have Nathalie Baye in New York. With two movies, we can make her an event."

Swaim: "What can we do about the problems I've mentioned?"

Furst offers a slight, crooked smile. "Does she want to be a star in America?"

Long, long silence.

"Like every French actor, she is . . . she is *drawn* to America," Swaim replies.

"This will be her best shot," Furst says in a tone that lets her collaborators know there will be no problem. "I'll talk to her."

A bombshell. Swaim says he would like to cut the picture slightly before the New York opening. "Then cut it now, before the first critic sees it," Furst advises. "Why do you want to cut it?"

"I think the opening is slow."

Furst: "That's sometimes true in European pictures. In Italian films it's okay to let the phone ring sixteen times. In America, they have a nervous breakdown."

Beath: "It's not like that, Renée. It's very fast. I don't think you should cut it, Bob." She hears herself and laughs. "This is reversed. It's supposed to be the director who doesn't want his film cut by the distributor."

Swaim: "About the title. My producer is a friend of the New York City police chief. He called him and said the American equivalent for *La Balance* is *Dime Dropper*, which means snitch."

Furst: "We should go ahead and call it *La Balance*. I fought for *La Dolce Vita* and I fought when they wanted to call *Cousin, Cousine Kissing Cousins*—have you ever heard anything so ridiculous?"

May 11, 1983:
Kathleen Carroll of the *New York Daily News* is walking along the Cannes beachfront avenue, the Croisette. "Have you heard about the American director Bob Swaim and his French movie *La Balance*?" she asks breathlessly. "Oh, you have. It's a great story, isn't it? A real American in Paris. I can't wait to see the movie, but it's only in French here. We'll have to wait for the subtitles in New York. Have you seen Bob Swaim lately? The last time I saw him he was with Annette Insdorf, from the *New York Times*. Before that he was with Renée Furst. She was deciding what parties he should go to."

December 1983:
Bob Swaim is forty years old when *La Balance* opens in New York, title unaltered. On a per-screen basis at the end of three weeks, it is a spectacularly solid number two. *Yentl*, starring Barbra Streisand, is number one.

The Frustration Factory:
Juan Travolta's Cuba

The style of the First International Festival of the New Latin American Cinema in Havana is High Khaki—Moscow, not Cannes, is the model. Opening night, there are ten to fifteen casual onlookers in shirts and jeans gathered at the front of the Cuban Film Institute's official theater, and they constitute the extent of public curiosity (and participation). There are no movie stars on a jury that will sift through dozens of Latin American entries—in Nobel laureate Gabriel García Márquez and writer Régis Debray (the last journalist to interview Che Guevara before his death in the mountains of Bolivia) there are familiar names, but the majority of the judges represent the Chilean resistance and the newly installed Nicaragua regime. Nicaragua is the year's cause célèbre, and then some; the audience's longest and loudest applause is reserved not for Márquez or Debray but for leaders of the Nicaraguan Film Institute, intense young men who one year earlier were hiding in the mountains of their country with cameras and firearms. The festival does not kick off with a new work by Tomás Gutiérrez Alea or Humberto Solas, Cuba's best-known feature-filmmakers. Instead, opening night is devoted to three short documentaries about Nicaragua, two directed by Cubans. In *Douglas y Jorge*, a pair of cherubic adolescents tell of their struggles against General Somoza, of their nights in the mountains, of their feelings as they watched friends killed by the military police; in *La Infancia de Marisol*, a female revolutionary talks movingly of her rape and torture by the same military police. The third documentary, *Noticiero Incine*, is directed by a Nicaraguan, Frank Peñada, who receives a standing ovation—his paean to the revolution is a straightforward interview with an elderly freedom fighter. The movies are introduced by Alfredo Guevara (no relation to Che), the Cuban vice-minister of culture, who was once a guerilla *compañero* of Fidel Castro when Cuba's revolution was in the mountains and who stridently attacks the non-Communist world in rhetoric the imperialist North American pigs in the audience dutifully, if somewhat uncomfortably, applaud.

Outside the cinema, neither the Nicaraguan revolution nor the films praising it engender quite the same enthusiasm—for some Cubans, Nicaragua is merely the latest place to avoid being posted to, and for some Cuban filmmakers, it is merely the latest cause one is expected automatically to espouse. The lionization of the Nicaraguan experience can border on the preposterous. Standing in a long line to exchange money, a French journalist finds his place abruptly usurped by a solidly built little woman who shoves in front of him with a one-word announcement: she points to her tunic and proudly declares, "Nicaragua!" The French journalist, a Communist in good standing, points to the thirty people behind him and says, "Line!" The women points again to herself and says again, "Nicaragua!" The journalist looks behind him, hoping to find support. *Nada*. He shrugs, mutters "Nicaragua, *si*," and allows the woman to precede him.

The novelty of the Sandinista regime in Nicaragua has proved in some ways convenient for Cuba's rulers, whose own revolution is an entrenched, ongoing fact of life and has therefore lost a certain amount of verve. Cubans in positions of power are often expert exploiters, as evinced by the festival's politically astute orchestration of a troubling division in American society. As all delegates to the festival arrive, they are presented with identification cards bearing their names and nationalities. But on the cards handed out to the large contingent of American Hispanic filmmakers (most are U.S. citizens born and reared in Los Angeles), the nationality is not "U.S." but "Chicano." Several Hispanics are flattered, others are amused, one or two are insulted. A Hispanic writer who speaks no Spanish whatever grins: "Oh well. So far, as a group, we've been represented in American films by *Boulevard Nights* and by that sweet little *gringo* Robby Benson in *Walk Proud*. They're doing better by us here than Hollywood is at home." And they are. The Cubans have organized a retrospective of films by and about Hispanics living in the United States, they have commissioned a striking poster (an American flag lies shredded on the spines of a bright green cactus), and they have made sure that every street leading into and out of the Nacional, the festival's official hotel, is plastered with it.

The festival itself has been organized to emphasize the didactic, the pedantic, and the politically correct, but the lessons are interspersed with levity breaks of a nature one is likely to find only in Cuba. As delegates leave the auditorium after an especially harrowing *film du jour*, a gruelling and finally gratuitous reconstruction of the torture of Chilean Marxists —the picture is a necessary catharsis for the victims, but an unwatchable document for everyone else—they are directed to buses that whisk them to the Tropicana, a nightclub dating from the days of Cuba's fame as "the brothel of the Americas." In the mind's eye, men are being strapped to iron beds while electrodes are being attached to eyelids and testicles, but on the stage of the Tropicana, the ghost of Meyer Lansky walks to a bossa nova beat and hundreds of Carmen Miranda facsimiles balance fruit-stands on their heads. The revolutionary government has mummified the club's pre-Castro elegance—forty years ago it was the most famous night-club in the world—but in lieu of wealthy Americans, the audience is composed of a potpourri of average Cubans, Soviet and eastern-bloc digni-taries, assorted Third World socialists, and overdressed delegates to the film festival. A director from Mozambique and a director from Angola are sitting together; both are flabbergasted by the decidedly non-Communist opulence of the place, and both are getting nicely tight on a bottle of Havana Club rum. Next to the man from Mozambique is a grandiosely inebriated woman from New York who is trying to decide, out loud, if she is a feminist-socialist or a socialist-feminist. ("This is her worst prob-lem?" Mozambique wonders with a shake of the head.) Next to her is a Parisian journalist writing a book on the Folies and the Lido. "This show," he says dreamily, "is the finest tits-and-feathers revue I've seen anywhere in the world. Outside Cuba it would cost between $8 million and $10 million to mount. The shows are sexier in France because there is more nudity, but everything else is superior here." And it's true that the presentation is a masterpiece of kitsch, somewhere between Disney and De Mille, a platform for a kind of gaudy spectacle absent elsewhere in Cuban culture. The choreographic concept was created in the fifties and it is in the fifties that the show remains; attending it is like being plopped into *The Godfather II*, the most popular American film—no coincidence here—ever screened in Cuba. To the left of the main stage is an ancillary platform of three levels shrouded by a curtain of steam. A hugely fat diva with the face of Pontiac and the voice of Birgit Nilsson on a bad night oversees the dancers and every now and then does some-thing that must be described as a shimmy. A male singer with the flat-featured smiley face of Don Ho throws his baritone to the skies and then all but cartwheels around the stage, narrowly avoiding lissome chorus boys toting sheaves of fabric sugar cane. A black woman in a Scarlett O'Hara gown shakes her antebellum bottom. Norma Torrado, one of the founders of the Cuban Film Institute, danced at the Tropicana twenty-five years ago and gets misty every time she returns. "It was closed after the revolution," she recalls. "Before the revolution, it was only for the rich. Today, to get in is free and Cubans pay only for drinks and dinner. It is very cheap. And when someone is being rewarded for something, they are sent and allowed to pay a reduced rate. They do not have to stand in line.'' Nor do they have to retire early. The second show begins well after 2:00 A.M.

Entertainment is one of the few things Cubans can spend money on, material goods being virtually nonexistent, and they spend it willingly. North Americans may be dismissed as capitalist warmongers, but the products of capitalism are eagerly sought. Castro's elucidation of the limits of freedom—"Within the revolution, everything; against the revolution, nothing"—is clear enough, but the limits of the allowable have expanded considerably. Not only *The Godfather II*, but movies such as *A Star is Born* (the Barbra Streisand version) and *Jaws* have been exhibited. A lot of young Cubans are *au courant* with the hottest rock groups because a lot of Cubans, young and old, listen to Miami radio stations. It is possible that at a time when the revolution must change or die—to die in this context means to become an ossified, repressive, totalitarian nightmare—entertainment is in the foreground of the effort to loosen things up. Not necessarily indigenous entertainment, for it continues on its politicized course, but North American and European popular culture, which offer different tunes scored for different drums. Because the variant of Communism adopted belatedly by Castro has proved in other countries to be puritanical and work-oriented, the admission of a movie such as *A Star is Born* assumes in Cuba a political meaning, if only because the film implies that not everything in life must be viewed as political, that not all enjoyment need proceed from onerous effort. Cubans are much less apt to find that message counterrevolutionary than, say, East Germans, in that Cubans are historically neither puritanical nor work-oriented. They may be Communists, but they are Latins. No one would argue that Barbra Streisand or the Bee Gees pose a direct threat to the revolution, but another argument does rage among Communist intellectuals: does popular culture imported from capitalist countries enhance or dilute the revolution?

Not open to public debate is the desirability of the revolution itself. Many Cubans are old enough to remember clearly what life was like "before the revolution" (the phrase most often uttered in Havana) and any Cuban who travels extensively in Latin American will return home with renewed respect for the revolution's achievements: abject poverty has all but been wiped out, illiteracy is virtually absent, health care is universal. If by the standards of the North American middle class Cuba is poor, and it is, then its poverty has been equalized. People neither starve nor beg. The embarrassment Cuba places at the door of capitalist theoreticians is not so much what Cuba has accomplished (there are those who maintain that Cuba cannot be compared to the rest of Latin America because it was always wealthier) but what the rest of Latin America, nourished economically by the United States and its multinational corporations, has not accomplished: to ameliorate to any significant degree the hideousness of daily life as experienced by a large percentage of the population. One of the most memorable films screened in Havana is a documentary from Colombia, directed by Ciro Duran, that follows a number of street children through the underbelly of Bogotà and reveals a nightmare existence utterly unknown in Cuba. The hero of *Gamin* is Pinoche, who is about seven years old and lives in a city that has grown from four hundred thousand in 1948 to a current population of well over four million. Pinoche smokes, when he can, sneaks into wrestling matches, when he can, and eats, when he can. He eats cotton candy, Coca-Cola, and popcorn. His ankles are swollen to twice normal size from malnutrition. Sometimes, when he is very lucky, he finds marijuana to smoke. Sometimes, when he has begged or stolen enough money, he buys a small can of gasoline—Esso—and sucks in the fumes. The older children in his *gallande* (the word for a family of children) get high on gas, hallucinate, play sexual games, masturbate. Pinoche, too young for that, plays with cars. Real ones. He crawls through the traffic on the street that is his front yard—he and his friends live on a highway divider in downtown Bogotà that serves variously as living room, bedroom, and toilet. His parents and the parents of his friends are for the most part dispossessed country people who occasionally visit the divider and bring parcels of food. If the children happen to be away from ''home'' it may be because they are at a funeral; one of their number, a girl named Mosquito, is hit by a bus during the course of the film. Had she survived she would probably have become a prostitute like Dora, who is stabbed on camera but is relatively lucky—she lives. Another prostitute involved in the same fracas dies. Duran films it all and again invites the audience to a funeral.

Castro's pronouncements on culture and its control were accepted by intellectuals—most of whom had supported the revolution with equanimity—until the Heberto Padilla case occurred in 1968. (Before the revolution, no books by Cuban writers were published in Cuba except at the writer's expense. Serious Cuban culture was of no interest to the regimes running the country under the de facto direction of the United States, which is one reason intellectuals rallied around Castro. Castro promised a censorious grip on art and journalism, but for a time that grip was relatively benign. Financially speaking, it was downright generous: the Cuban Film Institute was founded within three months of the revolution. Before the revolution Cuban contribution to cinema consisted of three notorious pornographic movie houses.) In 1968, Padilla published a book of poetry, *Fuera de Juego* (Out of the game), that was attacked as counterrevolutionary in a government literary organ. The critique led to the writer's arrest, an event that earned him the somewhat misleading sobriquet "the Cuban Pasternak." The conditions of Padilla's incarceration and release were in fact unique: he was required to apologize for his conduct, but he was permitted, once out of jail (technically, he was under house arrest), to continue to publish his work in the *New York Review of Books*. In his own country, however, he was indeed "out of the game": his poetry was never again printed in Cuba. No wonder:

> *The poet, get rid of him . . .*
> *He does not make his message clear*
> *does not even notice the miracles . . .*
> *He is even out of date*
> *He likes only the old Louis Armstrong*
> *Humming, at most, a song of Pete Seeger.*
> *He sings the* Guantanamera *through clenched teeth . . .*

As journalism the poem is more dyspeptic than descriptive. Louis Armstrong is not proscribed. Far from it. One night on Cuban television a modern dance company rotates to a Dionne Warwick hit and the next morning Billy Joel sings over the public address system at Jibacua Beach. Sixty-five percent of the population of Cuba is under twenty-five. The implications are endless. Sixty-five percent of the population is literate and remembers nothing of the era before the revolution: it does no good for the government to argue the past to people for whom the present *is* the past. One of those people, Spanish by extraction, Cuban by birth, and North American by desire, is Santiago Ortega Carabajal. He is exactly as old as the revolution: he was born in the second month of 1959. "I like very much this Barbra Streisand—I see her in the *Star Is Born* —and I like very much the *norteamericano* movies on the television. I like most Juan Travolta, but I have not seen his movies. He is very sexy, *que no*? I see a picture of him, with his shirt off. When all the rest of the world has seen something, then we see it here. My uncle lives in Miami, when he comes to Cuba, he tells me about this Travolta—my uncle, he knows I am gay, the only one in my family who knows. He tells me about this *Saturday Night Fever*. He says I have it, this Saturday night fever. I want very much to see. The life here, it is very difficult. I have two *petusa* (pants) and no cards for more this year. I can take a holiday to Moscow, but I want to go to California. Every morning, since I was a *muchacho*, I listen to Miami radio station. My favorite English word I learn there. It is the word 'fantastic.' I like this word 'fantastic' very much. It is fantastic in *Estados Unidos*, I think.

"I am going to be drafted, but the doctor write a letter, saying I am sick. I am not, but why should I go and die in Angola, Ethiopia, Mozambique? The people there, I know, have problems. The people in Cuba have problems. We should stay here, like *Estados Unidos* and Vietnam. I say this to an American I meet, he is mad at me, he is a Communist. One is right, one is wrong, he says. I tell him I am 'draft dodger' like Vietnam. He says it is different. He says my attitude is not good. It is not good, yes, true, he is right. I think his attitude, it would not be good, if he lived here, in fear for his gay life. I think very soon now if I cannot leave Cuba, I go crazy. I ask them to let me go.

"Maybe it is because I am gay. I want . . . I am young. It is hard on the young. There is only one life, yes? I do not want it to go to doing work, work, work, nothing but work, work, work. I want to dance. I want to drink. I want to make love. It is very difficult here to make love, I am living with my parents, my boyfriends are living with their parents, and if I meet a foreign man, he cannot take me to his hotel, because I am Cuban, and they will not let me in. It is the same with men and women. Worse for gays. In Cuba, there are gays, everybody knows the film director, O———, is gay, many ballet dancers, famous politicians, we all know, they can be gay, they have parties, but I cannot be gay, only in secret. Only in the big class, only the high-ups, they can be gay. They make me sick. I want to see gay movies, gay discos. Cuban movies I never see. They show me my life. For what do I want to see it, my life? I *live* my life. I want . . . *amigo*, I want to live."

Toward the end of the film festival, Santiago ("Call me Sam"), who has tagged after delegates in the streets "so my English, it gets better," is allowed into the lobby of the Nacional. A group of delegates led by Lynda Miles of the British Film Institute complains to the Cuban Film Institute that the staff of the hotel is harassing Sam and he is instantly left alone. For a few days thereafter he can be found in the lobby at all hours, sitting with groups of four or five Europeans or North Americans, eagerly asking questions and just as eagerly—and recklessly—informing the ignorant of the reality of Cuban life as he sees it. His presence is intensely irritating to straight (in all senses of the term) North American Marxists but intensely fascinating to other less doctrinaire delegates, such as the American documentary filmmaker Barbara Kopple (*Harlan County U.S.A.*) who, when asked if she has seen many good movies in Havana, looks around guiltily and whispers, "No." The final day of the festival, Sam shows up with several small gifts for a handful of friends. He gives me a paper pocket calendar. I thank him and say it will come in handy. "You do not understand," he says. "I can give you nothing else of myself. But this is mine. This is part of me. So when you take it, part of me is gone. Part of me, it is out of Cuba."

When Sam finally sees *Saturday Night Fever*, he may decide he is living in the biggest Brooklyn in the world—his experience, he may conclude, is different in degree but not in kind from the experiences of young people (some with more *petusa*, some with fewer) around the world. The real difference, for him, is that his experience receives no reflection in the art of his country because his experience does not officially exist. The experiences of women are another matter. Cuba's first overtly feminist film, *Portrait of Teresa*, directed by Pastor Vega, is playing commercially in Havana. In it, a woman gets involved with an "evening cultural group" against the wishes of her husband. Latin machismo is the film's target and the woman eventually dumps her mate. Castro has said, "In regard to women, we've had a revolution within a revolution." That revolution is especially impressive in a Latin country; if feminism can receive a fair hearing in Cuba, perhaps the grievances of the young, of homosexuals, and of other disillusioned groups will one day be addressed. As it is, Cuban intellectuals, a number of whom are gay, privately consider the government policy on homosexuality to have been a stupid mistake. (As recently as 1971, homosexuals were sent to "work" or "reeducation" camps along with criminals, counterrevolutionaries, and prostitutes.) Homosexuality is theoretically legal today, but any sort of open expression is flatly insane.

Tentative dissent in other areas is possible. There is a tremendously revealing snatch of rhetoric in a Cuban Film Institute leaflet describing a feature about housing: "The film shows how the revolution changes everything and even if it hasn't been able to solve the problem of lodging, it creates the only serious possibility of doing it." The thesis is resumed in a poster: "We do not say that in socialism man will not cry, we only mean that his tears will have a much more noble origin." I show the poster and the leaflet to Sam. "Tears are tears," he counters, and then adds, "This means they admit not everything is good. Certain bad things we can talk about. That is good. The Russians I meet, they cannot talk about bad things at all. But, still, in Cuba they do not let us talk enough." Several days later, I visit the mother of the cinematographer Nestor Almendros, the man who shot *Days of Heaven* and *Kramer vs. Kramer*; he has asked, through an intermediary, that a can of Nescafé (the coffee ration in Cuba is half an ounce a week) be delivered to her. Señora Almendros speaks Spanish and French, lives in a pleasant apartment, and is very guarded. It is her belief that the revolution runs the risk of fossilization and that its attempt to homogenize the population has been a miserable mistake—she predicts that many smart, creative people are going to leave, one way or another. "To have everyone the same is terrible," she comments. "We left Spain when Franco killed my husband, and we came to Cuba. We were hopeful. In Spain, we were leftists, you know." She pauses and indicates with one thin arm the Havana skyline visible from the window. "Here, everyone is a leftist."

December 1979

Postscript. *Gamin* never opens in North America; instead, Brazilian director Hector Babenco's *Pixote*, a dramatization of the lives of street orphans, becomes an art-house success. Heberto Padilla leaves Cuba and lives in New York. Señora Almendros leaves Cuba and lives in Barcelona. Nestor Almendros works as a cinematographer and co-directs the documentary *Improper Conduct*, an indictment of Cuba's treatment of homosexuals. Four months after the First International Festival of the New Latin American Cinema concludes in Havana, over one hundred thousand people leave Cuba from the port of Mariel in privately owned boats. One of them is Santiago Ortega Carabajal, who is at first shipped to a refugee camp in Indianola, Pennsylvania, and is then allowed to join his uncle in Miami. In March of 1985, Sam nears the end of his graduate studies in chemistry at the University of Miami, works part-time, and spends many hours dancing in gay clubs. He has seen *Saturday Night Fever* five times. "I have a boyfriend," he reports. "Things are not always happy, no, because I miss my family. But I am A-OK. I like very much my life. It is fantastic, I think."

The Patriot Factory:
Tom Wolfe's Washington, D.C.

And they all came together, in their formal suits (black and smooth, like the night sky) and in their southern belle gowns (sweet and layered, like magnolia blossoms), and they made their way to the Kennedy Center (Republican and Democrat alike, yea verily), and they paid big strong American bucks (betcha my currency can whip your currency) for their seats, and they heard Uncle Walter Cronkite orate mellifluously as the master of ceremonies, and they gazed out on the enchanted knights of the celestial round-table, four of the seven original Mercury astronauts (Scott Carpenter, Wally Schirra, Donald Slayton, and Gordon Cooper came; Alan Shepard, never a team-player anyway, and John Glenn, running for office, didn't: Gus Grissom is dead), and they gazed out on the actors who played them, and they gazed out on the movie in which they were played, the movie *The Right Stuff*, from the book with the same name by Tom Wolfe, and they saw that it was good, that it was all good, and that it was more than that, that it was MORE THAN GOOD—that it was *mighty* good, *real* good, gut-busting puke-all-over-your-shoes good—to be an American again. Praise God. Three or more cheers for Yankee Doodle Dandy, hot shit and hallelujah!! And the Hallelujah Chorus is on the soundtrack of *The Right Stuff*, to make a point. The point is that the Americans who went into space were God's own good guys.

America, America, God shed his grace on thee. (Old song)

When Tom Wolfe published *The Right Stuff*, that irreverent, hot-as-a-crotch history of the first seven American astronauts, he kept his cool-as-a-cucumber distance, he kept his white gloves on and he made sure his natty/nifty/neato white suit was unspoiled by even the tiniest drop/droplet/dropette/ of spilt sweat; *The Right Stuff*, about patriotism, was not intrinsically patriotic. Nossir. Just the facts, man, jazzed up to the stratosphere, wham bang and you better believe it, ma'am. When William Goldman, the screenwriter of *Butch Cassidy and the Sundance Kid*, decided he wanted to turn *The Right Stuff* into a movie, Americans were being held hostage in Iran and Goldman loved the tale of the enchanted seven, but he wanted to keep the Wolfe from the door; he didn't want to keep his distance, didn't want to be a journalist dandy, no thanks buddy: he wanted a chest-pounding, gang-bang, rave-up/party-down that would make Americans feel good again. Yessir. An EVENT that would make them proud—honored—pleased as punch—downright puffed up—to be American. As Bill Goldman saw it, it was about time to get Old Glory off the ass and up the flagpole. The sixties were very groovy and all that, with stars and stripes sewn on the butts of blue jeans, making a point and a pitch, don't you know, against the war that wasn't right, but enough was goddamned enough. The sixties were over already.

Now speaking of the sixties, into the big picture came a flower child of same, Phil Kaufman, the San Francisco filmmaker, the director of *Invasion of the Body Snatchers* (the remake), and he was hired on, and he was not—or so he said, at first, back then—interested in a patriotic movie about patriotism, he was not interested in winning the morale war with Teheran, let them do that in D.C., and good as his word he threw out Goldman's script, flat threw it out, and wrote his own, flat out, in early 1980 or thereabouts, and he wrote it when John Glenn, the Democratic senator from Ohio, had—at least when the good senator was in public—no more than an urge, a tickle, a whisper somewhere at the back of his brain, way off the record, that said John Glenn should get up and go for it, the big enchilada, the office of The President of those United States, and Kaufman decided, rereading *The Right Stuff*, that he liked John Glenn a lot, and he decided to make him a hero, whatthehell?, because every story needs a hero, and some stories need seven, and he decided, why-thehellnot?, to make them all heroes, and *The Right Stuff* worships its heroes for three hours and ten minutes without intermisssion.

This here, according to Tom Wolfe, who ought to know, is what "the right stuff" is all about: "The idea here (in the all-enclosing fraternity) seemed to be that a man should have the ability to go up in a hurtling piece of machinery and put his hide on the line and then have the moxie, the reflexes, the experience, to pull back in the last yawning moment— and then go up again the next day, and the next day, and every next day, even if the series should prove infinite—and, ultimately, in its best expression, do so in a cause that means something to thousands, to a people, a nation, to humanity, to God."

To God. A cause that means something to God. In heaven. The big Him. The old fart likes having His sound barrier broken; He likes having the fate He's put down in his big books stirred up and tested. He likes guys who fly high enough to give him the finger. God's a good sport and He can take a joke. 'Bout the only thing He likes more than all of that is a good ol' American movie that celebrates all of that. God likes good ol' American movies made the way they used to make 'em, with heroes and suchlike. God likes a good battle between good and evil: hell, God invented it.

The Right Stuff gets on the cover of *American Film* magazine. Peter Biskind, the editor, is at Kennedy Center the day after the big premiere, the day all the actors and a lot of the astronauts are going to meet the press over breakfast, and somebody tells Biskind, who's a smart lefty and a good egg, that it's kind of surprising that *The Right Stuff*'s on the cover, because it's such a gung-ho picture, but that maybe it makes sense, because it's *American Film*, and it's a story that'll mean a lot to Americans but maybe only to Americans. "Oh?" says Biskind, genuinely surprised. "Only Americans? You think so?"

Newsweek is the first magazine to review *The Right Stuff*. Innocent as apple pie, the writers of a cover story on John Glenn ask: "Can a movie help elect a President?" The man who is President of the United States the very second the question is being asked is Ronald Reagan. Can a movie help elect a President? A disgruntled Republican answers the magazine's question: "Well now, I don't know, but I do know that *Newsweek* cover stories asking questions like that sure as shit can."

Gary Arnold, the film critic of *The Washington Post*, is the first daily-newspaper man to review *The Right Stuff*. "I don't doubt for a second," he writes, "that *The Right Stuff* is going to make millions of people feel gloriously proud to be Americans, or to identify themselves with Americans . . ." Even to have touched the hem of His garment . . .

The cause of this commotion flies by faster than a plane snapping the sound barrier—there's rarely a moment in *The Right Stuff* that's not entertaining, and precious few that aren't eye-fillingly photographed and toe-tappingly choreographed (it's not a musical, but in a way it is, a musical without any songs), but if you aren't American all the excitement is in the celluloid, in the filmmaking. "The right stuff" by definition is stuff Americans have, stuff that goes into speedier machines, stuff they bring to their thing about conquering the environment, and if you don't feel a swell of nationalistic pride watching an American rocket lift off *because* it's American, well then, *The Right Stuff* has a big fat hole where a subtext should be. This is not a movie about the first time Man (or Woman) accomplished something, it's a movie about the first time *Americans* did it.

Kaufman's "history"—it's a history of the space program like *Gone With the Wind* is a history of the Civil War—opens up with test pilot Chuck Yeager (Sam Shepard) charging up to the big orange X-1 that he's gonna use to break the sound barrier ker-splat. The long and lean and good-lookin' Yeager is on horseback, like he'd just moseyed along in from the nearest John Ford Western, and he's a symbol of what America once was, strong and silent and steady as the Death Valley sun. He glows. He hangs out at a local flyboy bar run by a heavy gal name of Pancho (Kim Stanley, snapping like a pissed-off turtle) and he don't talk much; the right stuff don't come out of books, and it don't get gussied up with big words and educated ways. Yeager watches them astronaut fly guys fly by on the television screen and he's real unimpressed. "Spam in a can," he calls 'em.

Them astronauts are varied bunch, but the wrinkles that made a lot of 'em, including John Glenn, less than consistently likable in the book have been ironed right out. Worst they get is amiably eccentric, like somebody's weird uncle, and when they do act up they're rambunctious cuties, human versions of piddling puppies (and old Alan Shepard, the first American in space, does piddle, right in his spacesuit). No matter what they do they're great guys and no guy is greater than Glenn (twinkly-eyed Ed Harris), who's a little stuffy in the morals department and a little constipated in the religious area, but he gets good applause when he tells his stuttering wife (lovely, tense Mary Jo Deschanel) she doesn't have to let that blow-hard Lyndon Baines Johnson (Donald Moffat) into her house.

If the astronauts are squeaky-clean heroes, that means—good-and-evil time—they have to come in contact with something that tests their virtue and, boy, do they! NASA, the press, German scientists, politicians—every other group is unmercifully caricatured. NASA men are know-nothings. The ladies and gents of the press are neither ladies nor gents, and when they come into view the soundtrack fills up with what sounds like bug noises (and, it will be revealed later, *are* bug noises, the sounds of munching locusts mixed with the noises of three women eating carrots). Press people are pricks. German scientists are fools. Politicians are assholes. Why would a savvy guy like Kaufman—he also made *The White Dawn*, *The Wanderers*— go for cartoons? Maybe because denigrating the people around the astronauts is the only way to make them look as good as they need to look (in the country of the blind, etc.). It takes no special acumen to see that using human specimens in the early Project Mercury flights was dictated by public relations—it's all laid out in Wolfe, who shows that chimpanzees could do all the tasks, rudimentary as they were, required to fly the Spam cans. Sam Shepard's Yeager, desperate to make a distinction between man and beast, announces that the astronauts deserve to be heroes because they, unlike the chimps, are conscious they may die. This is known as democracy in action: by this definition, the entire cognizant planet is heroic every time it goes out the front door. As if realizing the absurdity of the position, the movie's definition is eventually narrowed: a hero is a man willing to undergo physical hardship, a man not afraid—or a man who pretends not to be afraid—of danger. *Boys' Life* swells up into *Soldier of Fortune*.

Then there is the symbolism: a black-suited figure arrives to sing at funerals and spends the rest of his time hanging around, looking grim—he's Mr. Death, the G. Reaper. Then there is the mysticism: the sparkly "fireflies" Glenn saw during his orbital flight are attributed to "magical sparks" from the fires of Australian aborigines—Kaufman's been watching too many Peter Weir movies. None of this is enough to get everybody ready for the film's climax and conceptual nadir, a production number that comes off in Houston. As the boys are greeted at a giant barbecue by L.B.J. and sit down to watch an interpretive dance by Sally Rand, Kaufman cuts from the stripper's fans to Yeager's parachute—he's after another record—and back to the faces of the chosen seven. Big Chuckles Yeager is demonstrating the right stuff while the fraternity of seven celebrates it. The boys smile knowingly at each other, their faces outlined in a shimmering golden light. Haloes, yet.

Laughable in psychology and sociology—except the psychology of myth and the sociology of nationalism—*The Right Stuff* is nonetheless impeccable in its technology. (Aggressive and self-confident, silly but mechanically adept, *The Right Stuff* is the European cliché of what "American" means.) The soundtrack rattles the chest when the rockets take off, the outer-space effects by San Francisco avant-garde genius Jordan Belson are lyrical and subtle, and John Glenn's quiet flight is positively pastoral, a welcome respite from the noisy jingoism. But when Glenn goes back to earth, everything falls to earth: as he hurtles into the atmosphere, heat shield a-sizzle, he's humming *The Battle Hymn of the Republic*.

✩

Kaufman is a West Coastie in more than geography. On the morning after the night of the ritzy rustle, when satin moved against silk like new money against old, he is using words like "mojo." As in: "You have to find the mojo that works for the actor." He is "curious to see how John Glenn is going to respond to it." (It takes John Glenn a long time to respond to "it," the best free PR in the history of the Republic; when he does, he is coyly approving.) Barbara Hershey, the actress who plays the wife of Sam Shepard's Yeager—he's Gary Cooper to her Ava Gardner —arrives at the table at the Kennedy Center for breakfast with Kaufman. "I think," she opines, her arm through Kaufman's, "that it's a real flattering picture of Glenn. He was a great astronaut. The question is whether a great astronaut makes a great president." Hershey long ago changed her name to Seagull and then changed it back; some years later, she let herself be supernaturally abused in *The Entity*, so she's obviously no stranger to tough questions. As in: "What's the career-wise down-side of getting fucked on-screen by the devil?" Kaufman's no stranger to tough questions, either: he gets asked about a highly sympathetic and totally made-up scene in which Glenn, portrayed in the book as an insufferable moralist, a kind of Pat Boone of the ozone ("the flying monk," Wolfe calls him), worries to his charming wife that he might be "too gung ho" while she nods and sucks up to him. Kaufman says, "I'm sure something like that might have happened."

Lance Henriksen, who is Wally Schirra, says of actor Ed Harris, who is Glenn, "Ed is one of those guys who really gets into his part. He was John Glenn all the time. I had to listen to it, all this 'Gee whiz!' and 'Golly!' " A woman who handles historical films for the National Space Museum later comments that "it is impossible from the very beginning of Project Mercury to find footage where Glenn is not aware of the camera and smiling. And it's impossible to find footage where Alan Shepard *is* smiling." (Everybody thought John Glenn would be the first American into space, especially John Glenn, but that Alan Shepard got there first is all half-assed and academic anyway, in that the Russians really got there first, and *The Right Stuff* has to end with narration about how a pilot is flying higher and faster than any American ever has.) Scott Carpenter—the real Scott Carpenter—also comes to the meet-the-press breakfast and says of Glenn's presidential campaign, "He's been by his own admission aiming at this for a long time. It would have been evident to you, if you knew him, even if he did not admit it." Carpenter, dressed casually but expensively, as if preparing for a crisp autumn golf game at the local country club, is angry about one thing: that the funding for the space arsenal has slowed down. "We hoped in those naive days"—he's talking about the sixties—"that we would keep weapons out of space. But man is a warring animal, and in war high ground is valuable. Space is high ground." His pause is portentous. This is important stuff, this right stuff, make no mistake about it: in the race to fill the skies with death, it is possible that the people with the patent on the right stuff may go soft, pussy-out, and fall behind: "The Russians don't have the technology but their resolve will soon give them the technology unless we get cracking." How's about peaceful coexistence and cooperation? Carpenter has the look of a man who's just opened a tin of rancid fish. "We gained very little and the Russians gained a great deal with Soyuz-Apollo."

☆

Other voices in other rooms. What happens now is that a group of journalists gathers at groups of tables here and there while people from *The Right Stuff* are passed around; after this is all over, after the notebooks are full of notes and the tape recorders are full of sounds, notes and sounds that will go back to newspapers in Cleveland and Spokane and New Orleans to herald the arrival of *The Right Stuff*, everybody will go out and watch an air show led by Brigadier-General Charles A. Yeager, Mr. Right Stuff himself.

Pamela Reed was Belle Starr in *The Long Riders*. In *The Right Stuff* she is Trudy Cooper, the wife of "Gordo" Cooper (Dennis Quaid). "I'm about as far left as I can get," she says. (In the U.S., this means you would not rule out socialized medicine.) "But I think *The Right Stuff* is very American. I think it captures a time when we were proud to be Americans; people had a sense of unity." (Especially in Birmingham and Little Rock and—oh, never mind.) "Watching it gave me a warm and good feeling."

Scott Paulin is astronaut "Deke" Slayton. "Space exploration is nonpartisan nationalism. It doesn't draw lines across party lines. *The Right Stuff* is patriotic but it doesn't celebrate racism or colonialism. It's hard to find a project that supports Americanism."

Actor Henriksen (a.k.a. Schirra): "This thing is being released at the right time. I think it's a great thing for the country."

Mary Jo Deschanel, Mrs. Glenn in the movie and Mrs. Caleb Deschanel (cinematographer of *The Right Stuff* and *The Black Stallion*) in real life: "It's important to feel good about yourself. The people we played have the right stuff, whatever it is."

Kaufman, on the people his people played: "They're all mavericks. America has nourished that spirit. It's in danger of being forgotten." (Or elected President.)

Hershey, on being told by a representative of *The London Times* that *The Right Stuff* may be an essentially American document: "The true human spirit is not just American. To say this is 'just American' is almost offensive. It's about people in all countries."

Now everybody goes out to watch the fly-by. The woman from *The London Times*, still dumbfounded by Hershey's ethnocentrism, looks up at the planes and then down at her notepad. "All I'm getting from this," she says, "is a crick in the neck. All I got from the film was a headache. Americans are wonderful people, charming, except when they go on about themselves, which they will do."

☆

And then there is Yeager, who don't go on about himself or nothing else.

Chuck Yeager was born in 1923. He was the first man to break the sound barrier. He broke it with broken ribs: he'd been thrown from a horse two days before, told no one, and went to Mach 1 with a sawed-off broom handle jammed in the X-1's door because he was too sore to come up with the leverage to close the hatch. More than anyone else, Yeager, who acted as technical consultant on the film and has a small role as a bartender, is held up as an exemplar of the right stuff. "Every single person in the cast is crazy about Chuck Yeager and I think ninety percent of the people in the film disagree with his politics," actor Paulin reports. "His politics are to the right of Attila the Hun."

Brig.-Gen. Yeager, a high-school graduate from West Virginia, is wearing powder-blue slacks. He is drinking a Coke. He looks like a peaceful farmer, a decent man with a weakness for fishing. He is surrounded by reporters in a small room at a District of Columbia Hilton. He is asked about his derring-do. "It was my job. There was a great deal of dedication back in the forties. That's the way we were trained. It was my job. That's about it." He smiles. He means it. Case closed. So someone wants to know what it's like, *really* like, to put your life on the line. Shrug. "I've had a few close calls." The movie implies he was sorry in the end, "Spam in a can" notwithstanding, that he didn't become an astronaut. He says he doesn't think he came up with the phrase "Spam in a can" and he doesn't know who did. He says he was not sorry. "I was transferred to Germany. I didn't know the space program was going on. The film takes liberties. I liked it very much; I think the whole thing goes through real good. You have to take liberties. You gotta flower it up to make money, I suppose. You see all these colors when the planes are flying in the movie. Well, you never look outside of an airplane when you're flying—you're too busy looking at the panel—that's where your neck is. But if you're gonna pay five dollars you gotta see somethin' besides the inside of a cockpit.'' Does he have political ambitions? ''Being a U.S. senator wouldn't enhance me personally, financially, ego-wise or any other way.'' The message of *The Right Stuff*? ''It's entertainment. The white hats win and the black hats lose. You don't have to think.'' And the right stuff itself—what is it, the stuff he has so much of? ''I think it's a heck of a lot more important that a guy be at the right place at the right time and be a little lucky. I waste about as much time thinkin' about 'the right stuff' as you wasted askin' the question.''

October 1983

The Sadomasochism Factory:
Rainer Werner Fassbinder's Germany

In the last week of August 1981, Rainer Werner Fassbinder, arms crossed over his distended belly, was smiling for photographers at the Hyatt Hotel in a conference room rented by Montreal's World Film Festival. He had spent the afternoon in a limo snorting coke and cruising boys, but the baddest bad boy in movies was now meeting with the Canadian press and he had resolved to be exemplary, even angelic. Grinning madly and occasionally rubbing the black leather of his vest, he came across as a Hell's Angel pixie—grinning madly and occasionally scratching his crotch, he resembled an obscenely flirtatious Toad of Toad Hall. Then suddenly he lowered his head, placed it on his hands, and glared. The photographers applauded: *now* he looked liked a German director. *Now* he looked like Rainer Werner Fassbinder, *wunderkind*, *enfant terrible*, and all the rest. The performance began. What do you think of Montreal? "Montreal seems to me the highest point of hope for culture in the Western world." What do you think of *Lili Marleen*? "I saw the film for the last time a year ago. You've just seen it. I should be asking you the questions." Why are so many of the women in your movies whores? "From now on, I'm going to make only films about emancipated women journalists." What is the general situation in Germany? "The general situation in Germany is very dangerous. Young people in Germany today are older than the old people." What directors do you admire? "Pasolini and Visconti. Only directors who are dead." A friend of Fassbinder's reviewed the show from the back row. "I suppose he's not a nice man," he snickered. "He's just a genius."

No one expected the genius to live long, least of all the genius himself. And not many people liked him, least of all the people who knew him best. "After I saw *Lili Marleen*, I was ashamed ever to have worked with him," his ex-wife, Ingrid Caven, snarled of the 1980 Nazi extravaganza starring Hanna Schygulla. Caven had never cared for Schygulla, either—at the mention of Schygulla's name, Caven would put her hands to the side of her face, palms out, and purr, "You mean, 'Make Pretty'?"—but now she muttered, "Hanna's always been a cow, I know; still, Rainer didn't have to do that to her." Schygulla was one of the few artists in the ensemble Fassbinder gathered from several Munich theater groups in the late sixties—an ensemble he would transform into one of the most effective the film world had ever known—to largely escape Fassbinder's wrath, one of the few members of that intensely unhappy but phenomenally efficient Fassbinder family who did not have horror stories to tell regarding her abuse at the hands of his satanic majesty. Over the years Fassbinder's pre-eminent discovery, the star of *Effi Briest* (1973) and *The Marriage of Maria Braun* (1978), felt very little coming her way, good or ill, from the director she acknowledged—to co-star Piotr Lysak, on the set of Andrzej Wajda's *A Love in Germany* (1983)—as "the man who made me what I am." Passing through Toronto in October 1979 en route to a rendezvous with one of her lovers, a Navajo woman she had met during a five-year hiatus from Fassbinder (the collaboration that began in 1969 with *Love is Colder Than Death* and ended more than ten films later with *Effi Briest* did not resume until *The Marriage of Maria Braun*), she reminisced happily about her Svengali: not only was she the star of *The Marriage of Maria Braun* that year, she was in the *The Third Generation* and the monumental *Berlin Alexanderplatz* was in the offing. Even so, her emotions were muted. "We met when we were in our twenties," she said, "I think my first reaction was that he was talented, but I should not get too close. I never have. Our relationship is kind of strange. We don't talk much to each other. He came to New York but I didn't see him much. We don't"—here the word was spat—"chat. But the chemistry between us is strong. If people would see us together, though, they would think we'd had a fight, because there is so little normal contact between us. There is so little normal contact between Rainer and anyone."

Fassbinder was born in the small Bavarian town of Bad Wörishofen on May 31, 1945. He maintained, proudly, that his upbringing was "unbourgeois" and the appearance of his mother, Liselotte Eder, in his most brazenly confessional movies, where she was billed as Lilo Pempeit, supports the claim. True, his father, Hellmuth Fassbinder, was a doctor, but many of the doctor's patients were prostitutes: in the more than forty movies Fassbinder made before his technically non-suicidal death from a combination of drugs, booze, and exhaustion on June 10, 1982, prostitution was invariably viewed as the essence of all human relationships, as the fulcrum for every interpersonal seesaw: for Fassbinder, love was about dominance, power, and payment. In *Katzelmacher* (1969), his first significant, formally rigorous film—each sequence is a discrete unit uninterrupted by editing—Jorgos, "a Greek from Greece" played by

Fassbinder himself, disrupts for a time the carefully ordered world of the movie's gelid Germans with his aura of hot Mediterranean mystery. But only for a time: one of Katzelmacher's oft-quoted lines is, "Where there's money, you can do everything," a "moral" that emerged once again in Fassbinder's corrosive *Fox and His Friends* (1975), the movie that proved Fassbinder was an equal-opportunity satirist and pessimist. In *Fox*, Fassbinder plays a homosexual prole, a gay carnival worker who wins a lottery, makes bourgeois "fag" friends, and is deserted by them when his good fortune deserts him. (The contempt felt by Fassbinder and his coterie for the bourgeoisie was bottomless. "When in New York, I once stayed at the Algonquin Hotel," Schygulla frowned. "I hated the super-bourgeois mentality of that place. Everyone is dead.") In a lucid enunciation of his principles, Fassbinder declared, "I stand firmly behind this thought: You must show the victim with his qualities and faults, his strengths and his weaknesses. The really terrible thing about oppression is that you can't show it without showing the person who's being oppressed and who also has his faults. For example, you can't talk about the German treatment of the Jews without evoking the historical Jewish rapport with money, but when you do this, it seems as if you're explaining or accounting for the oppression. But oppression allows very few possibilities of reaction if you are to survive. When I made *Fox*, homosexuals only saw homosexuals making mistakes. They wanted to be exhibited as good, kind, and friendly people, and that would have been a lie. I'd have been saying that they didn't have any problems. If everything's fine, great—you've got nothing to change."

In the majority of his movies (in toto, they could be called *Notes For a Post-Ideological Critique of Life*) the structure was a revival of Hollywood melodrama, particularly the melodrama of Douglas Sirk, director of *Written on the Wind* (1956) and *Imitation of Life* (1959). Fassbinder combined the plushly plotted, fatalistic Hollywood form with a stiff dose of Brechtian alienation techniques that depended increasingly for their effectiveness on an avalanche of self-conscious kitsch in the form of stylized performances, grandiloquent lighting, and evocatively bizarre decor. Fassbinder's composer, Peer Raben, mastered the use of music as a self-reflexive character in its own right, a character with an archly cynical point of view—Raben's sawing violins remind the spectator that what is being watched is "only" a movie, "only" a melodrama—and this intentionally intrusive wall-to-wall sound, both homage to and satire of lush Hollywood scores of the forties and fifties, accomplished for the ears what the "Stop staring romantically" signs Brecht put in his theaters were meant to accomplish for the eyes. Fassbinder augmented Raben's work with perversely but brilliantly chosen snatches of popular music; the most extreme examples were probably Johnny Horton's "The Ballad of New Orleans" ("In 1814, we took a little trip, along with Colonel Jackson down the mighty Miss-iss-ipp") as the background for the death of Veronika Voss in the 1981 film of the same name and the croonings of Elvis Presley and Dean Martin (singing "Silent Night") in the apocalyptic dream-sequence epilogue of *Berlin Alexanderplatz*. "I think melodramatic films are correct films," Fassbinder said. "The American method of making them, however, left the audiences with emotion and nothing else. I want to give the spectator emotions along with the possibility of reflecting on and analyzing what he is feeling." As Robert Burgoyne wrote in his perceptive essay on Fassbinder, "Narrative and Sexual Excess," "Melodrama projects no ideal future in which its protagonists gain awareness, only an uneasy and contradictory present in which they suffer from a failure to be at one with a patriarchal society. . . . The 'happy end' of melodrama is the result of an acceptance, rather than an understanding, of repression." (One of the few "happy" endings in the Fassbinder canon is the hellishly ironic conclusion of *Lola* [1981], in which the ex-hooker becomes a comforted creature of the despicable bourgeoisie.) Wim Wenders, then a critic, wrote of *Katzelmacher*, "The gruesome thing about this film is that down to the smallest detail, it is lifeless" (and then went on to make several of the most gruesomely lifeless "new German" movies extant).

Lifelessness was not a charge that would be levelled against Fassbinder again—though misanthropy would be—and he was successful in large measure at the task he set for himself: "The best thing I can think of would be to create a union between something as beautiful and powerful and wonderful as Hollywood films and a criticism of the status quo." As his personal life (documented in deadeningly unintelligent detail by Ronald Hayman's scandalous 1984 excuse for a biography, *Fassbinder Film Maker*) continued on its druggily self-destructive course, the films, shot at the famed feverish pace, were gaining in complexity and technique, in part because Fassbinder's cinematographer, Michael Ballhaus—who remained with him until *The Marriage of Maria Braun*, when he was replaced by the flashier Xaver Schwarzenberger—was perfecting a graceful yet emphatic method. *Beware the Holy Whore* (1970) was an introverted examination of Fassbinder's own ensemble, a movie about making movies, with close connections to Wenders's later *The State of Things* (1982), but the next important film, *The Merchant of the Four Seasons* (1971), was a true departure. Set in the Adenauer era, it detailed with unexpected sympathy the reasons for the death of a fruit-seller, Hans Epp (Hans

Hirschmuller); Fassbinder thought it "more universal" than his preceding work and it was the first of his films to be greeted warmly by German critics. The stars of *The Bitter Tears of Petra von Kant* (1972), an unloving look at male power struggles in lesbian disguise, were the decor and the prowling, elegant camera. (Ballhaus's swirling style reached its flamboyant apogee in *Chinese Roulette* [1976], Fassbinder's sadomasochistic response to Jean Renoir's *The Rules of the Game* [1936]. As the revellers embark on destructive parlor games, glass bookshelves serve as metaphors for the solid yet see-through divisions between them. Ballhaus's camera moves with such seductive stealth around and through shelves and mirrors that his technique confounded American director Philip Kaufman. "That camera!" he said, "I don't know how they've done it.")

Fassbinder's best films between *Merchant of the Four Seasons* and *Chinese Roulette* were very good indeed: *Ali—Fear Eats The Soul* (1973), *Effie Briest* (1973), *Fox and His Friends*, and *Mother Kusters Goes to Heaven* (1975). *Ali*, arguably the gentlest of all Fassbinder films, featured one of the director's lovers in the lead—El Hedi Ben Mohammed Salem M'Barek Mohamed Mustafa as the Turk whose romance with an aged widow (the exceptional Brigitte Mira, who reappears as Mother Kusters) turns her neighbors against her; she finally—inexorably, horrifyingly, realistically—turns against him. (Salem was in reality a Berber Fassbinder had met in a Paris sauna, and although *Ali* gave him both notoriety and respectability, he was told not long after the film was completed that Fassbinder had finished with him. He re-embarked on a life of petty criminality and prostitution out of Jean Genet and eventually hanged himself in a jail in Nîmes; with ghoulish appropriateness, Fassbinder dedicated his final film, *Querelle* (1982), from the Genet novel *Querelle of Brest*, to the man who had lived the fiction.) *Effie Briest*, a long, leisurely film in black and white of Fontane's 1895 novel about a seventeen-year-old girl (Schygulla) who marries a much older rich man and comes to grief, was another impressive departure, a "Masterpiece Theatre" approach to moviemaking that Fassbinder never again pursued. With *Mother Kusters*, in which the title character, a working-class woman, becomes the darling of leftists after her factory-worker husband runs amok and kills himself, Fassbinder returned to hostile form. This time his target was the left, a movement he saw as having been fatally co-opted by the dreaded bourgeoisie. Commenting on a scene in which Mother Kusters's Communist champions apologize for their silver tea service, he said, "That's not sarcasm, that's reality."

Chinese Roulette behind him, Fassbinder embarked on what until *Ber-*

lin Alexanderplatz was his finest film for television and one of the finest films in his oeuvre, his adaption of Oskar Maria Graf's 1931 novel *Bolweiser* (1976), retitled in North America *The Stationmaster's Wife*. Working close-up and indoors (when the camera strays outside, it comes as a pleasant shock), Fassbinder claustrophobically evokes the stultifying existence of the German lower middle class of the twenties. The melodrama outlines the adulterous story of the diffident, unimaginative Bolweiser (Kurt Raab) and his restive wife Hanni (Elisabeth Trissenaar), a woman in the literary and psychological tradition of Madame Bovary. The passive Bolweiser, on one level a symbol for the subservient pre-Hitler masses, allows himself in the aftermath of an affair Hanni has undertaken with a beefy butcher (Bernard Helfrich) to be manipulated into a court case that destroys him. His tragedy reignites his passion for his wife, but their lovemaking is bitter, savage, without release; when Hanni asks him to hurry, he snarls, "You're . . . my . . . property. I can do what I like with you." Once again, Fassbinder's model for the love between men and women is sadomasochism and once again he is an egalitarian satirist—in varying degrees, both Hanni and Bolweiser are admirable and disgusting. The movie's method is exacting, as if an important autopsy is underway, but rarely grim, as if the doctor conducting the autopsy has become so intent on his investigation he has ceased to notice that the thing he is cutting is a corpse.

Despair (1977), Fassbinder's first film in English, adapted by Tom Stoppard from Vladimir Nabokov's novel, is a curiosity. The opening hour marries the opulent decorator kitsch of Josef von Sternberg's Paramount peroid with an acute study of disassociation in the person of Dirk Bogarde, as the operator of a chocolate factory in Berlin. "I am," he announces, " a connoisseur of soft centers." His Art Deco apartment might have been designed for one of the brothers Warner, and his girlfriend (the Rubensesque Andrea Ferreol, of the oblong bottom) is the stereotypical starlet, a "sexual Disneyland" with a Mickey Mouse mind. "Intelligence would take the bloom off your carnality," Bogarde teases her. And then: "We're a perfect couple. I like literature, she likes trash." But he watches, sadly and silently, as his life falls apart; in order to retain control, he dons a modern black motorcycle cap (an intentional anachronism, symbol in the gay world of S/M) and directs his mistress, game for any game, to lick his boots. In the corner, another Bogarde—the disassociated, interior Bogarde—watches the scene, grimly bemused. "The things I do!" his smile seems to say. The second hour of the film, in which Bogarde sets out to trade identities with a working man, to find himself by becoming someone else, is derivative to a fault; Stoppard sets

unfortunate thriller mechanisms in motion; and the *Sunset Boulevard* ending with Bogarde at last ready for his close-up is irritatingly smug—there is
something cheap about this highfalutin literary enterprise that calculatingly castigates the cheap while exploiting it. Fassbinder's sensibility
was foreign to much of the eclectic lavender bitchery of Stoppard's script,
but he was preparing to address directly several of the issues raised by
implication in *Despair*—it's no accident that Bogarde's sardonic sadomasochism was the one deeply felt aspect of the picture. "Rainer wasn't
into heavy leather, despite all that stuff he wore," a close friend said.
"He was into more than that. He was into heavy metal. A couple of
times, guys he picked up wound up in the hospital." Swiss filmmaker
Daniel Schmid, who directed Fassbinder and Caven in *Shadow of Angels*, a
1976 cinematic treatment of Fassbinder's play *The Garbage, The City
and Death* (Fassbinder appears as a pimp, Caven as his whore), revealed
that the design for the picture was inspired in part by The Mineshaft, a
New York bar devoted to S/M. Fassbinder was never coy about this: he
constantly wore clumps of keys clipped to his left hip, a signal to all gays
that he was a homosexual who took a dominant sexual role, and a signal
to gays in his own S/M subculture that he was a sadist, or "top." In the
unforgettable episode he contributed to the 1977 omnibus documentary
Germany in Autumn, an effort by German filmmakers to warn the country
of the insidious methods used by Bonn to erode civil liberties in the wake
of the mysterious prison deaths of three members of the Baader-Meinhof
gang, he argues with his politically reactionary mother about terrorism
and enacts a savagely sadomasochistic relationship with his lover of the
time, Armin Meier, who committed suicide on Fassbinder's birthday in
May 1978—shortly after the director had taken *Despair* and another lover
to the Cannes Film Festival. The double thesis of Fassbinder's daring
and moving contribution to *Germany in Autumn* is that fascism begins at
home, and that the fascism at home is accentuated and symbiotically pro-
moted by the fascism outside it. The sequence is one of the most unsparing acts of self-criticism in the history of movies. Fassbinder's response
to Meier's suicide resulted in an innovative masterpiece, *In a Year of
Thirteen Moons* (1978), one of three movies—the other two were *The
Marriage of Maria Braun* and *The Third Generation*—he took to Cannes
in 1979. The film was an act of penance, a leap of empathetic imagination,
an ego trip (Fassbinder served as writer, director, executive producer,
cinematographer, art director, and editor) and a document that metamor-
phosed a wake into a work of art. Elvira (Volker Spengler), a transsexual
beaten under the credits by a homosexual pickup for having posed as a
man, is an outcast rejected by outcasts; the film follows with terrible,

tranquil inevitability Elvira's slow slide into suicide. At each station of Elvira's cross, there are long monologues of clotted, operatic prose. One of the nuns who reared Elvira (the nun is, significantly, played by Fassbinder's mother) theorizes that "the order human beings have made ruins them." Robert Burgoyne has captured precisely the effect of the film: " . . . the death of Elvira enacts a kind of group fantasy; each of the characters betrays Elvira, to no particular end. Like a pinball, Elvira rebounds from one character to another, lighting them up as they tell their stories, momentarily delaying her extinction. The suicide . . . fails however to elicit a sense of moral elevation, of the character achieving a kind of 'moral sainthood.' The character departs with the same ignominy with which she was introduced. Elvira is the excess which must be repressed in a patriarchal society. The melodramatic form of *Thirteen Moons* reveals both the necessity of this imperative and the consequent and irreparable suffering which it entails."

The third film at Cannes in 1979, *The Third Generation*, was by Fassbinder standards a comedy, a postmodernist essay on a theme stated unambiguously by a police chief: "I dreamed capital invented terrorism to force the state to protect it better." (This is the film the producers of *Germany in Autumn* must have thought they were getting.) Satirically if superficially Godardian, the picture is a heady confluence of Luchino Visconti's *The Damned* (1970) and Robert Altman's *Nashville* (1975). Most of the fourteen major characters are addicted to the electronic media: in the opening scene, a Berlin computer magnate is watching a film by Robert Bresson on video and his terrorist puppets—they have no idea they are being exploited by their ostensible enemy—have as a condition of membership in their gang possession of a video recorder. The movie is full of jokes, puns, references, parodies: the terrorists play keep-away with a volume of Bakunin it might do them good to read, their password phrase is "World as Will and Idea," and someone chooses as an alias Oskar Mazerath, the hero of *The Tin Drum*. The incredible, promiscuous overload of media material—televisions are always running; the film's six sections are divided by tasteful green titles that reproduce scatological graffiti found in public washrooms; the soundtrack is layered in an abstract expressionist sludge of words and music—is thematically germane to what is, in the last analysis, a rumination on the effects of icons and talismans, of bromides and clichés, televised and otherwise, on political and psychological reality. The "third-generation" terrorists are visual and aural sophisticates of a post-literate McLuhanesque culture, but they are also conceptual dunces, free of consistency or calculation: they dynamite buildings because it is expected of them. They are acolytes of the evening news, plugged permanently into a ceaseless collage of gibberish. Fassbinder saw these media-monster terrorists as near-morons, but he was frightened of the excuse they afforded governments anxious to expand their powers of control and surveillance, and he believed gloomily that the West "is becoming just a little more totalitarian with each passing day." He refused to allow the tone of *The Third Generation* to reflect that gloom, however; he wanted the audience to laugh until it cried.

The Marriage of Maria Braun did more than engender international mass-market popularity for Fassbinder and it did more than make Hanna Schygulla an international star: it began a trilogy that, taken with *Thirteen Moons* and *Berlin Alexanderplatz*, constitutes Fassbinder's firmest hold on immortality. *Maria Braun* is a parable of progress, an analysis of the price of surviving the peace, and a giddy party that actually begins with a blast: Maria (Schygulla) marries Hermann Braun (Klaus Lowitsch) in a slapstick ceremony while American bombs fall, and then, when Hermann is listed as missing, takes a job in a bar where, her hair piled high on her head—"I look like a poodle," she sniffs at the Otto Dix reflection of herself in a mirror—she becomes the in-house siren. She parlays her sex appeal into a career as a businesswoman, Rosalind Russell division, but she selfishly uses her proto-feminist influence primarily to maintain and augment her power base—she becomes, in her own words, "the Mata Hari of the economic miracle." Clearly the personification of a postwar Germany that embraced American capitalism and in the process sacrificed morality to "progress," Maria Braun is the sanguine symbol of an exsanguinated era. "It's a bad time for emotions," she shrugs.

It gets worse in *Lola* (1981), the second instalment of the trilogy, a candy-colored satire played out in a nameless German town in 1957. The pink, green, and blue titles announce the visual scheme, which positions characters Visconti-like under theatrical pastel lights. *Maria Braun* ended elliptically—did Maria kill herself, or was her death an accident? (although Fassbinder originally wrote a suicide, Schygulla argued against it and won a concession to ambiguity). But there was nothing ambiguous about the context of the heroine's death: Maria Braun's mansion blows up on the day West Germany wins the world soccer championship; on the day, in other words, that postwar Germans first permitted themselves a public display of nationalism. For Fassbinder, that day marked the end of the swing-shift liberation women had achieved during the war: Maria's death was coldly preordained as a metaphor for the restoration of the conventional sexist power balance. (It's typical of Fassbinder that Maria, forced at first to battle up from under, should embrace without qualms the very system that worked against her; in Fassbinder, everyone identifies with the aggressor.) In contrast, the eponymous Lola (Barbara Sukowa) is a singing whore working in a tony brothel frequented by the town's ruling class; she is the uncritical, fundamentally powerless plaything of a cartooned elite who combine the creatures that slither through Sinclair Lewis's novels with the monsters that move through George Grosz's caricatures; these conniving power-brokers, these amoral architects of the economic miracle, spend hours in the bathroom, washing their hands. The tone is essentially a burlesque of *The Blue Angel* (1930)—a stolidly honest building commissioner (Armin Mueller-Stahl) falls under the spell of the Lola who gets what she wants—but if the debt to the von Sternberg film is obvious, Fassbinder has other folks to fry; there is little interest in the pathos of the lovers' predicament and a good deal of interest in how they contribute to their own misfortunes. "People here have an inner life and an outer life and the two have nothing to do with each other," Lola warns the building commissioner, who naively fails to listen until it's too late. "The building commissioner," Fassbinder explained, "condemns the basic principle of capitalism from a moral point of view but realizes that without that principle the country can't be rebuilt. He has a liberal/social democratic attitude which assumes that this sort of politics can somehow be contained. In the end he realizes it cannot be stopped. This is exactly what happened in Germany."

Prior to *Lola*—the concluding film of the trilogy, *Veronika Voss*, will be discussed later—Fassbinder reached a peak with *Berlin Alexanderplatz* and a pit with *Lili Marleen*. Inspired by a 1929 Alexander Doblin novel Fassbinder read in his teens, *Berlin Alexanderplatz* is a fifteen-and-a-half-hour howl of hatred at the way things are. Well into the thirteenth hour, the narrator says, "And I turned and saw the injustice of everything under the sun," and that is what the director proffers, a celluloid encyclopedia of the race's wrongs, a bestiary of humanity's beastliness. The violence, the angst, and the anger of Doblin's prose branded it unmistakably as a product of the waning years of the Weimar Republic, the interlude that of course gave birth to the didactic furies of Brecht, the stinging portraits of Grosz, the swirling torments of Expressionism, and the starkly photographed cinematic nightmares of Lang, Murnau, Wiene, and Boese: Fassbinder has maintained the texture of the times. Each episode opens with an identical newsreel collage of the twenties backed by Richard Tauber singing "Oh Signora, Oh Signora." The title of Part One is Teutonic in its leaden irony but incontestable for Fassbinder in its truth: when Franz Biberkopf (Gunter Lamprecht), who killed his wife four years earlier, is released from prison, "The Punishment Begins." This small-time

Everycrook squeezes his round and fatly undistinguished features between his hands and emits a silent scream, which he repeats many times.
"Whining," the narrator notes crisply, even sadistically, "is cheap. A
sick mouse can whine, too." The first episode is distanced—analytic and
comic—in its emphasis on irony and injustice. Franz meets a beautiful
woman, Lina (Elisabeth Trissenaar), against a backdrop of tawdry bars
and apartments in the vicinity of the Berlin subway station Alexanderplatz,
against a human backdrop of assorted cripples hampered by society and
victimized by the limitations of their own psyches. Vowing to be a good
man, he works at odd jobs, selling sex books and a Nazi newspaper, but
virtue fails and he is gradually reduced to alcoholic madness until, in
Part Four, in the most theologically sophisticated apostrophe of Fassbinder's
career, he becomes a modern Job, M to God's S. "The world," God's
slave screams in his letter from the earth, "is full of filth and madness."

Franz recovers, which for Fassbinder means he regains the gift of seeing
things as they are *not*, and in Parts Five and Six, he accepts the cast-off
women of the other major character, Reinhold (Gottfried John), a promiscuous crypto-Fascist gangster at once Franz's best friend and worst
enemy. Reinhold is also Fassbinder's image of the dark side of himself,
an alter ego who bears the same relation to the filmmaker that Travis
Bickle in *Taxi Driver* bore to Martin Scorsese, and Paul Snider in *Star 80*
to Bob Fosse. But there is an element of narcissistic homoeroticism in
Fassbinder that is absent in Scorsese and Fosse, for it is now Reinhold,
and not God, who is the S/M master of Franz's slave, and the erotic
frisson between the two theoretical heterosexuals is extreme. (Albert Camus in *The Stranger*: "Ah, *mon cher*, for anyone who is alone, without
God and without a master, the weight of days is dreadful. Hence, one
must choose a master, God being out of style.") Franz's final girlfriend,
Mieze (Barbara Sukowa), a representation of innocence and purity in a
tradition that goes back to D.W. Griffith's Mae Marsh, hasn't a hope of
surviving in this heavy-leather arena; when she confronts and attempts
to control the evil embodied by Reinhold in a shimmering wood in Part
Twelve, Fassbinder sorrowfully stages her murder with a ravishingly
eerie delicacy that is the summit of his career. But nothing, not even
the death of Mieze, is sufficient to diminish Franz's masochism: a title
repeatedly states he loves two people, "One is Mieze and the other is
—Reinhold." Franz, the masochist, has no self-definition in the absence
of his sadist, a point clarified when Reinhold and Franz slug it out in a
boxing ring in the ninety-minute, surreal epilogue ("My Dream of Franz
Biberkopf's Dream") that concludes the heretofore conventional narrative of *Berlin Alexanderplatz*. The epilogue parodies Hans-Jürgen

Syberberg and pays homage to Pasolini; it also revives and expands an abattoir metaphor from *In a Year of Thirteen Moons* in which cattle were equated with humanity, but this time Fassbinder himself, eyes hidden by dark glasses, solemnly witnesses the evisceration of non-metaphorical humans. The bemused smile that Bogarde adopted watching himself en-act gamy sexual psychodramas in *Despair* is gone; the games are by now real, matters of life and death, and Fassbinder's expression recalls the dictum of Spinoza: "Not to laugh, not to lament, not to curse, but to understand." Understanding is as close to redemption as Fassbinder could imagine, as close to heaven as he would allow.

And then, immediately following the sublime, there was the ridiculous: *Lili Marleen*, Fassbinder's audacious bid to wed the kitsch of Hollywood and Nazism in his own Anaheim-on-the-Rhine. In the end he knew he had failed, and when he accompanied the picture, the fictionalized story of the singer Lale Andersen (impersonated as a Teutonic Lana Turner by Schygulla) to Montreal, he insisted that the brand-new and as yet unsub-titled print of *Lola* be screened in simultaneous translation. "*Lili Marleen* is a stage in my development," he explained. "I wanted a second film here to show that it was only a stage and that I have developed past it." The original *Lili Marleen* was shot in English, but the line readings were so maladroit the American distributor had the soundtrack re-recorded in German (the same procedure would be followed with *Querelle*)—a pity, in that the English version at least accentuated Fassbinder's goal of unit-ing the excesses of UFA and MGM.

What he failed to do in *Lili Marleen* he achieved in *Veronika Voss*, a film that is four things (at minimum): the conclusion of the iconoclastic trilogy; a crystalline black and white remake of *Sunset Boulevard*; a re-telling and critique of Christianity's central myth; and a melodramatic biography of the actress Sybille Schmitz, who had been a star for UFA before and during the Second World War and who died a drug addict in the fifties. The film opens with a prologue at the height of the actress's career—she is in a vehicle entitled *Creeping Poison* and her on-screen character is begging for an injection. "I have nothing to give you but my death," the woman pleads piteously to her pusher. Cut to the film's present, 1955: Voss (Rosel Zech) has been forgotten when a sports reporter, Robert Krohn (Hilmar Thate), meets her one rainy evening, looks into her life, and discovers that the fiction of *Creeping Poison* has become fact. Voss is in the thrall of an unscrupulous physician, a lesbian named Katz (as usual, no minority is spared) who numbers among her other clients an aged and "darling" Jewish couple, camp survivors and drug addicts, who quip of the Germans, "They are polite these days, but it's still no reason to forgive them everything.'' Katz runs a white-on-white clinic where pop music from the American-operated armed forces radio station is a constant reminder of Germany's loss (''They've colonialized our subconscious,'' a character in Wenders's 1976 *Kings of the Road* grumbled of Top 40 tunes) and where one of Katz's cronies in crime is a black American soldier (it's a blessing he's not also a midget —and gay and lame). Fassbinder's summation of consumer society has never been harsher and his attraction to death has never been stronger. ''It must be strange to die,'' the actress conjectures, then corrects herself, ''Nonsense, life is just as strange.'' When Katz determines that Voss can no longer afford the price of ''happiness'' (morphine), a going-away party is planned at which she sings ''Memories Are Made of This''; while the camera circles the room, the faces of Voss's disciples and betrayers, past and present, are systematically framed—this is The Last Supper in an obsidian deep-freeze, a fête surrounding a savior who can save nothing, a canonical rite (the German title translates as *The Passion of Veronika Voss*) for a saint whose face is both a pristine porcelain death-mask repulsive in its resignation and a radiant icon flush with a rush of morphine. Voss dies horribly on Good Friday, ending Fassbinder's death-deifying pageant, a ''passion'' draped in jewels and makeup and mirrors and melodrama—Stations of the Gloss. His history of postwar Germany snaps shut, embalmed in an icy ode to extinction. *Veronika Voss* is the glistening product of a love affair consummated in a coffin.

''When I met him, I was sure he was going to die soon, though I didn't think it would be so soon,'' Laurent Malet, one of the stars of *Querelle*, said. ''He was working fifteen hours a day and freaking out the rest of the time. He was addicted to work much more than to any drug; he could not spend a day without work, he was always saying, 'I will do this, and I will do this . . . if I live long enough.' He was very lonely, very scared of being alone, and I think the only way for him not to be alone was to work. His lifestyle was decadent but he was not himself decadent. *Querelle*, I think, is the one movie at the center of his work.'' It is, and it isn't: it is the one film in which the psychosexuality that elsewhere serves as a locomotive entrusted with a varied cargo revolts and deserts the train. *Querelle* is out of control, but Fassbinder knew what he wanted and what he was getting, according to Malet: ''Each day he would screen for us— Brad Davis, Franco Nero, Jeanne Moreau, me, whoever was there—what had already been shot, but these were not rushes. As he went along, the movie was put together, edited, so as we watched, it came together. He finished shooting on Saturday and the rough cut, edited, was ready by the following Tuesday. It was amazing.''

As imagined by Fassbinder, Genet's fantastical seaport of Brest is a phallotocracy—the enormous statues of penises that adorn the set are merely the most unmistakable indicators of the film's operative principle. The gorgeous sailor Querelle (the American actor Brad Davis inappropriately suggests a chesty elf in the role) packs Franz and Reinhold into the selfsame narcissistic sex machine, a strutting masochist who submits sexually to other men and regains his dominance through murder—and who finds that in being fucked by other men, he has magically become a manlier man. (There are sadists who suspect the masochists they ostensibly dominate in fact control them.) Querelle is the fantasy apotheosis of the masochist, the passive-aggressor borne into a heaven of self-sufficiency where S and M unite. But for the devotee of this most demanding and rigid of sexual disciplines, there is only one such heaven: the grave. The ritual is tolerant of role-switching, but of role amalgamation —never. That would be . . . *normal*. As a testament to Fassbinder's search for an unreachable unity, the film is problematic in more ways than one. What is strongest in Genet's novel, the language, can't be filmed, and what is accessible to cinema, the crude and cruel melodramatic posturing, the unremitting sadomasochism, is already extreme enough to be read as a parody of Fassbinder. Both Genet and Fassbinder were concerned with the links between sex, dominance, and society, but Genet was withal a romantic and an acolyte of the cathartic powers of physical violence. Fassbinder was never a romantic and his belief in the efficacy of violence as catharsis was nonexistent. Despite everything, Fassbinder ploughed into Genet, forsaking his own intelligence as he did so, and he remained remarkably faithful to the alien vision. But the substitutes he devised for Genet's mythopoeic language—chunks of narration (as awkward as those in *Berlin Alexanderplatz* were eloquent), interruptions of the action by titles (quotes from Plutarch, from Genet), frieze-like compositions (who would have thought Fassbinder would imitate the Fellini of *Satyricon*?), a Sparkle Plenty lighting plot (even dirt gleams), an unexpectedly unsuccessful Peer Raben score (snatches of everything from Penderecki to Porter), and thoroughly silly casting (there is a mustachioed mannequin on screen where Franco Nero is reputed to be)—were pitifully inadequate compensations. And for the first time in a major work by Fassbinder, there is open approval of those who identify with the aggressor; heretofore, corruption was regrettable, if unavoidable; it was understood but not condoned. In *Querelle* it is celebrated. "The thing I admire in them," Querelle remarks of the corrupt of Brest, "is their stature, their power, their authority *over* moral authority." He is speaking for Fassbinder: in *Querelle* Fassbinder, the proud anarchist, no longer recoils from the lash of authority or the shackles of debasement. "Life is pessimistic in the end because we die, and pessimistic in between because of the corruption of our daily lives," he said around the time of *Veronika Voss*, but he continued to argue until *Querelle* that what saved him from total pessimism, not to mention corruption, was his revulsion at the way things were. He thought his relentless need to expose reality kept him honest, and his matchless dedication to the art of the exposé obviously allowed him an occasional and precarious but nonetheless authentic state of esthetic grace. ("At least," said Maria Braun, "if you know you're unhappy, there's hope.") *Querelle* is—tries to be—a "happy," lyric film: it exposes nothing and sanctions everything, and it submerges Fassbinder's intellectual precision in the depths of Genet's turbid adoration of homicidal bullies. In falling over the spiny altar of Genet's words, Fassbinder eviscerated himself; the notoriously anti-altruistic iconoclast left behind as his final word a film that was an act of self-abnegation, after all. At the end of his life, Fassbinder found in Genet a master and he attempted desperately to become his slave, to deliver himself up as a victim to the authority he had spent so many years eluding and deriding. In giving everything to Genet—in giving everything, he must have thought, to his art—he paradoxically annihilated that art. In giving the sum of the energy he owned (and the sum of the energy he could borrow from drugs) to filmmaking—in giving everything, he must have thought, to his craft—he paradoxically annihilated the possibility of continuing to practice that craft. And then—there no longer being any distinction between his life, his art, and his craft—he annihilated himself.

The Jes Folks Factory:
Dolly Parton's Texas

"I'm from New Jersey but I like Texas," says the guy played by Dom De Luise in *The Best Little Whorehouse in Texas*. "It suits my style." (The way he really says it is like this: "Ahm from New Jersey but Ah lahk Texas, it sooots muh style.") And Hollywood likes Texas, too, it likes it a heap, and for a couple of days in Austin, where you can find the L.B.J. library and the bar where Janis Joplin hung out, Hollywood's been throwin' a party just about larger than anybody in these parts can recollect, a Hollywood fiesta thrown Texas-style, and that's about as big and berserk as life on earth is ever gonna get.

Day One, Part One
Out to Shepler's Western Wear, they're all agog. Jim Nabors, who's makin' his movie debut in *Whorehouse*, has been tryin' on boots. Shepler's is a humungous place, and they've got everything from cowboy boots on keychains that cost less than five bucks to ostrich-skin cowboy boots that cost more'n a thousand. Jim is real friendly out to Shepler's, real down home. He says, "Goll-eee!" just like Gomer Pyle, then he laughs at himself. ("That Gomer's over there laffin' at hisself!" says one of the help.) Jim's takin' his time 'bout things, givin' everybody a chance to get a good look at a real star. ("That Gomer's goin' slower'n a snail on a freezer door," says one of the help.) Jim says he's been doin' Burt Reynolds's dinner theater down in Florida with Florence Henderson, he's been doin' *The Music Man*, and he's livin' in Hawaii on a ranch where he's planted an orchard of macadamia nuts. "I'm plannin' on my nuts takin' care of me in my old age," he giggles, high-pitched, jes like a girl. He says he don't have a radio or a TV out here in Hawaii and he don't miss Hollywood none but he does love Gomer Pyle, always has and always will, and he says Gomer's "the nicest guy I ever met." There's a guy in Shepler's, young guy, wearin' a tank top, showin' biceps and tattoos, and Jim squeezes the guy's muscles like he was testin' ripe fruit, and then he says, "Nice arms." He don't buy no boots, though.

Day One, Part Two

Out to the Austin airport, all hell's fit to break loose. Dolly Parton and Burt Reynolds are comin' in.

"You seen Dolly yet?" the boy at the Hertz counter hog-hollers to the boy at the Avis counter.

Avis ain't seen her yet. "But I'm on the lookout," he says.

"She'll be hard to miss," Hertz yahoos, movin' his hands in front of him like he's turnin' the knobs on a giant TV set—over the next little while there's gonna be more Dolly Parton bosom jokes than there are tits on a pig, an' Dolly'll tell a mess of 'em herself. But right now they gotta get Dolly and Burt out to the house that played the whorehouse in the movie—it's out near Pflugerville, home of the Pflugerville Pflyers—where Austin Mayor Carole McCellan, a jolly fat gal with bad skin, is hostin' a barbecue, nouveau-Texas style. There's ribs drippin' with sauce, and there's avocado stuffed with an embarrassin' amount of li'l black fish eggs, and there's deep-fried chili peppers hotter'n hell's backroom, and there's fresh watermelon colder'n a repossession. Folks at this shindig paid $500 a head just to be part of it all. Country singer Jerry Reed, who's got a grin wider'n the Texas plains, and who's gonna call Burt Reynolds "my main man" so many times durin' the next few days it's gonna remind folks of Sammy Davis Jr. and Frank Sinatra, is up on a stage near the house rehearsin'. Everybody's eatin' everything in sight, not payin' Jerry Reed much mind, when Burt and Dolly drive up in a limo longer'n time on a hot day, and all hell *does* break loose. Burt and Dolly are loved down here like nothin' this side of Southern Comfort— these oil-rich Texans in their $350 Domingo Goat Lucchese cowboy boots turn right into star-struck teenagers, squeakin' with excitement, and when Burt and Dolly head on up to the stage, you can hear the roar they let out all the way to Tulsa. Jerry Reed has been rehearsin' for hours, seems like, and has been pickier'n anything about everything. He stops in the middle of his first number cuz he says his guitar's outta tune. "Who's he think he is?" grunts a good ol' boy who's been East, "Teresa Stratas?" Dolly ain't picky. Burt introduces her by sayin', "She's workin' her way up here, she'll be here long before she gets here," then Dolly introduces Jim Nabors, then some problem or other keeps Jerry Reed from comin' back up on stage like he's supposed to. "I don't want to stand up here lookin' stupid," Dolly tells the folks, "I'd rather stand up here and *sound* stupid," so she sings a rough, blister-makin' "Rocky Top" with Reed's pickers. Still no Jerry. So Jim sings "Your Cheatin' Heart" an Dolly comes in singin' backup with a sound sweeter'n honey on a bun.

"Do you wanna foller that?" Dolly turns and asks the air where Jerry Reed should be.

Day Two, Part One
At seven in the A.M. Austin's main drag, Congress Avenue, is already blocked off. The parade before the world premiere of *The Best Little Whorehouse in Texas* won't start until five in the P.M. It's already hot —it's gonna be more'n a hundred today. Lookin' out the window at the folks plannin' to barbecue hours and hours for a glimpse of Burt and Dolly, the headwaiter at the Driskill Hotel, where Burt and Dolly are holed up, says, "Ah think it's downright ridiculous. It goes to show ya how bad times have got that people need somethin' like this to take their minds off their troubles."

Day Two, Part Two
By the time the parade starts up, thousands of people wantin' to forget their troubles are cheerin' as the South West Texas Marching Band and the South West Texas Strutters, Rockettes in Stetsons, go by. Amanda Blake, Miss Kitty on "Gunsmoke," allows as how she knew Burt would be a star even as far back as his "Gunsmoke" days. Cactus Prior, a local media celeb, introduces Miss Kitty, singer Mel Tillis, and a pile of politicians, up to and includin' Governor William Clements. "You notice how the right side of the street is applaudin' more loudly for the Governor?" Cactus crows. Governor Clements is a famous man, famous for tryin' his damndest to get Texas cops unlimited wire-tap privileges. He keeps tellin' everybody he's not the governor who caused the Chicken Ranch (the real-life whorehouse the movie whorehouse is based on) to be shut down, 'long about 1975. The governor who did that was not re-elected. The Chicken Ranch had been in La Grange, Texas, for years and years—it could've catered to your daddy and to your daddy's daddy, all the way back before the First World War. When Dolly and Burt reach the front of the theater, comin' along in the parade in big white Caddies, Cactus asks the crowd not to "surge." Maybe Cactus has seen *The Day of the Locust*. Don't matter none, cuz if he has or he hasn't, either way that's what this afternoon is like, a little bit, Nathaniel West with a drawl. Governor Wiretap gives a speech, a long one, about makin' Texas a film center, and some folks pass right out from all the heat, but that don't stop him, he just keeps tricklin' right along, like a no-account crick 'bout to dry up. Burt finds some lookers out in the crowd and puckers up at 'em and they 'bout faint from two kinds of heat.

Day Three, Part One

Burton Leon Reynolds, at this minute the world's most popular male entertainer accordin' to some poll or other, is givin' interviews. An ostrich-skin cowboy boot, just like one of the ones at Shepler's, is resting real casual-like on its mate, and he's saying, "I think we've become a bunch of people interested in a bunch of crap." But he doesn't mean the crowd that roasted all day yesterday—he doesn't mean for a minute that bein' interested in Burt and Dolly is "crap." What he means is that some people are interested in the wrong things about Burt and Dolly. They're interested in private things.

Now it's good to remember before Burt gets goin' on all this that Burt is the same guy who was once on "The Tonight Show." He was on with Judy Carne, who'd once been one of Burt's girls. Burt was the guest host of "The Tonight Show." He was goin' with Dinah Shore at the time and everybody knew it.

"Going with anybody?" Burt asked Judy Carne.

"Yes," she said.

"A younger guy?" he said.

"Yes, Burt, you know me," she said, then she gave him a look, real slow-like, and said, "I hear you've gone older."

And this is the same Burt who put his long-limbed furriness in *Cosmopolitan*. This is the same Burt who talked about a lot of his romances to Johnny and Merv. But there is also another Burt, a real person, not a star, the Burt who's the half-Cherokee, half-Italian son of a police chief, the balding Burt with the nickname "Buddy," the hungry kid from south Florida. ("Hunger," Burt says, looking at his taffy-colored thousand-buck boots, "has nothing to do with money.") This Burt is a kid still easy to hurt. This Burt is hurt that *Playboy* printed an article by Larry King, co-author of *Whorehouse*, that compared LBJ's ego to Burt's and gave Burt's the edge. But Burt turned a cheek. Then King published a whole book, *The Whorehouse Papers*, that expanded the *Playboy* piece. Burt turned the other cheek. Then Burt came to Austin and the local rag, on the very week of the premiere, started up a six-part series of excerpts from the book. And Burt finally blew up. "What I said was that I wanted to hit Larry King so hard his parents would die." Burt looks rueful. "When I say something humorous it has a way of flattening out on the page. I'm embarrassed I acted the way I did. I lowered myself to a high-school level, which is exactly what he wanted. Mr. King is a kind of Addison Dewitt in cowboy boots. I made a star out of him. It hasn't been a real happy experience for me, down in Texas."

It don't get no better, neither. At his press conference, somebody asks why the newspapers would print there was trouble on the set if there wasn't any, like the stars say. "You are incredibly naive," Burt growls, and goes on to allege that major newspapers pay crew members for gossip. "Rona Barrett used to have people like that, union members working for $200 a tip, on every film, and most newspapers do." (This is not true. Most newspapers do not pay for any kind of news. And most newspapers certainly do not pay for news about the shenanigans on movie sets.) "Nobody bothers to check up on the tips. We have gone from the *National Enquirer* to *People*, which is for people who can't read the *National Enquirer*—*People* is only pictures—to where there is gossip in reputable newspapers such as the *Los Angeles Herald Examiner*, and they don't check. The most popular section of our major newsmagazine, *Time*, is the People section. Carol Burnett wins a suit against the *Enquirer*, but the circulation, and the circulation of all the smut peddlers, goes up. In twenty years, all I think we're going to have in print is that kind of stuff. Why? I think people *like* sitting on the john reading the *National Enquirer*. People actually come up to me in airports and ask me to sign it. *Rolling Stone* loves to attack, murder and destroy anything that seems in any way commercial, square, Americana. I've turned them down seventeen times for an interview, so they're waiting in the weeds for me."

Day Three, Part Two

Sooner or later, everything's gonna be written about the way Dolly Parton looks, and she's writ a lot of it herself. (She once said, "The public thinks I'm a joke, but the joke's on the public.") On her newest albums, she's peekin' out, smilin', like to say: "My, ain't I a big girl, though! and ain't this silly?" On *The Best of Dolly Parton* she's against a red background in a spangly, buttery pantsuit, smilin' innocent as the honeysuckle that grows near the homestead down in Georgia, and her torso's swivelled to the right. Profiled. She looks like the front end of a canary yellow 1959 Cadillac. She looks like Jayne Mansfield, the girl who couldn't help it. She looks like Diana Dors. Fact is, she looks like a parody of the way a lot of women looked in the fifties. Fact is, there's nothin' at all original about the way Dolly looks, except that nobody else wants to look like that now, except maybe a drag queen.

"Hi y'all!" she hoots. She's standin' in a room at the Driskill and she's tiny as can be; she's planted both feet wide apart in stilettos that look like baby booties on little stilts, high heels on a midget party girl, and she's cinched her silver lamé belt tighter on a waist no bigger around'n a beer can, and she's took a deep breath and pointed herself toward the door, comin' at ya, like to say: "Why beat around the bust?" She gets goin' on 'bout how she's got too fat, but she says, "The legs're still good," and she hikes her skirt right on up to the very top of her thigh with the flirt of a little girl just walkin' around the playground at recess time with her dress over her head. "See?" Absolutely. The legs are real fine.

The meetin' with Dolly is not at all like the meetin' with Burt. One complains, the other doesn't. The shock of meetin' Burt is that he's not very funny and that he can be petulant—leastways on this Texas trip. The shock of meetin' Dolly is that she's what she's always said she was —shrewd, sexy, ambitious. ("It's *nice* ambition," Jim gurgles in the Gomer voice.) Dolly knows why she does what she does and she doesn't get real complicated about it. "It's a desire to be loved," she says. (Norman Jewison, who directed the Oscar show the year Reagan was shot, tells this story about Dolly. She was on stage rehearsin' *Nine to Five* when Jewison got word of the assassination attempt. "Dolly, Dolly!" he said, cuttin' off the rehearsal, "the President's been shot." Dolly put both hands on her hips and said, "Well, Ah didn't do it!") Dolly always has a lot to say, and here's a sampler of quotations from chairperson Parton writ down during one hour in Austin:

On the raunchiness of *The Best Little Whorehouse* script: "I was afraid it might offend my people. My granddaddy is a preacher. I read the script to my granddaddy and my mom and they both laughed a lot. My granddaddy said, 'If God can forgive you, so can I.' "

On God: "I feel like I have a good communication with God. I'm not sayin' I'm anything extra because of it. He gets all the credit for the good things I do, so sometimes when I screw up, I ask him why He let me do it."

Relaxing with her husband: "We like to camp out and stay in cheap hotels."

How she manages to get into those cheap hotels without being recognized: "I look cheap when I go there."

Wanting to be a movie star: "I didn't. I didn't grow up with the movies. I was more impressed with trash and *True Confessions* magazines."

Trash: "I was influenced by the trash in my own home town. I felt I looked like trash. I wanted to look like trash. I was the most popular girl in my high school, for all the wrong reasons. The teachers thought the way I looked was tacky and the girls' mothers didn't want their daughters to run with me. Funny thing was, I didn't do anything, and those girls were screwin' everybody.''

Getting down: "When you do as much as I do, you leave yourself wide open to every emotion. I do get depressed. But I don't have a depressed nature, except one time when I was having female and hormonal trouble. I get depressed but I will not allow myself the luxury of wallerin' in it. You gotta work at bein' happy like you work at bein' sad. You gotta work out what's makin' you unhappy, then get the hell out of there.''

Bosom humor: "My frank reaction is, I play it up, so I deserve it. It's made me a lot of money. It doesn't bother me unless it's like, well, once on Merv Griffin, he couldn't seem to get to nuthin' but the boobs. So I said, 'I do have a brain beneath this hair and a heart beneath these boobs.' ''

Dolly Parton look-alike contests: "Boy, some of the hogs that come through there! It's like a livestock show a lot of times.''

Stardom: "Superstardom to me is continuin' to do what I'm doin'. I just want to be loved.''

Weaknesses: "Shoes are the thing I spend most money on. And makeup. I buy everything on the market.''

Working without wigs and makeup: "I would, I would do it. I'd have to be blonde, but I'd work with my own hair. My feeling about makeup is, you can have a good barn, and if you paint it, it looks a little better, but if you take the paint off, it's still a good barn.''

Country music: "I'm partial to the old country sound, but if you're gonna make a livin' in this business, you gotta do what you gotta do.''
An unreleased album with Emmylou Harris and Linda Ronstadt: "It just wasn't good enough.''

Broadway: "I'm workin' on a play I'd like to see on Broadway. But I wouldn't want to do it a long time. I get bored at sit-down jobs.''

Burt's nemesis, the *National Enquirer*: "I have to say I like it. What they print about me is bull, but all those stories—"I was Trapped in a Tank For Fourteen Years!''—it's fascinatin' stuff.''

On Dolly: "I feel real safe in myself. That's because of God; I can lay the burdens on somebody else. I wouldn't change a thing about my life.''

Day Two, Part Three
At the world premiere of *Whorehouse*, right after the parade, everybody

laughs and claps. Dolly is real good, and she has a sorrowin' tune, "I Will Always Love You" (a sorta "My Man" with Hawaiian guitars) that's a killer, and Burt's little duet with Dolly is purty cute, and Charles Durning does a dance step, "The Side Step," that brings down the house for real, not just for polite, and Jim Nabors is so soft and gentle up there on the silvered screen he could be a stuffed toy. Dolly has to say in the movie she dreamt of bein' a ballet dancer but gave it up cuz if she jumped up and down, "I'd black both my eyes." Burt has to say, "Jesus was a real good man and a heck of a speaker." There's an endin' tacked on to the real endin'—the love 'tween Dolly and Burt has no place to go but o-u-t after he closes her cathouse up—and the tacked-on endin' is a crowd-pleasin' endin', which means individuals are too smart to fall for it but mobs just might.

After the world premiere, Burt and Dolly and members of the $500 club go off to the Hyatt Regency for a "Supper with the Stars." Jerry Reed introduces "my best friend." Burt say he thinks he sang better'n Marlon Brando did in *Guys and Dolls*. Dolly, lookin' back on *Nine to Five* and on up to *Whorehouse*, says "I think I made a better whore than I did a secretary." When Burt has an emotional reunion with Miss Kitty, who is nowadays a fairly elderly party, and Miss Kitty mouths from the floor to the banquet hall to the big stars at the head table, "You look great!", Dolly chirrups, "You look good, too. You look better all the time. Miss Kitty lives forever!" Dolly and Burt sign autograph books. Dolly says, "I hope you liked the picture and if you didn't, I don't want to hear about it." Cathy Lee Crosby, who does a TV show of some description, is hangin' around in a black and yellow dress—if Dolly wore it, it'd ruin her image—and is nuzzlin' up to some good-lookin' drink of water. Outside the hotel, dozens of folks with Instamatics are waitin' for the stars to finish supper. Security guards are high and low. It's almost midnight, and it's still hot. The stars are eatin' oysters with spinach, anisette and rock salt; they're eatin' shrimp and squid and fettucine; they're eatin' almond mousse. Burt is in a silky, tight black tux—it has a crotch on it like a pair of nylon swimmin' trunks—and Dolly is in a mustard cowgirl outfit with more gold to it than a block of pavin' stones in heaven. (For Dolly, a gilded lily is just a good start.) Out front, the folks are eatin' too—munchin' warm apples and glurpy candy-bars, and they're wearin' T-shirts and cutoffs, and most of 'em have powerful awful sunburns, like they washed in red raspberry juice, and some of 'em are reading the *National Enquirer*. A bunch of 'em give up and go home, they're plumb tuckered out from all that standin', all day and now half the night. They're sorry to give up, though.

"Lordy, I wanted to see that purty li'l Dolly just one more time," says a blue-headed lady in a beehive that looks like a cone of wrong-colored cotton candy at a state fair. "I do love that Dolly, I love her voice all right, but I do love 'specially her hair. I'd love to work on her wigs, I tell ya!"

An almost teenaged security guard, pullin' his hat back off bangs that stick to his sweaty forehead like a mess of soggy spaghetti, comes on over. "They're jes folks," he says, "like you and me. But they got lots more money than you and me. Who cares about 'em?"

"I do," the cotton candy woman says, lookin' offended. "They're good people and they worked for what they've got, 'specially Burt. He's done some fool things, but I think he's gettin' smarter. I really think he is." She looks at her watch. "Tarnation, y'all gotta excuse me, I gotta get up 'n' go to work in the mornin'." The pimply kid security guard wants to know what the cotton-candy lady does for work. "Well, I'm real lucky, I got a good job at a beauty parlor, I'm a beautician, and it's just the right size. We got the nicest regular customers you ever did see. I thank God every day for my good fortune." She gives the kid the old up 'n' down, real motherly-like. "Wouldn't hurt you to do the same, honey," she says, pattin' his cheek.

July 1982

The Burnout Factory:
Canada's Hollywood

Prologue and Epilogue: December 15, 1980
Prime Minister Pierre Trudeau, in black tie, a blood-red rose ever so slightly wilted on his satin jacket collar, looked pensive. A journalist had gestured toward the ballroom at Toronto's Four Seasons Hotel, the scene of Canada's most elegant and expensive movie premiere party to date. As usual, the party was better than the movie to which it paid tribute, which was *Tribute*. Taking in the furs, the diamonds, the hairdos, the journalist had commented, "Your government is in some sense responsible for all this." The prime minister smiled. "It's amazing what a few tax laws can do," he said. Then he added, with a shrug, "There are now many Canadian films. But there aren't too many good ones, are there?"

In fifteen words, Trudeau not only summed up the state of the Canadian film industry, he also implied that the Canadian Film Development Corporation, charged with creating a film industry in Canada, and the Film Festivals Bureau, charged with promoting that industry, were less than truthful. For months, they had been telling the world that Canada was the Australia of North America. And now the man whose government had made an unprecedented movie-production boom possible— by allowing passage, in 1978, of a liberalized tax-shelter law for film investment—was joining the critics. A year after the offhand comments at the *Tribute* party, the Trudeau government would announce substantial revisions to the tax-shelter law—revisions clearly designed to control what had become a flood of con men, carpetbaggers, and some folks with real ability (such as Louis Malle) to the "Hollywood of the North." From 1979 to 1981, a staggering one hundred and thirty feature films were financed in Canada (compared with fifteen a year in the mid-seventies); as 1981 drew to a close, almost half had yet to see theatrical release.

The future of the industry in Canada remains uncertain. What is beyond doubt is that the government is determined not to repeat the wildest weeks of the past few years—weeks when movies where being made from coast to coast, when second-rate American stars were being paid fabulous sums to appear in disaster films shot "entirely on location in Montreal," when inexperienced producers sent the negative and only print of a $5-million picture through the luggage system of a commercial airline, when to comply with government regulations Canadian personnel were listed in movie credits while the real jobs went to Americans, when Dennis Hopper would say, "Canada's a positive place, maybe I'll move there," and when Canadian actress Colleen Dewhurst, disgusted by it all, would recall her first day on the set of a thriller fittingly entitled *Final Assignment*. "It was supposed to be in Russia," Dewhurst said in her inimitable growl. "I walked up and fingered the set. It wiggled. I was to perform in front of a *cardboard Kremlin*. Dear God, I knew then we were in trouble. It was another Canadian film that was supposed to fool the audience into thinking it was an American film. We Canadians are *people*. Surely our stories are as universal as French or German stories."

Dewhurst's complaint has been the most common criticism of the New Canadian Cinema—that there *is* no New Canadian Cinema, that there is instead a New American Cinema on Canadian soil. The Australians make movies about and usually with Australians. The Canadians make movies about and often with Americans. *Middle Age Crazy*, starring Bruce Dern, was set in a Toronto disguised as Houston, and *The Changeling*, starring George C. Scott, was set in a Vancouver disguised as Seattle. A continual, cavalier disregard of their topography, not to mention their culture, infuriates many Canadians.

Outfitting New York as Paris on a movie set might not bother Americans, but Americans, insecure about so much, are not insecure about their identity. The very definition of Canadian identity, however, is that it is too insecure to be defined. And Canadians have noticed that the quality films of other countries do not go out of their way to grossly curry favor with the Americans. The filmmakers of Italy do not seem terrified that a film with an Italian locale will be dismissed out of hand by an American audience merely for being *set* in Italy. But Canadian producers were convinced, for a time, that American audiences would bolt from the theater should the words Winnipeg or Toronto or Ottawa fall from actor's lips, save in jest; Canadian designations were permitted only when used as representations of the names of impossible, colorful, comic places.

Roots I: The Old New Wave

Canadian cinema—what there was of it—came into the seventies carrying naught but goodwill. John Grierson had made the National Film Board the toast of the civilized cinematic world, and animator Norman

McLaren was its in-house saint. It was true, as writer Robert Fulford remarked to critic Martin Knelman, that "English-speaking Canadians grew up believing they would eventually *graduate* from Canada. Real things happened elsewhere." But it was also true that Canadians were trying to understand the reasons for that phenomenon and that in so doing they would soon release a remarkable series of films. At the end of the sixties and in the early seventies, there were, for example, Don Shebib's *Goin' Down the Road*, about two hicks in the big city of Toronto, and Claude Jutra's *Mon oncle Antoine*—widely thought to be the greatest Canadian film ever made, a study of a mining town seen through the eyes of a child, a politicized version of *The 400 Blows*.

Goin' Down the Road and *Mon oncle Antoine* were the strongest examples of the new wave; strength to Canadians meant that the Jutra and Shebib films opened in New York to good reviews. But there were others. William Fruet's *Wedding in White*, with the then unknown Carol Kane as a pathetic child-woman trapped in a Second World War prairie town, was one of them. Today Fruet, who also wrote *Goin' Down the Road*, directs horror movies of execrable quality (*Death Weekend, Cries in the Night*, the forthcoming *Death Bite*). In 1972, Gilles Carle's *La vraie nature de Bernadette* contained the dazzling debut of Micheline Lanctôt. Today, after embarrassing himself with *Fantastica*, a self-indulgent ecological musical that mercifully vanished after opening the 1980 Cannes Film Festival, Carle has returned to prominence with *Les Plouffe*. Derived from a popular novel of a French Canadian family, it has been made into no fewer than three popular movie editions (and Canadians are not an extravagant people)—one for Quebec, one for English Canada, and one for an international audience.

Allan King's 1969 cinéma vérité record of *A Married Couple*, ninety-seven minutes in the bickering lives of Billy and Antoinette Edwards, anticipated *An American Family*. Today King is the director of Ellen Burstyn's *Silence of the North*, an inept paean to a pioneer women, and a box-office flop. Don Owen in 1964 directed *Nobody Waved Good-bye* —"Marvelous," wrote Brendan Gill in *The New Yorker*. Today Owen has become a sadly familiar fixture in Toronto, reduced to talking about projects he may never be allowed to realize. In 1970 Paul Almond caused nationwide controversy with *Act of the Heart*, in which Geneviève Bujold set herself aflame to protest the way we were. Today Almond is famous as the director of *Final Assignment*, which is famous for its cardboard Kremlin.

Most of the old new wave came to grief, on the beach. The reasons are various, most traceable to money, the rest to bad timing. After the surge in the early seventies, directors were left without outlets, unless they wished to work for the National Film Board or the Canadian Broadcasting Corporation. The days of independent shoestring movies were all but over. By the end of the decade, when tax-shelter productions were going strong, it had been years since many of the old guard had worked. But their services were frantically sought, and they were perplexed recipients of big stars and big budgets from producers who often had no experience with either. There were exceptions—Garth Drabinsky, producer of *The Silent Partner, The Changeling*, and *The Amateur*; Denis Héroux and John Kemeny, producers of *Atlantic City* and *Quest for Fire*—but they were of the rule-proving sort.

Worse, in conforming to the demands of "international production," directors who did work under the tax-shelter laws were wrenched from subjects they knew, in order to direct ersatz American product. They were asked to move comfortably in genres and styles hopelessly alien to them. Paul Almond's cinema is personal and mystical—ergo, he is hired to helm an international thriller. Jutra's greatest achievement is the stylized celebration of a specific rural French Canadian milieu; he is therefore restricted to other people's scripts in a language not his own (English). The tax-shelter laws appeared on the surface to be great equalizers: everybody got a chance. It was the exact nature of the chance that was the problem; for some of the old new wave, being given a chance meant you never had one.

Roots II: The New New Wave

In the mid-seventies, two Canadians were busy imitating American movies to commercial, if not esthetic, advantage. Ivan Reitman made something called *Cannibal Girls*. David Cronenberg made *The Parasite Murders* (a.k.a. *Shivers* and *They Came From Within*), which Reitman produced. Then Reitman co-produced *National Lampoon's Animal House* and directed *Meatballs* (the most successful Canadian film of all time). Then Cronenberg directed *Scanners*. Now Cronenberg is completing *Videodrome*, starring Deborah Harry, the ice queen of another kind of new wave.

Back in 1975, Bob Clark made an effectively nasty horror flick, *Black Christmas*—and went on to *Murder by Decree*, with Christopher Plummer as Sherlock Holmes and to that glossy $8-million Jack Lemmon fan letter, *Tribute*. Daryl Duke made *Payday* in the early seventies and *The Silent Partner* in the late seventies.

Ted Kotcheff (*The Apprenticeship of Duddy Kravitz, North Dallas Forty*) and Norman Jewison (*In the Heat of the Night, Jesus Christ Superstar*), proud of being Canadian and prouder still, perhaps, of getting regular work in the United States, became the elder statesman of Canadian film.

One of the upstarts unexpectedly fell short: Richard Benner, the American expatriate who directed *Outrageous!*, the $167,000 Craig Russell picture that in 1977 caused a sensation in both New York and Toronto with its robust profile of an outlandish female impersonator. Benner moved back to New York and brought a version of the Albert Innaurato play *Gemini* to the screen. The result, *Happy Birthday, Gemini!*, was greeted in most quarters as a harbinger of herpes.

Where Were The Youngsters?
Where Were Their Elders?

1. Where one of the elders could be found: a demonstration of what could go wrong in Hollywood of the North.

Claude Jutra was hired by Toronto producer Beryl Fox (who did the Vietnam documentary *Mills of the Gods*) to direct *Surfacing*, based on a novel by Margaret Atwood. The book is in the we-are-the-Swedes-of-North-America tradition of Canadian literature; it is a bleak, allusive, metaphoric interior odyssey in which the unnamed heroine comes to terms (maybe) with her dead father, with the Americans she nationalistically despises, with the land that begat her (the lake country of northern Quebec), and with the land to which she has repaired, the dank terrain of her own self-destructiveness. Imagine *The Bell Jar* in the bush.

Fox hired an American screen writer, Bernard Gordon, best known for *55 Days at Peking*, of all things, to adapt the book. She hired the American actress Kathleen Beller as the Atwood alter ego, and the American actors Timothy Bottoms and his younger brother, Joseph. Canadian actors, who in general respect Fox and the feminism she stands for, were furious—but privately. (When the elder Bottoms dropped out, though, the Canadian R.H. Thomson took over.) Jutra, when it was all over, intimated he was enamored of neither novel nor screenplay; what he did not need to intimate was that he needed the work. When *Surfacing* finally emerged, an intransigently Canadian, intransigently anti-American novel had become an astonishing thing: a film *with* Americans, a film somewhat *by* Americans, and a film almost *for* Americans—a film in which anything that might offend an American audience was carefully excised. (Canadians have yet to recognize a law to which the British have profitably adhered for years: Yanks will queue up for highbrow insults.)

2. Where one of the youngsters could be found: a demonstration of what could go right in Hollywood of the North.

Francis Mankiewicz is a relative of Herman (*Citizen Kane*) Mankiewicz and Joseph (*All About Eve*) Mankiewicz. He is in his early thirties, he lives in Montreal, he is bilingual. He is the director of *Les bons débarras*, a film that won for Marie Tifo the best-actress award at the 1980 Chicago Film Festival and that won virtually every Academy of Canadian Cinema award possible. And it did mighty fine in its New York release.

Les bons débarras is as Canadian as self-doubt. The film, set in a small Quebec town, was written by Réjean Ducharme in a poetic French Canadian patois impossible to translate adequately—consider a Gallic Tennessee Williams by way of Flannery O'Connor. (Mankiewicz was anxious to see John Huston's adaptation of O'Connor's *Wise Blood* and said of Huston's *Fat City*, "It's a perfect Quebec movie.") *Les bons debarras*'s conflict is between a woman (Tifo) having an affair with a cop, and her preternaturally mature thirteen-year-old daughter (Charlotte Laurier). The daughter reads *Wuthering Heights* and greets *mère*'s announcement she is pregnant with, "A baby cop? You make me sick!" The picture was made on a minuscule, $625,000 budget without taking advantage of the tax-shelter laws. Thanks to the expertise and artistry of Mankiewicz and Ducharme, and thanks to the genius of cameraman Michel Brault (director of the galvanizing 1975 documentary *Les ordres*), *Les bons débarras* has become one of the most honored Canadian movies in history.

Why Some Stories Have No Endings, Happy or Otherwise

Mankiewicz was lucky: *Les bons débarras* was distributed. Zale Dalen was not so lucky. He is a Vancouver filmmaker whose first picture, *Skip Tracer*, a tough portrait of a bill collector, has been a staple on the festival circuit. His second film was *The Hounds of Notre Dame*, based on the renowned (in Canada) exploits of Père Athol Murray, who ran a school for boys on the prairies during the Second World War. As stunningly brought to larger-than-life in the film by actor Thomas Peacocke, Murray is a cross between Jean Brodie and Mayor Daley. In accepting his Genie for best actor, Peacocke thanked the cosmos and then noted ironically, "No one's seen the movie." *The Hounds of Notre Dame* opened briefly in western Canada; it has never played Vancouver, Montreal, or Toronto.

Most of those sixty-odd Canadian films that have failed to find distribution are dreck. But as Margo Raport, editor of *Filmworld*, the Canadian trade paper, observes, "They should be sold somewhere. There are all kinds of markets." The federal government's Canadian Film Development Corporation (CFDC), which invests in both commercial and arty films, with an unfortunate emphasis on the former, has been supremely successful at getting movies made. But its mandate is sadly sketchy as to what it can or cannot do once they are in the can; the CFDC refused, for example, to assist in underwriting *Les bons débarras*'s New York opening.

Without Hands: The Post-Tax-Shelter Future

Jean Pierre Lefebvre is Canada's most accomplished filmmaker, director of some twenty features, among them a sympathetic study of an act of high-school vandalism, *Avoir 16 ans*; a look at the commercialization of human emotion by late-night phone-in shows, *L'amour blessé*; and the finest film extant on the subject of Canadian identity, *Le vieux pays où Rimbaud est mort*. Conceptually indebted to Godard, Lefebvre has refined his minimalist technique. *Avoir 16 ans*, his most recent feature, which critic Peter Harcourt has described as combining "the human feeling of Renoir with the formal austerity of Michael Snow," was shot in color in 35 mm. It cost approximately $100,000. "You can make movies for ten people," comments Lefebvre, whose visual essays are admittedly "difficult" and are rarely distributed outside art galleries. "But if you make movies for ten people, they better cost ten bucks."

There are and probably will continue to be funds for films perceived as sure things: for Ralph Thomas's drama about Moonies, *Ticket to Heaven*, which got greater critical and commercial acclaim in New York than anywhere in Canada; for Charles Jarrott's *The Amateur*, a thriller with John Savage filmed in Toronto and Vienna. Nothing else is predictable. Lefebvre's economy works well for him, but the nurturing of a nascent Francis Coppola in Canada is unthinkable right now.

"We are in a third era," Margo Raport says. "The first was pre-tax-shelter, the second was tax-shelter and now we have entered the post-tax-shelter era. That means that new ways of financing will have to be sought, and I think you will see co-ventures with the major studios. The French will be less affected, because they never used the law much. Ironically, they were just getting ready to, but the revisions make it worthless for them. Pay television is going to determine to a large degree the direction of feature production. With Ottawa's Canadian content regulations, at least twenty-five and up to forty new films have to be produced in this country every year for pay television. That's at minimum two a month, in a country of twenty-two million. How?"

There is no answer to Raport's question. The metaphor most often employed for Canada vis-à-vis the United States is of a mouse sleeping next to an elephant: The elephant can move with impunity, but each twitch is for the mouse a potentially life-threatening situation. Many Canadians—French and English—think that the United States' cultural colonization of their nation may be, with the advent of pay television, a fait accompli. The tax-shelter law was seen as a last-ditch effort to create a film industry nearly sixty years too late; for everyone but the producers, the result was a deluge of disappointment.

Shortly before the law was set in place, Pierre Berton looked at the development of Canada's image of itself at the movies. He entitled his witty book *Hollywood's Canada* in recognition of a bizarre paradox: from the twenties on, Canadians bought at American movies an image of themselves that had nothing to do with their own reality. But given the opportunity to bring their disparate experiences to the screen, to engender their own dreams and to immortalize their own mythologies, they opted in most instances for a slavish imitation of American dreams, for a crude approximation of American mythology and its attendant iconography. The recent record of the Canadian film industry might be called *Canada's Hollywood*. (*March 1982*)

Without Minds: The Post-Tax-Shelter Past

Margo Raport was right, but not about pay TV—about television in general. They changed the name of the Canadian Film Development Corporation to Telefilm Canada and that said it all: the new "thrust" would be toward hybrid productions, toward the creation of amphibious monster mutants meant to bask equally well in the lights of two environments, the television tube and the silver screen. The misunderstanding displayed by this policy toward the craft of television, let alone the art of film, was beneath contempt, if not comment. So the sequel to *Les Plouffe* showed up in no less than four failed editions: as a two-hour feature in French and subtitled English, and as a six-hour mini-series in French and dubbed English. Denys Arcand directed the feature, which became the last two hours of the mini-series; the other four hours were directed by Gilles Carle. Said Arcand, "Now the trend is TV. If you don't have a story that will fit neatly into six hours, forget it." Of his labors on two versions of *Joshua Then and Now*, Mordecai Richler said, "I had to write fat and thin at the same time. It's a contradiction. For the television series, I had to extend a scene beyond its natural length. I don't think it's going to work very well. It will be destructive to both TV and film. You will have ersatz versions of both."

There were suprisingly few films shot for pay TV, which turned out to have a more circumscribed future than anyone had predicted. One of the successes, the winner of the 1984 best-picture Genie (it beat *The Wars*), was *The Terry Fox Story*, produced by Robert Cooper for Home Box Office. Cooper affected shock and indignation when the film failed in Canada, the country it was about and the only country in which it was theatrically released. How dumb did Cooper suppose Canadians to be? They knew the film had been made for TV and they knew where they could see it free in a few months. Besides: they knew how it came out. *The Terry Fox Story* opened in every second theater across Canada on Friday, May 27, 1983—it opened in *four times* as many theaters as did the other moderately well-known film that premiered the same day, an adventure flick called *The Return of the Jedi*. Directed by *Ticket to Heaven*'s Ralph Thomas, *The Terry Fox Story* was a gritty look at the reality behind the press clippings of the Marathon of Hope undertaken by the kid from Vancouver with the athlete's muscles and the cupid's curls, the kid who lost his leg and then his life to cancer. In trying to explain Terry Fox, the media, the Great Explainers, had rendered him inexplicable: they had transformed an alternately angry and tranquil, frightened and courageous, self-centered and compassionate, manipulative and ingenuous kid—a dying boy—into a living doll. The film, starring amputee Eric Fryer, reversed the process: in cutting the kid down to size, it returned the myth to the land of the living and paradoxically increased the boy's heroic stature. ("Terry's real heroism," Fryer, himself a cancer victim, confided to his director, "was not running across Canada, it was going back to take chemotherapy a second time.") But the marketing of the movie was insane: treating it as a preordained blockbuster and opening it in every shopping mall guaranteed that it would look like a failure. Even if every theater had attracted a substantial audience—*Jedi*'s audience —the auditoriums would have remained half-full and the picture would have continued to carry the taint of failure. (*Gandhi* and *Chariots of Fire* originally opened in one theater each in Toronto, guaranteeing line-ups and the appearance of a hit.) Cooper complained one morning on the record about the mistakes, but when the story appeared in *The Globe and Mail* he telephoned angrily and announced, "You've killed the film." How? "You've made it look like a failure." Prime Minister Trudeau meanwhile snubbed the opening of *The Terry Fox Story*; the ingrate was photographed taking his children to *The Return of the Jedi*.

Sandra Gathercole, the most consistent and intelligent critic the government's various film policies have had, wrote in 1984 that "pay television and the one-hundred-percent Capital Cost Allowance have come and gone as the great white hopes for financing Canadian production." In English Canada there were no new hopes to replace them, but in the ever-irascible and -ingenious Quebec a new law, Bill 109, the Cinema Act, looked good. This law required that distributors invest a certain percentage of their revenue in Quebec films. It also attempted in various complicated ways to beef up Canadian distributors by obtaining American films for them to distribute. (Canada is technically a foreign market for the United States, but the major American studios have long treated the nation as a fifty-first state; the Americans distribute their own movies in Canada, movies they are required by law to sell to local distributors in other countries. Furthermore, every one of those other countries imposes taxes or quotas or both on American product. Good neighbor Canada imposes neither.) The lack of a secure distribution base, Gathercole said, meant "Canadian production will perpetually prostitute itself to the American market. There is no point in pouring public funds into production without corresponding measures to open domestic distribution." The funds that would be used to finance production in Quebec as the result of Bill 109 were particularly important in that the population base was no longer substantial enough to support its own cinema—the cost of making movies had grown so excessive that even many minor independent features had to look to markets outside the province to recoup their investment. The Academy of Canadian Cinema's Maria Topalovich estimated in the spring of 1985 that the Americans took $500 million a year out of Canada—directly, through the box office. "They return," she charged angrily, "next to nothing." Bill 109 was a first step at containment, a beaver dam at the bottom of Niagara.

Where Were the Bureaucrats?
Where Were the Artists?

Over at the National Film Board, some good films were being made. Some. But the NFB was beleaguered as never before, and it was hard to care: *Not a Love Story*, an inept and dishonest documentary that benefited from the pornography controversy, was instantly definitive of what happened to feminism when it became both bourgeois and fascist. The men at the NFB, presumably distressed by the attention the women were receiving, emitted a movie about male consciousness-raising, *The Masculine Mystique*, that received favorable reviews from Americans who thought it was a put-on. Few of the documentaries produced between 1982 and 1985 by the NFB were distinguished (*Incident at Restigouche* was an exception) and many were considerably less than that; the NFB had developed a house style at once pedantic, melodramatic, and patronizing, a way of seeing things that reduced the most complicated material to simplicities full of sound and fury. All too frequently, participating in a screening at the NFB was an experience in ghostliness that would leave spectators feeling they had joined one of the ghastly card parties attended by the faded faces in *Sunset Boulevard*.

Why Some Stories Have a Happy Ending

The tax-shelter years gave a bad name to carpetbaggers and co-productions, but a few worked out after the fact. The French director Jean-Jacques Annaud (*Black and White in Color*) came to Canada to make his lively caveman tragi-comedy, *Quest For Fire*, and the American director Richard Pearce (*Heartland*) came to Canada to make *Threshold* with Donald Sutherland as a heart surgeon in a film shot by Michel Brault, a film that captured exquisitely the politics and the egos in heart surgery, not to mention the unearthly submarine beauty of an act on the heart itself.

Roots III: The Tidal Wave

Jean Pierre Lefebvre made three movies in two years: *Wild Flowers* (1982), *To the Rhythm of My Heart* (1983), a black-and-white "film diary," and *Le jour S . . .* (also 1983), a quirkily self-indulgent comedy (this small delight, in which Marie Tifo plays all the women in Pierre Curzi's life, ironically became the first Lefebvre film to open commercially in English Canada). The triumph of the trio is *Wild Flowers*, which is two hours and forty minutes long, won the International Critics' Prize at Cannes, was shot in fifteen days for $350,000, and covers a week in a Quebec summer when three generations—Simone, who is seventy, her daughter Michèle and Michèle's husband Pierre, and their two children Claudia and Eric—get to know one another a bit better. "It was a short, simple week in our lives," one of them says, but *Wild Flowers* is a long, complex film—"difficult," said Lefebvre, "because it is so simple. I wanted it to be simple. I wanted everything in it to be true." It is a masterpiece. The editor, Marguerite Duparc, Lefebvre's wife, died of cancer in March 1982, and the movie is very much about mortality and the immutability of personality. As the aged Simone, Marthe Nadeau gives flawlessly formed life to a woman who has come to complacent good terms with her own existence. "Like it or not," she mutters, "things never change." But they do change, a little, during her week with her family. "I don't believe in artificial transformations," Lefebvre said. "But if it is impossible to transform some things, such as the gap between generations, it is possible to transform our way of looking at it. The premise for the movie was: for those who cannot talk to each other, a movie about what might have been said."

In less exalted forums, William Fruet was still making horror films: his *Bedroom Eyes* was nominated for a minor Genie in 1985. Jean Beaudin, whose stately *J.A. Martin . . . photographe* had won a Cannes best-actress award for Monique Mercure in 1977, returned to the prize circuit in 1984 with *Mario*, a gorgeously photographed film that fostered a rather bewildering sentimentality toward autism and death, and that won a Genie for cinematographer Pierre Mignot. Gilles Carle followed the first *Plouffe* with *Maria Chapdelaine*, which treated the 1914 Louis Hémon novel of unfulfilled love and everlasting fortitude in the north woods—Edna Ferber in the outback—as the libretto of a musical on the order of *Oklahoma!*, a kind of *Kay-Bec!*, in which the cast pops like toasters and perks like coffee pots but never actually breaks out into song. The two leads, Carole Laure and Nick Mancuso, are blankly glossy beauties, but the love between them is never consummated and that's a blessing: watching them go at it would be like trying to make fire by rubbing a pair of magazine covers together. Don Shebib meanwhile directed *Running Brave*, a sensitive and convincing story of the Indian Olympic runner Billy Mills and then demanded that his name be removed from the credits because he was dismayed by what the producers had done to the film. The director on record was a fictitious "D.S. Everett"; D.S. Everett was a man of considerable talents. Nothing was heard from Allan King, Claude Jutra, Paul Almond, Daryl Duke, Zale Dalen, or Richard Benner. Don Owen at last was permitted to make a sequel to *Nobody Waved Good-bye*, but *Unfinished Business* was a disappointment, a Crunchy Granola irrelevancy about the sixties disguised as the eighties. Bob Clark (*Turk 182!*) joined Ted Kotcheff (*First Blood*) and Norman Jewison (*A Soldier's Story*) in the ranks of the fat cats, directors capable of making Americans come to them—they are an affluent trinity cognizant of commercial success and artistic integrity (at least occasionally). Ivan Reitman surpassed all three in the former department by directing *Ghostbusters*, the most successful comedy ever made (Clark's *Porky's* meanwhile surpassed *Meatballs* as the most successful Canadian comedy ever made). In 1985 Reitman received a special lifetime-achievement Genie award; the buck talks here.

Look Back in Glory

In 1984, Toronto's festival polled Canadian and international critics on the subject of the best Canadian films of all time. The results, in order of preference:

1. *Mon oncle Antoine*, Jutra, 1971;
2. *Goin' Down the Road*, Shebib, 1970;
3. *Les bons débarras*, Mankiewicz, 1979;
4. *The Apprenticeship of Duddy Kravitz*, Kotcheff, 1974;
5. *Les ordres*, Michel Brault, 1974;

6. *The Grey Fox*, Borsos, 1982;

7.-8. (tie) *J.A. Martin . . . photographe*, Beaudin, 1976; *Pour la suite du monde*, Pierre Perrault and Brault, 1963;

9.-10. (tie) *La vraie nature de Bernadette*, Carle, 1972; *Nobody Waved Good-bye*, Owen, 1964.

Roots IV: After the Deluge

As the years went on, the youngsters fared as their elders had, from great to gruesome. Francis Mankiewicz's follow-up to *Les bons débarras*, *Les beaux souvenirs*, never opened in English Canada, a small mercy for Mankiewicz. Micheline Lanctôt's second film as a director, *Sonatine*, is divided into three parts: the first, in which a girl carries on an innocent flirtation with a bus driver, is charming; the second, in which another girl has a similar communication with a sailor, is dreary; and the third, in which the two girls decide to kill themselves by taking downers on the Montreal Metro—they announce their intention with a placard and wait in vain (and vainly) for someone to notice—is a preposterous and vapid spasm of social criticism dramatized by a situation only an actress could have dreamed up: it's no coincidence the girls perish from receiving too little attention. They go on stage, as it were, to better the world, and no one applauds. So they drop dead. The clever, dynamic Lanctôt, who had a history of winning weird awards—she was the recipient of the lifetime-achievement Genie on the occasion of the release of her sweet first film, *The Handyman*—received the best-director Genie for *Sonatine*. She said she was surprised.

There were debuts of promise. Léa Pool made a wonderfully assured, self-reflexive film about filmmaking, *La femme de l'hôtel*, that had the international jury at the 1984 Toronto film festival agog over her talent. *Une journée en taxi*, shot by the welcomely ubiquitous Pierre Mignot (*Maria Chapdelaine*, *Streamers*, *Come Back to the 5 & Dime Jimmy Dean, Jimmy Dean*) was an amazingly confident study by Robert Ménard of the relationship a convict strikes up with the taxi driver who takes him away from prison. After years of wrangling, Robin Phillips's film of Timothy Findley's *The Wars* presented to Canadians for the first time an intelligent feature set in the hearts and minds of the English-speaking ruling class. And Philip Borsos's *The Grey Fox*, the pre-eminent legend of Canadian film production in the eighties, proved again to those who required proof that Canadian stories *were* important and that Canadians *could* tell them beautifully, if given a chance. *The Grey Fox* and *The Wars* were long overdue, films hailing from the heart of Canada's Canada.

March 1985

The Fountain-of-Youth Factory: Ron Howard's Florida

Flo Jebb, who is seventy years old and was one of the last of the Ziegfeld girls—she was in the Follies of 1943—is sitting quietly on a metal folding chair near a big pink house near a dock on the bay. Tampa Bay. Flo is sitting in St. Petersburg, across the causeway from St. Petersburg Beach, where Maureen Stapleton is staying. Stapleton has already told a New York gossip columnist that St. Petersburg is "God's waiting room" and that "eight weeks here is like eight years." ("Shot my big mouth off, didn't I?" she hoots.) But this is the movie business, a business about waiting, about everybody waiting all of the time. At the moment, the waiting is about midnight. Flo has been perched on her chair for five hours, off and on. A muscular young man in full Florida flower—the tan is the creamy texture of butterscotch pudding, the Ocean Pacific shorts are tight, the chest is bare, and the hair is worn flyaway in a sun-bleached Beatles cut—ambles by. He nods at the old woman and solicitously asks, "How are you?" Flo winks: "I'd like some action!" He winks right back: "Wouldn't we all?"

Flo smooths out her print dress. "I'm one of the few older professionals hired from the St. Petersburg area, you know," she confides haughtily, gesturing toward a beach house containing an assortment of elderly people dressed in bubble-gum pinks, hibiscus magentas, and bird-of-paradise blues. "Those are extras. I have a speaking part. I came to St. Petersburg thirty-five years ago and just stayed, but I've always stayed in show business. I've done dinner theater. My husband and I had a nightclub. I still do my one-woman show. 'The Mistress of Mirth' is how they bill me. In between, I've been campaigning for Reagan and William 'Bill' Young. He's local. I was going to do a movie this November with Jeanne Crain, but she had to have a biopsy. She's a lovely girl. I worked with her in dinner theater. Every year at Christmas she sends me a bouquet of seven lollipops, with the names of her seven children. She wanted to have eight, you know." Don Ameche walks by and tips an imaginary hat to Flo. "You know who's aged?" she whispers cattily behind a liver-spotted hand. "Him. Oh, he was so handsome! Now he looks elderly." She fluffs her wig of tight, pewter-colored curls and sighs. "I don't know how some of these people, the *old* people, bear up."

Dom Ameche is seventy-six. He does not look young. But he looks pretty good. "That Flo, she's a character," says the man who invented the telephone in *The Story of Alexander Graham Bell*, the man who —dubious honor—was the partner of little Alice Faye in all those romantic musicals. "She loves doing this movie, she loves acting. I enjoy acting, but acting has not been my life. I have always had few friends in the business because I have always been avid for knowledge. If I associated with show people, I found that show business was all they talked about." Ameche is one of the half-dozen aged stars hired for *Cocoon*, a $17-million sci-fi comedy drama that has been shooting on Florida's Gulf Coast since the beginning of August. It is now late October and the cast is bored out of its well-paid mind. Director Ron Howard, long ago the cow-licked little Opie on "The Andy Griffith Show," less long ago the clean-cut kid on "Happy Days," and just yesterday the director of *Splash*, is intentionally oblivious of the complaints. "I know for the actors it seems like we're poking along," he sympathizes. "They feel it's slow, but I'm scrambling for every shot." Ameche snorts. "I've never worked with anyone who shoots the way Ron does." He shakes his head, wonder tinged with admiration tinged with bewilderment. "He will do twelve takes, print five, and encourage us to use different dialogue each time. We don't know what's in his mind. He must feel it's right. He's very kind to the performer and will listen to you, but what he's firm about, he's very firm about." Howard is aware of Ameche's discomfiture. "It's been a little trying for Don. He told me, 'I don't quite understand what you're doing, but it seems to be working.' What he's referring to is what I call the George Lucas–*American Graffiti* tack. I like our script, but I always felt it didn't quite come to life for me. Some of our actors, such as Hume Cronyn and Wilford Brimley, are comfortable with improvising and I've taken advantage of that to get some spontaneity. It has been uncomfortable for others. Sometimes the actors don't even know if the camera is on them."

Lest he appear ye olde curmudgeon, the courtly and self-contained Ameche adds that the movie business has always been berserk and that he has nothing but respect for actors who live to act. "Henry Fonda lived to act. He stayed alive until after the Academy Awards—he might have died earlier if he had not been nominated for *On Golden Pond*. I just wasn't like that. Don't misunderstand me. I do enjoy acting. But I have continued to act, quite frankly, because I have never been able to find anything else I was equipped to do." Detractors, Pauline Kael among them, have suggested he was not equipped to do that: for *The New Yorker*'s critic, he was "the zero that sings" and in a double role in *That Night in Rio*, "that's twice nothing." Ameche laughs kindly at the assessment and then fixes his interlocutor with a basilisk gaze and adopts a set-the-record-straight tone. "There were awfully good directors back then, but not many. So many of the directors at that time didn't know anything about making a quality motion picture. An actor's job used to be to learn the lines and try to figure out how to get around the director. Let me give you an example. There was a director named Roy Del Ruth who did many of the big musicals at Warner Brothers. One morning I walked on the set, Roy walked over to me and handed me a seven-page scene. He asked what I thought. I read it and told him I didn't think it was very good. So he went over to his secretary and they rewrote it, before we started shooting. He had got the scene from the writer the night before, but he hadn't bothered to read it. This was not an odd thing, not at all. On one picture, I forget which, we had to wait on the set for dialogue to come from the writers; they didn't know who the characters were, what the situation was—nothing. It wasn't as stressful as it sounds because we were used to it. It was a question of trying to do the best you could. The big stars were treated this way and the directors depended entirely on them. This is not the way to make a class picture. Ernst Lubitsch was an exception. It was a great joy to do *Heaven Can Wait* for him. He had worked with his writer polishing the script for eight months before shooting and on the first day he asked us, 'I beg you, do not change anything.' When I made *Trading Places* for the young John Landis, he was the same, sure of what he wanted. In my opinion John Landis is a great director. I know my career was not all it might have been. If my face had aged earlier, I might have been able to work in more interesting parts. I think I did passably good work. There are two kinds of stars, Spencer Tracy was one of them, a real actor and the greatest performer I ever saw, and Clark Gable was the other kind, a personality. Gable couldn't act hardly at all, but he drew people to him. I was a little of both, actor and personality. I was never a top star but I was a legitimate star, a lesser one. I saw *The Story of Alexander Graham Bell* a few years ago and I thought I did an okay job on it. I've never had a dry spell and now I can do what I want. Anyway, I've had a wonderful life."

A wonderful life is what the majority of the elderly men and women in the *Cocoon* cast feel they've had, but they are not the gracious pink-cheeked grannies and grampas who flit through the fantasies of greeting-card companies. The distinguished stage actor Hume Cronyn is seventy-three and his equally distinguished wife Jessica Tandy is seventy-five.

"When we started *Cocoon*," he remembers, "the assumption was that out of respect for our limited energies—and they are limited—filming would start early and finish early. Not only for us: there are a great number of people in their seventies in this film. Well, that's become a joke. Our days have been fifteen-hour days. The actual work isn't hard, it's the sitting around and waiting that's killing. This sounds like one long bleat of complaint. Our older extras tell me that they had no idea moviemaking would be like this. Making movies is boring. You can write it down, but no one will believe it. They think it's a romantic occupation, but it ain't. Getting old ain't romantic, either. I'm trying to think of what the compensations might be. I'm afraid I can't. I'm afraid I have no thoughts on the subject. I am very aware that I grow older and I resent it. I resent the fact that my eyesight is lousy. I get angry about it. Which doesn't help. I am not an unhappy old man, however; I've had a hell of a good life. I've always lived hard, played hard, and felt professionally driven. The only compensation of growing older that I can think of is perhaps that I am not so driven—if I am asked to do something, I can just skip it and know the sky will not fall. I think Jess and I have been so damned fortunate."

"We *have* been fortunate," Tandy agrees. "Though not at the moment. On this set, I am doing very little and it is taking a very long time." She picks up a copy of a Ken Follett novel and brandishes it. "You see? Any trash will do. If I were busier I would be happier. I walk on the beach and do my exercises but this is a long time to spend in Lotus Land. This is not a place I would wish to retire. I think one can have life *too* easy. So I think, probably, I would pick New York City. I would prefer going to theater, to museums. I certainly do not want to retire to playing shuffleboard or whatever the hell it is they do here. Hume wanted to do *Cocoon* and I came along with him for the trip. Ron Howard obviously knows what he's doing but it's a very fragmented script. Maureen Stapleton told me she envied us because Hume and I actually had scenes to play. Yes, we did have a scene to play. It was two weeks ago, I think. I really don't like making movies and I like seeing them even less. I get riveted on myself and hate every minute of it."

"There is some truth to what Jess says, that she did this for me," Cronyn nods. "But there is something else. Jessica goes from here to a play for Joseph Papp at the Public Theater, where the top salary is $450 a week. That will perhaps pay for a car to take her to and from the theater; that's all. One hand washes the other. Films are easier than theater, but not nearly as stimulating except economically. You cannot always do what you want to do. We are very handsomely paid on this film. We just bought a house; we have to pay for it. Also, we are working with a lot of young people, which I like, I find it keeps us in touch. As we get older, I think we spend as much time in memorial services for our contemporaries as anything else. That can be very depressing.''

''Well, I wouldn't retire here, either,'' Gwen Verdon winks a little later over lunch. ''A lot of our extras are from the Sunny Shores Nursing Home. They are the ones in good shape. After I saw what was going on there, I flew back to New York and had papers drawn up that will make it impossible for me to be kept alive by extraordinary measures. I will *not* wind up in one of those places. If I were a writer like Colette, to be bedridden would not be too horrible, but for me, because I've been so active—I don't call it being alive. Even if my brain were working.'' Verdon, the long-legged gal who was the Lola who got what she wanted, the Charity who was sweet, the Roxy Hart who sang ''Sophie Tucker'll shit I know/to see her name get billed below/foxy Roxy Hart,'' winks again. ''It's also made me feel good about being older. About not trying to hide it. What a lot of effort! When I tried out for this part, they told me I was too young. I'm fifty-eight! They asked me, 'Would you object to looking older?' I play a woman who starts out old and then gets dunked in this swimming pool that's a kind of fountain of youth. 'It's a character part,' they warned me. Lola was a character part; every part I've had was a character part; I've always been the town's naughty lady. Apparently, they saw other people who *did* object. I happen to know of one movie actress who is, minimum, twelve to fifteen years older than me. She went in to talk to them only to tell them how insulted she was to be considered for the part of the older woman.'' Verdon will not divulge the woman's name; she approves of dish, but can't stand indiscretion.

Which is why the assumption that she is the model for the character played by Leland Palmer in Bob Fosse's autobiographical *All That Jazz* has always bothered her. ''People think it was us, because Bob and I were married so long, but that was not my relationship with him. There was only one scene taken from our lives together, and that was the scene where the choreographer, Roy Scheider, asks her what she thinks of the Air Erotica number and she tells him, 'I think it's the best thing you've ever done.' And that's not even about Broadway, it's about the *movie*. Bob was choreographing that dance and the producers were uptight because he was using just about every kind of erotic situation people or groups could get into. He was really getting undermined by the brow-beating of the producers. So he called me and asked me to have a look at it. And then we went off in a little room and he said, 'I'm going to have to give it up.' I said, 'You can't give it up, it's the best thing you've ever done.' '' She chuckles. ''So Bob put *all* of that into *All That Jazz*. I think it's an *extraordinary* film. But he's always been extraordinary. And controversial. Always. He's always been the first one to take risks that other people come along and use after he's broken the ice. They say he's concerned with death and eroticism. Everyone's involved with things sexual. Work, eroticism, death: that's what he's been involved with, that's what all men are involved with. For women, family is in there, more strongly than for men, I think.'' She gazes out at the water. ''Oh,'' she moans, ''I cannot stand to look at that Gulf another minute. I think this weekend I'll go to another hotel. Just for a change.''

Much later, at 4:00 A.M., Maureen Stapleton is in the lobby of the St. Petersburg Beach Hilton Inn. A glass of white wine is in one hand; the other is caressing a Trivial Pursuit game laid out seductively in front of her. ''She'll proposition you if you don't watch out,'' hisses a desk clerk. ''She's after everybody to play that game.'' Stapleton hoists her goblet. ''I keep waiting for a new batch of cards for this thing. Jessica's whupped me, but I've whupped her. There's a guy who works here who was real good—beat me at the Silver Screen Edition, which I thought was *mine* —but he got tired of playing. I never do. You know, if you play with two people, you can go on for *four hours*? I've had a game almost every night right here in the lobby. The food and beverage manager's pretty good, but he bought his own set and now he plays with his mother.'' She frowns. ''I'm addicted. Severe. But I *hate* the Baby Boomer Edition. Makes me feel stupid.''

Stapleton loved Trivial Pursuit before coming to Florida, but in St. Pete it has become her bulwark against boredom. ''Oh, I was so bored, I did make that joke to Marilyn Beck about eight weeks and eight years and God's waiting room— but that *is* what they call it here—and it was all over the papers. It was a dumb thing to do. I have nothing against St. Petersburg. It could have been Rome, if I'd had to be there for eight weeks. Now it's twelve weeks. I didn't realize how long twelve weeks was. I was only on *Reds* for six, though the rest of them were on it for years. I remember asking Warren Beatty if I could rehearse a scene just a little. So we rehearsed after work at night, and we rehearsed Saturday, and we rehearsed Sunday, and that was the *last* time I opened my mouth to Warren. I love him, but he's a *very* hard worker. You know what my Oscar for Emma Goldman got me? I got fewer offers for less money. I have no idea why. I don't think it's supposed to work that way. It's just I'm not a sunshine freak or a sand freak and that cuts out a lot. I tried in the beginning to be positive and I did all the positive things, but I ran out. I once made a movie with Art Carney in Vancouver. That was better than here, more to do. There was no Trivial Pursuit then, but we managed.

Art plays the piano by ear and he knows, like, eight songs, and his big number is 'Autumn Leaves'. One night as a joke he's in the hotel lounge and we put out a glass cup on the piano for donations. This sweet man comes up and puts a hundred bucks in the jar. We all went and tried to give it back to him. Art kept playing. The guy wouldn't take the money—we had to give it to the waiters to split up. 'No, no,' he kept saying, 'that man gave me so many years of pleasure on the television, and if he has to do that to make a living now, I owe him at least that much.' '' Stapleton chortles. ''Somebody must owe me a game of Trival Pursuit, don't you think?''

Earlier that same night, midnight, Flo Jebb is still on her chair and Ron Howard is on a fake boat, a boat that floats but has to be towed: any time now, most of the cast will board it for a complicated crowd scene. ''Has Maureen asked you to play Trivial Pursuit yet?'' he wonders. Howard is thirty but retains the soft, peachy patina of an eager undergrad cramming for an exam. He quickly outlines the *Cocoon* plot —aliens inadvertently invest a swimming pool with restorative powers and try to set things right—and then says, ''*Splash* had its complications, with night shooting in New York, and we had a little chase scene that was challenging, but here we combine many more elements, real dolphins, puppet dolphins, special effects, action, the young cast, the older professionals.'' (The company ranges in age from twelve-year-old Barret Oliver, the kid in *The Neverending Story*, to Tahnee Welch, daughter of Raquel, though she looks more like Ali MacGraw, and Tyrone Power IV, who looks so much like the namesake he never met it's eerie, and on up to Tandy and Cronyn and Flo. The eldest is Charles Rainsbury, who retired to St. Petersburg decades ago, who will be one hundred on February 12, 1985, and who says being in a movie is ''no big deal.'') When directing his first film, *Grand Theft Auto*, for Roger Corman, he was intimidated by the action scenes, Howard continues, ''But I took it—'' He is called away to consult with his cinematographer, holds a ten-minute conference, returns and picks up his conversation in mid-sentence: ''—one shot at a time, no matter what you're shooting, you break it down—'' Another call, another conference, back again, again in mid-sentence: ''—and shoot each part.'' Opie was fairly quick, but this is ridiculous. How does he do that? ''Growing up on the set, I guess,'' he shrugs. ''I had a great teacher on 'The Andy Griffith Show' who wouldn't put up with any 'cooling down' after I'd been in a scene. I had to go straight from Don Knotts to mathematics. Watching those shows now is like watching home movies for me.'' Howard's two favorite directors are John Ford (''Not a very original answer, is it?'') and Frank Capra (''Nip 'n' tuck with Ford'') but the career he craves is the career of Billy Wilder. "When he was really cooking along, he crossed back and forth between comedy and drama. *Cocoon* is a baby step for me in that direction because there is some touching and serious drama in it, though the movie is not reality. I admire Wilder because he never got typed. Everybody seems to settle in and find out what they can make a lot of money at and just keep doing it. Maybe that'll happen to me, too. I hope not. It's a good time for me now. I hope it lasts a while."

Beverly McDermott, who is over fifty-five and is a true Hollywood blonde—she lives in Hollywood and her hair is bleached (true Hollywood blondes are never natural)—has dropped by and says hi to Flo, who beams. McDermott is the *Cocoon* casting director and she doesn't mind St. Pete a bit. Not only did she find the extras, she found the "atmospheres," the non-union elders who get paid less. ("Elders," advises a representative of the Gray Panthers visiting the set, is the preferred term. "The others are all right, but senior citizen is to elder as Negro is to black.") McDermott reports she visited nursing homes throughout the area and came to some definite conclusions. "I cast *Scarface* in Miami and we had a lot of elders in that movie. They really look old in Miami, maybe because they are richer retirees and they do like their sun. It might be diet, smoking or drinking. St. Pete is the only place I've ever been in the world where the elders are in such good shape, and are so happy. They all attribute their health to the same thing, hard work. They're mostly Protestants from the Midwest in St. Pete. They share amongst each other on the set, which the rich retirees in Miami never did, maybe because so many of them in Miami are from New York. Anyway, I went to the shuffleboard courts, the Coliseum—the big dance auditorium here—and the rest homes, and picked those I thought would hang in there after they found out the 'glamor' of making a movie is so-called. After thirty years at this job, I can tell. I found Charlie on the street, literally. He was walking by. He fibbed about his age. He told us he was only ninety-four."

Producer Lili Zanuck, who is thirty years old (like Howard, she looks ten years younger) and is responsible for getting *Cocoon* made, dreamed of a movie that would star Cronyn and Tandy; she dreamed of "an oldsters' *Big Chill*." But she realized as she worked with McDermott on casting that she faced an insuperable problem. "Even with Jessica, who is seventy-five, and Hume, who is seventy-three, no one was old enough to play our roles. We saw Rudy Vallee, and he's not young, but he didn't look or act very old. At the beginning of the movie, even the actors in their seventies are acting older than they are. Then they get younger because of the pool—a lot of our actors took scuba-diving so they could do their own stunts underwater, Hume went para-gliding (dangling from a parachute pulled by a boat) on his own, and Don Ameche is going to do some break-dancing in the movie. Maybe our profession keeps people young. Or maybe a lot of people just don't get old, in the way of the traditional stereotype."

"Oh, there are a lot of elders who need help and are pitiful," Flo retorts when quizzed on the putative St. Pete paradise. She has gone back to waving and winking at the bemuscled Florida hunk in the Ocean Pacific shorts—he has come up to tell her she is needed at last for her scene on the phony yacht, where Flo's "cute Ron Howard" is chipping out his career, shot-by-shot. "I'm involved in raising funds for down-and-out showgirls, you know," Flo says. "It's no fun to get old. My husband died of a cerebral hemorrhage and was in a coma for seven days and six nights, and it broke your heart to see that handsome man reduced that way. But I'm almost seventy-two and I sure don't feel it. I swim every day and do aerobics in the water. As long as I'm around show people, I'm great. Show business keeps me young. You know, there's a man in there who will be a hundred in February and he's spry as anything. They found most of these people in rest homes. They've been doing real well. I'm supposed to be the one to show them age is all in your mind, but I haven't had to. We drink coffee all night and never even have to go to the bathroom if we're on the set. Usually, most of us have trouble holding it." Flo's smile is beatific. "It's the magic of movies."

October 1984

The Teen Factory:
Francis Coppola's Tulsa

The Arkansas River, which cuts through the center of oil-rich Tulsa, is wide, shallow, and sluggish, and one afternoon in August 1982, when the temperature had been hitting over a hundred for weeks, it moved imperceptibly under the heavy, humid air; even at that, it moved faster than some of the life along its banks. For a lot of people, people attracted by year-old magazine articles touting a long-since vanished unemployment rate of 2 percent, life had pretty much stopped that summer. These were people on welfare, people whose kids ran in packs, people caught in a modern *Grapes of Wrath*—looking for heaven, they found hell—and people who at their most extreme lived without benefit of permanent residence, outside, in crannies under freeway bridges. Their children were the subjects of one of the most unusual movies ever made, a Francis Coppola "art film for teenagers" inspired by a self-proclaimed S.E. Hinton "art novel for adolescents."

Rumble Fish was the third film to be inspired by a Hinton novel, and the second to be directed by Coppola. Tim Hunter, director of the first Hinton movie to be released, *Tex* (a Walt Disney production that was invited to the 1982 New York Film Festival), bought the book in galleys after hearing about the Oklahoma writer from what seemed like every kid he knew, every time he turned around—"I was researching another movie, *Over the Edge*, and was interviewing about a hundred kids," he said, "and the only common denominator was that they all knew and loved the Hinton books." *Tex* is a character study of an Okie farm boy (Matt Dillon, star of all three instalments of the Tulsa Trilogy) with a grin wide as the western sky and a dispositon sweet as spring peas. But there's no mistaking the truth in the words of the carnival fortuneteller who softly lets him know, "There are people who go. There are people who stay. You will stay." *Tex* is one of Hinton's sunniest novels, but it's about being whipped before you start; it says there's not a darned thing wrong with that, and not a damned thing you can do about it. Hinton's first novel, *The Outsiders*, written when its author was seventeen (it sold five million copies between 1967 and 1982), was more sentimental about its heroes but even tougher regarding their fates. "I could picture hundreds and hundreds of boys living on the wrong side of cities, boys with black eyes who jumped at their own shadows," *The Outsiders'* kid-narrator wrote. "Hundreds of boys who maybe watched sunsets and looked at stars and ached for something better . . . they were mean and tough and hated the world, and it was too late to tell them that there was still good in it, and they wouldn't believe you if you did."

Coppola had never heard of Hinton when his producer, Fred Roos, intercepted a letter from a high-school class "nominating" the director as the most likely candidate to bring the beloved book to the screen. "You made me cry—on a plane," Coppola teased Hinton when he finally met her. Roos had forwarded both the book and the letter; in the expensive wake of *Apocalypse Now* and *One From The Heart*, the "ringmaster," as Coppola would sometimes call himself, was intrigued by what he presumed would be a quick and profitable project. He corralled some of the most talented unknown actors on earth (Patrick Swayze, Ralph Macchio, C. Thomas Howell, Rob Lowe, Emilio Estevez, Tom Cruise, Diane Lane), took them to Tulsa, and then predictably permitted himself to be sucked into grandiloquence: he decided to make Hinton's simple, gritty story a teen *Gone With The Wind*, and shot the entire film as if the burning of Atlanta were taking place outside each burnished frame. The resemblance to the Civil War epic was inspired by the fact that the runaway kids, the outsiders of the title, dip into the tale when they're on the lam. (Why would male juvenile delinquents read Margaret Mitchell? Hinton: "I was reading *Gone With The Wind* at the time. I just put it in. Parts of *The Outsiders* are embarrassing to me now.") The movie was arty but uneven and Dillon's magnetic performance in the role of the decadent Dallas undercut the rest of the film; when he left the screen, the movie collapsed into a cloudy haze of over-directed special effects and goldenly photogenic busts of barely post-pubertal icons. Beverly Walker, the film's publicist, said Coppola realized what was happening and "desperately" edited "more and more Matt" into the movie; but she believed Coppola had at one point assembled a cut of *The Outsiders* that was "a great movie." It was not the cut he finally delivered to Warner Brothers.

There was no possibility of making the same mistake in *Rumble Fish*: from the beginning, the plan was to drop Dillon into nearly every shot. The novel, an expressionist parable of coming of age, is held together by stylistic links to Hemingway, Chandler, and James M. Cain: "I had to worry about money, and whether or not the old man would drink up his check before I got part of it . . . and I had a cop itching to blow my brains out. . . . So I didn't have much time for serious thinking about my life," writes Rusty-James, the narrator-hero. And earlier: "She had blond hair with dark roots. I like blond girls. I don't care how they got that way.'' Hinton claimed ignorance of Hemingway, Chandler, and Cain; she said her hard-boiled teenybopper tough guys, with warm but not soft hearts thudding gently under black leather carapaces, were her own inventions, and she wanted to keep them that way. Coppola was profligate with comparisons—with its *Caligari* camera angles, its *Cat People* fog, and its *Citizen Kane* chiaroscuro, *Rumble Fish* made him think of ''an *Apocalypse Now* for teenagers''—but Dillon joined Hinton in eschewing them. ''Marlon Brando?'' he sniffed, snapping a studded headband between his fingers. ''When I was in *Over the Edge*, someone told me I was like Brando. I didn't take that as a compliment. I thought he was a fat old man—the only thing I'd seen him in was *The Godfather*. Then I saw *A Streetcar Named Desire*.'' The black eyes narrowed. ''That was . . . interesting.''

''I know this sounds like Lana Turner in Schwab's,'' chuckled Hunter, who had co-written *Over the Edge* with Charlie Haas, ''but when our director on *Over the Edge*, Jonathan Kaplan, asked me to review Matt's audition tape, we took one look at him—he was fourteen years old—and said, 'This is a movie star.' He had so much magnetism, we *had* to use him.'' Hinton recalled being ''horrified'' when Hunter asked her to consider Dillon for *Tex*. (Hinton didn't know it then, but one of the reasons the movie had been given the go-ahead was Dillon's probable participation.) ''Tex is a sweet little unworldly cowboy and here was this guy who said, 'Like, man,' and told me *Rumble Fish* was his favorite book. When I get a letter from a kid who says *Rumble Fish* is his favorite book, he's usually in a reformatory.'' In time, Hinton's about-face was total and led to a singular symbiotic relationship between the writer of children's books and the pre-eminent star of children's movies. ''All of a sudden,'' Hinton remembered, her baby-blue Mercedes speeding by the huge bronze praying hands that adorn the entrance to the Oral Roberts hospital and university, ''I thought, 'I made this kid up.' He was exactly the kid I was writing about and for—really bright, doesn't fit into the system, has possibilities beyond the obvious.'' As the filming of *Tex* drew to a close, she fell in love. ''Susie was *really* in love,'' her long-time friend, the late *Village Voice* columnist Arthur Bell, reported dreamily. ''I think they kept it innocent, though—they kept telling themselves it was all maternal, mother–son.'' Hinton was distressed to find there was no interest in using Dillon, known until then primarily as a teen idol for his work in *My Bodyguard* (1980) and *Little Darlings* (1980), in the Coppola films; that he'd done the Disney movie was actually a disadvantage—the studio wanted fresh meat. Hinton petitioned Warner Brothers without success.

"So," she smiled, "I went to Francis myself. I *do* love that kid. It may be as close as I'll ever get to being a parent. Though it isn't an entirely pleasant experience. You worry a lot. But if anyone can handle stardom, he can. You should have seen him handle Dennis Hopper, his father in *Rumble Fish*, on the set; not even Francis could handle him like that. I was so proud of him I wrote his mother." "Susie," shrugged Dillon with typical teenage reserve, "is great." And then, a bathrobe covering the skimpy undershirt he wore in most of the movie, he excused himself to go off to his dressing-room with his current girlfriend.

Stylistically and thematically, *Rumble Fish* amounted to a revolution in teen movies. The allegedly inarticulate Dillon—the smart-ass mumbling is a defense against interviewers—commented cogently, "Most movies similar to it are about a kid from a small town who has problems but turns out to be a good guy and gets somewhere. The way Susie and Francis are making *Rumble Fish*, there are no good guys, no bad guys. The characters are not going anywhere." "*Rumble Fish*," Hinton added, "may be bleak, but that's life. It's adults who object to books like *Rumble Fish*, not kids." "Of course you know *Rumble Fish* is glorified," Dillon countered, "I read it when I was fourteen and it was my favorite book, but I never got my head smashed in by a crowbar, like Rusty-James does. Kids I knew really got into the book, but it wasn't their life. We weren't poor. Sometimes being from the middle class is not great, either. You're in the middle again." He let loose a what-the-hell laugh. "You can't complain that you've been too spoiled and you can't complain that you've never had anything. Susie understands kids who feel that way. That's why it says in *The Outsiders* that things can be rough all over for all kids."

They've always been rough all over for most kids, at least in the movies, but never with the savage severity and mind-numbing frequency of teen movies in the eighties, the decade in which films about the problems of adults are a statistical novelty. The force propelling this megatrend is demographically irresistible—kids are the only people going to movies on a regular basis—but the filmmaking response has been anything but simple, anything but uniform. Producers exploit the audience: they pander to it by glamorizing it, they deride it (though subtly—it carries a big stick), they subject it to socioeconomic and psychoanalytic analysis, they explain it politically—left, right, and center—and they in general feed it and feed off it with the ferocious ambivalence Hollywood once brought to its relations with the American public as a whole.

The producer seeking a precedent—the magic key to unlock the magic market—will find none. Until the seventies, pictures about (but not necessarily for) youth fell into cleanly defined categories, pro and con. It all began, perhaps, with Lillian Hellman, who left no doubt as to where the blame for youthful misbehavior should be placed: with the environment, and with the political system that created it. She adapted a Broadway play by Sidney Kingsley and, along with William Wyler, Joel McCrea, Sylvia Sidney, and Humphrey Bogart, gave birth in *Dead End* (1937) to the enduring mythology of the Dead End Kids, the hard-luck guys whose hearts would migrate to the right place if they were given an even chance. Even more softly sentimental were the Dickensian kids successfully re-formed by Spencer Tracy's Father Flanagan in *Boys Town* (1938). Most youth movies of the period shared a faith in the kids' basic decency. Times were tough, but optimism was high. This was the era when many of America's intellectuals embraced, in one form or another, the determin-ism of Marx and turned their backs on a heritage that had emphasized individual autonomy. To be sure, American Marxism concentrated on the redemption of the individual rather than the mass (Americans have never been good at envisioning ''mass'' unless the word ''market'' is attached), but the effect was still to remove direct responsibility for criminal behavior from the slim shoulders of the screen's slum children.

Youth movies went into hibernation during the Second World War —young men, and young women, were otherwise engaged—but when they returned in the fifties, it was, as dad would say while dragging ju-nior to suburban Little League practice, ''a whole new ball game.'' The landscape, cultural and geographic, was altered overnight. By money. By automobiles. By television. There were lots and lots of movies. There were drive-ins. But movies were not yet purposefully targeted at kids. The baby boom, which began the decade in diapers and ended it in elementary school, wielded no power; when *Rebel Without a Cause* was released in 1955, the oldest baby-boomer was only nine. It may well be, as Sal Mineo used to say, that James Dean ''invented'' the teenager in *Rebel Without a Cause*, or it may be that the first potent expression was Marlon Brando in *The Wild One* (1954), but these were not movies for youth. Teenagers of the time, however, did adopt Brando and Dean as icons for what leaked out around the edges of the tightly moralistic stories in which they were trapped—getting around constrictions was something teens knew a bit about.

Throughout the fifties, films that were sympathetic to kids argued that the reasons for their failings were psychological and could be traced back to mom and pop. James Dean, in *Rebel*, won the audience's allegiance in part because he suffered the burden of bad parenting and longed for a happier home life. While *Rebel* took juvenile delinquency out of the slums,

The Wild One set the pattern for the "gang picture," a genre that has proved astonishingly durable; and although this film evoked new possibilities for kids, it also acted as a pacifier for parents. Freud had usurped Marx, and the new psychologizing often took a conservative turn. Culpability had been internalized: troubled kids were no longer troubled because the enviroment was awry, but because their glands made them do it. A few fifties movies did blame parents, but most blamed kids, and in neither case were sympathies for children particularly profound.

Films that were unsympathetic to kids (movies could afford to risk alienating the youth audience in those halcyon days when adults were still their major audience) claimed that the evil resided within. *The Bad Seed* (1956) was a gruesomely popular success in which a genetically homicidal child played by Patty McCormack killed a playmate and was then herself struck by lightning: as if that weren't enough, at the end of the film the actress was trooped out to be paddled during a "curtain call." But *The Bad Seed* was cinematically and mythopoeically outclassed by *I Was a Teen-age Werewolf* (1957), in which the pangs of puberty were expanded into rampageous outings of absurdist destruction.

Probably the most viciously anti-youth movie ever made (until *A Clockwork Orange*), *Teen-age Werewolf* was nonetheless embraced wholeheartedly by the people it put down: it expressed, in exaggerated dimensions, one of their deepest fears. Just as children who saw *The Bad Seed* wondered if they, too, might not have been implanted with a character-warping kernel that would keep them mean for the millennium, kids watching *I Was a Teen-age Werewolf* wondered if they might not follow in the dank pawprints of star Michael Landon. Would the anger and aggression of adolescence surge hairily out of control and lope, frothing at the mouth, through the streets of quiet, well-ordered subdivisions? (Kids need not have worried: they would grow out of it, Michael Landon would grow out of it, and everyone would live happily ever after in a little tract house on the prairie.) *I Was a Teen-age Werewolf* was a solo dance of teenage death. Fifties gang pictures, despite their inevitable exhortations to straighten up, at least gave the comforting warmth of community to teenage anger. *Werewolf* was a movie for alienated children ready to believe the worst of themselves, but *The Wild One* was a movie about a subculture with potential, a potential extravagantly tapped in the picture that domesticated and musicalized the genre, and served as the transition from the youth-loathing fifties to the youth-loving sixties: *West Side Story* (1961). Doc, one of the nonsinging adults in *West Side Story*, screamed, "You kids make this world lousy!" and the audience was engineered at that second to agree, but the movie, with its weepy *Romeo and Juliet* romanticism, proved him wrong in the end. *A Summer Place* (1959), in which

Sandra Dee bestowed her nubile favors on a boyfriend, and the rock-star musical *Bye Bye Birdie* (1963) tried to have it both ways: they idealized and satirized simultaneously, hoping to attract teens without repelling adults. *Beach Party*, with Frankie Avalon and Annette Funicello, also released in 1963, didn't bother: it was unapologetically for kids. Flicks for and with teenagers became a staple of cinematic life. Nothing was ever quite the same again. The youth movie came into its own.

A screen vision of the ideal American teenager was relentlessly promulgated: she was stacked, he was well built, and they were horny (but not lascivious), studious (but not bookwormish), concerned (but not mushy), out for a good time (but not hedonistic), and, most of all, free, white, and living in California. They had tans. They had Disneyland. But within a few short years, *Beach Party* was rained out. Kids who had attended the pictures dismissed them as "teenybopper." Annette and her accoutrements became objects of ridicule. The phrase "Mickey Mouse" was a new pejorative. Vietnam and the emergence of the counterculture caught Hollywood short. The movies it made to capitalize on events dividing the country were at best flaccid, at worst absurd. *Getting Straight*, *R.P.M.*, and *The Strawberry Statement* (all 1970) and *Bless the Beasts and Children* (1972) were perceived as exploitive—and straight—and were rejected. *Easy Rider* (1969) and *The Graduate*, (1967) were antipodal hits. In *The Graduate*, Dustin Hoffman, whose misbehavior was blamed on the adult environment, learned that the system, although a mess, could be handled under the right circumstances: you had to find a nice, rich girl your own age and settle down. (Twelve years later, in *Kramer vs. Kramer*, the nice rich girl would dump you, but that's another story.) In *Easy Rider*, Peter Fonda maintained that the system was a killer; there was no exit. Tom Laughlin's do-gooder half-breed Vietnam veteran—*Billy Jack* (1972)—echoed the social sentiments of the thirties with a new, violent twist: change could be had if your heart was pure and your fists were sure.

Delinquency pictures died—in an age of youthful civil disobedience, the concept lost its meaning—but gang pictures did not. Not exactly. They were transformed into the concert film. *Woodstock* (1970) was the biggest, grandest gang picture of them all, the "good"-gang picture; the documentary *Gimme Shelter* (also 1970), in which a stabbing took place on screen at a concert, was the "bad"-gang picture, the "real" version of *The Wild One*. The next year brought *A Clockwork Orange*, which, like *Bye Bye Birdie*, wanted to satirize, sentimentalize, and idealize all at once. Stanley Kubrick's horrific, misanthropic fantasy of the future was bipartisan; the psychopathic kids deserved the corrupt authorities they got.

Sometime in the mid-seventies, the popular rock group the Beach Boys noticed that although they grew inexorably older, the average age of their audience remained forever young. Weird. And then, as the decade plunged into recession, Hollywood noted the same phenomenon: although the baby-boomers were getting older, the movie audience wasn't. Collectively, the young soon became the true terror of Tinseltown. Their demographic demagoguery was so well documented that their depiction as garishly attired mayhem machines in *The Warriors* (1979) could have been taken as an indication of Hollywood's *real* view of its new audience. Paul Morrissey's film about boy prostitution in New York, *Forty Deuce* (1983), put the ambivalence Hollywood harbored toward the dictatorship of the pimply rather well when Orson Bean told one of his kiddie tricks that buying the bodies of the young was a distancing device: "We can't admit to being in your power."

Like it or not, Hollywood conceded the power of the pubertal with an endless string of cheesy exploitation movies (*Zapped*, *Hollywood High*) and equally cheesy horror movies (*Halloween 3: Season of the Witch*, *Friday the 13th Part III*). B-movies have always been made, but the subject matter and tone have shifted to appeal to a narrower audience. The best of the Bs may be esthetically lacking, but they are usually instructive, energetic, and often thematically innovative. *Porky's* (1982), a B-plus, mythologizes the teen years by exploiting the hormonal hell of adolescence. Nothing in the pantheon of pics on teens is preparation for this film, which opens in 4/4 time to the rhythm of one of its heroes masturbating and goes on to become a group grope, a comic case of heavy petting between audience and filmmaker; director Bob Clark has invented canny, concrete metaphors for the chaotic repression-release cycle of adolescent sexuality. What *Porky's* did for guys, *Little Darlings* attempted for girls. In this farcical confection, two teenagers, Tatum O'Neal and Kristy McNichol, take bets as to who will part with her virginity first —the ubiquitous Matt Dillon is the implement employed by the winner —and then simmer down and learn that sex brings with it responsibility. It's doubtful the audience paid much attention to the moral: photographs of the doe-eyed Dillon were soon spread seductively across the pages of teen magazines. Dillon epitomizes a new breed of teenaged actors who appear in films that represent kids as they are (or as they could be): *Taps*, *My Bodyguard*, *Hard Feelings*, *Tex*, *Foxes*, and *Fast Times at Ridgemont High*—each pays dues to kids' movies of the past, and each departs from convention. In *Fast Times at Ridgemont High* (1982), the kids, who perform vaudeville routines in high-school halls and shopping malls (they apparently live nowhere else) and who fumble at sex for real, owe allegiance to *American Graffiti*, but they are tougher, stripped of the glaze of nostalgia. Based on experiences in a real high school, *Fast Times* was close enough to the truth to make money but too close to become a block-buster like *Porky's*.

Movies of the thirties preached that violence was unnecessary for the upstanding kid; movies of the fifties followed suit; movies of the eighties stop short of suggesting karate, but not by much. (And in 1984's *The Karate Kid*, not at all.) The terrain in *Tex*, *My Bodyguard*, *Hard Feelings*, and *Foxes* is mined with mortal menace. In *Tex*, the stage actor Zeljko Ivanek shows up as a homicidal, hotheaded con right out of *The Executioner's Song*; by then, naive Tex has already been wounded during a foiled drug deal. In *Foxes* (1980), an anomaly among teen pictures in that its point of focus is female, high school is shot in a style that could be called High Transylvania—the girls (led by Jodie Foster) move though a smoky environment stuffed with peril, including but not limited to drugs, abortions, and unbalanced parents. *My Bodyguard*, directed by Tony Bill, and *Hard Feelings* (1983), directed by Daryl Duke, take an opposite tack —the enemy is other kids. The hero of *Hard Feelings*, set in 1963, spends much of the movie running from a crew-cut jock sadist, and in *My Bodyguard* the plot pivots around the vicious internecine warfare of high-school halls. Matt Dillon (again), the school's chief bully, has organized his subalterns into an extortionist claque patterned after the Mafia; the movie's hero, Chris Makepeace, busts up the gang with aid of a big, slow kid who looks like Lurch. The Dillon villain is a funny variation on a familiar theme: the audience can see that he's learned how to be bad from watching *The Wild One*, *Grease*, and maybe even Sha Na Na. He's also watched the *Godfather* saga; he's a new-style, corporate thug, a teen bully who franchises his hate. The problems faced by these kids are resolved in a fashion peculiar to the seventies and eighties. Teen viewers are taught that they must fend for themselves, that they can't depend on adults for help. They are told additionally that when survival is at stake, it sometimes comes down to a matter of muscle. The hero of *Hard Feelings* finally beats the hell out of the bully, one of the parents in *Foxes* is profitably roughed up, Matt Dillon gets his in *My Bodyguard*, and gives as good as he gets in *Tex*.

But in *The Flamingo Kid* (1984), one of the oddest kids' movies of the eighties in that parents are not only present but accounted for, Dillon's character, Jeffrey—a gauche but decent boy from Brooklyn who goes to work at a beach resort, El Flamingo, in the summer of 1963, when pedal pushers were tight and doo wop was tops—*learns* from his parents; their integrity is taken seriously. The easy life of a used-car salesman (Richard Crenna, in the performance of his career) who drives a candy-apple Porsche is contrasted with the unglamorous existence of Jeffrey's poor but honest plumber father (Hector Elizondo), who wants his kid to go to college; in the course of the summer at El Flamingo, Jeffrey learns to see through sleaze. But for all its pastel charms—they include Dillon's performance as a relatively non-tortured teen—*The Flamingo Kid* feels like what it is, a nostalgic period piece.

Baby, It's You (1983), another exception, is similarly nostalgic and of a period—the late sixties—but it's much more ambitious than any of its pubertal peers: writer-director John Sayles attempts to kiss the teen genre goodbye much as Peckinpah ruined the western in *The Wild Bunch*. He succeeds. The teen movie grows up in *Baby, It's You*—the coming-of-age movie comes of age.

The film's mismated lovers, the affluent Jill (Rosanna Arquette, who brings to the role a trace of the high-necked, well-bred goosiness of Audrey Hepburn) and the working-class Sheik (Vincent Spano, unrecognizable from *Rumble Fish*, where he was Dillon's WASP friend, Steve), travel the barrier that separates high school from real life; their romance gets tougher as time goes by. Sayles sketches by-now familiar vignettes in high-school halls, but if nothing is fresh (growing up in North America is becoming as standardized as the production of the Big Mac), nothing is stale. There are no easy victims: in films that pander to kids, the enemies have faces, but in *Baby, It's You*, the enemies are abstractions—class, money, taste, and education. The good times experienced by the Sheik, with his Valentino profile (though in a typical Sayles joke he's named after the prophylactic), and Jill, with her dreams of academic excellence at Sarah Lawrence, depend on their differences. "You're crazy!" she purrs in admiration. "I've never met anyone like you!" he murmurs in loving wonder. When the picture should by all commercial rights come to an end, the lovers graduate; he goes to Miami, where he finds a job mouthing Frank Sinatra records, and she goes to Sarah Lawrence, where she learns to groove to Procol Harum and throw up in restaurants. What both lovers learn when they reunite in this miraculous combination of ruthless realism and high spirits—this is a picture that tells the hard truth about growing up without bringing on the blues—is that high-school students are to be envied. Envied? Because, Sayles thinks, "high school is the last bastion of the true democracy, the last place where you sit down to lunch with the guy who's going to be taking out the garbage." High-school students usually perceive graduation day as independence day. In Sayles's ironic world, the end of high school is the end of independence and the beginning of real, rather than symbolic, servitude. *Baby, It's You* pushes the teen factory over the edge with a swan dive: at the end, knowing they will part, the Sheik and Jill fall into each other's arms at a Sarah Lawrence dance. For one brief moment, they recapture the enchanted euphoria of their classless love, their high-school high, the time when they believed everything was possible for everyone.

Baby, It's You did not stem the production of teen movies any more than westerns were banished by *The Wild Bunch*, but Sayles did set a new standard: before long, there were a handful of honorably executed movies in the C-plus to B-plus range. *The Breakfast Club* (1985), the teen *No Exit*, written and directed by high-school specialist John Hughes, whose *16 Candles* (1984) introduced two of *The Breakfast Club*'s most promising stars, Molly Ringwald and Anthony Michael Hall, and Australian director Bruce Beresford's thoughtful, feminist *Puberty Blues* (1984) are typical of movies that tried diligently to get behind the patronizing *Porky's* facade. (Jodie Foster's mother in *Foxes*, Sally Kellerman, defined that facade handily: "You look like kids, but you're short forty-year-olds, and you're tough ones.") As contrived as the "truth games" it plays, *The Breakfast Club* nonetheless cleverly delineates the stereotypes that exist in high school and even more cleverly turns them into the material of memorable one-liners. When Molly Ringwald's Princess (the other stereotypes include "a Brain, an Athlete, a Basket Case and a Criminal") opens a box of sushi, the Criminal (Judd Nelson), a standard-issue disturbed kid and the film's catalyst, wants to know what's inside. The Princess: "Rice, raw fish and seaweed." The Criminal: "You won't accept a guy's tongue in your mouth and you're gonna eat *that*?" The Athlete (Emilio Estevez) asks The Brain (Hall) why he needs a fake ID. The Brain: "So I can vote." *The Breakfast Club* may not be what high-school kids are, but it's what they'd like to think they are—witty, smart, capable of surmounting prejudice. Adults are obstructions (the single teacher in the film is a miserable martinet blackmailed by a janitor) too peripheral to shoulder much direct blame. At first, the kids blame themselves; then they learn to blame the system, to assign black marks to high school itself. This is the antithesis of Sayles's contention that public secondary schools are fundamentally democratic: even as *Baby, It's You* emphasizes the ease with which love flows across socioeconomic barriers when hormones run high, *The Breakfast Club* dramatizes the sturdiness of those barriers—student bodies mingle in *Baby, It's You*, but the student body in *The Breakfast Club* is rigidly segmentalized by class, looks, physical abilities, interests, and intelligence. High school and later life are seen as identical, which is why the intensely honest communication between the stereotypes toward the end of the film feels forced: it is so rare. One of the few venues in adult life where a demographically representative sam-ple of the sort convened in *The Breakfast Club* can be found interacting in all honesty is a meeting of Alcoholics Anonymous.

Puberty Blues is less calculated and much less commercialized in its depiction of an Australian beach culture seen through the eyes of "surfie chicks," young women who eventually rebel against their men. Hinton's novels and the films made from them are justifiably greeted as advances in a genre that until the seventies was bereft of reality, but their maleness is both thorough-going and old-fashioned: except as addenda to men, there are no Hinton Little Women, and a movie such as *Puberty Blues*, which criticizes the sexist attitudes romanticized in Dillon's relationship with Diane Lane in *Rumble Fish*, could not be drawn from anything in Hinton's oeuvre. "I like boys. And when I was a teenager, I didn't understand what the girls were talking about," she explained defensively. "They were always waiting for something to happen; they got to stand in the john, rat their hair and outline their eyes in black. I liked bikes, football and drag-racing. It's not that I don't like women, but is there a book somewhere that deals with girls' society, without boys as a catalyst? Even now, when I go to baby showers, I still feel I'm an anthropologist at some weird rite." Hinton wanted to write about teenagers because "It's an interesting time of life. Feelings are more dramatic, ideals are slamming up against the walls of compromise. They have more feelings than any other segment of society, but they are more afraid of showing their feelings than any other segment." And she planned to keep writing about them. "But if I forget what it was like, well, I'll stop. I must say, though, it is getting harder to remember what it was like to want to commit suicide over the length of your hair." *Puberty Blues* remembers, and it remembers more than Hinton ever cared to know about the problems of being female, about the reasons—other than the length of hair—that might inspire thoughts of suicide: the misogynist behavior of the boys Hinton likes so much, for instance.

The rule-proving exception of *The Flamingo Kid* aside, it's not hard to see why the individuals or organizations that took care of kids in movies of the past are either absent or perceived as enemies. It begins at home: the modern game of musical marital chairs has removed the few pitiful props that used to shore up the precarious security of childhood. Self-reliance is seen not as a virtue, but a necessity. Hinton never apologizes for the relative bleakness of her books, in which a kid's only friend may be another kid (who may turn out to be his enemy): "I don't think there's anything wrong with telling kids that things sometimes get broken that can't be fixed. If that's reality, why tell them any different?"

Risky Business (1983) told them different, but in dreamy erotic fantasy. Again, parents are absent, allowing the hero, Joel (Tom Cruise), to face and fight many of the specters haunting high schools. Writer-director Paul Brickman's premise is simple: what if *The Graduate*'s Benjamin Braddock were to get out of high school in the eighties? Ben had the luxury of rejecting the materialistic push and pull of the guy who accosted him poolside and whispered into his unreceptive ear the single world, "plastics," but Joel does not. "Today," Brickman says, "kids are praying for someone to walk up to them and say 'plastics'—or 'computers,' or 'marketing.' " Hence, *Risky Business* offers a surreal crash course in getting youthfully rich, and while Brickman's generalization may or may not hold, his demonstration of the theory is supple and sexy. Joel, ambitious and cute in a pink-gummed Ivy League way (he was probably born with an alligator stitched to his chest), meets up with a hooker (Rebecca De Mornay) one night when the double doors of his parents' affluent manse fly open to admit more blowing leaf action than there's been in a movie since Bernardo Bertolucci buried his camera in autumn in *The Conformist*. Joel sets himself up as the hooker's representative in the suburbs and before long his house is filled with horny teenaged boys anxious to spend their allowances on whores. Joel's resourcefulness impresses a recruiter from an Ivy League business school and the film leaves no doubt that regardless of where Joel chooses to go to college he will make out in more ways than one.

All of these pictures, exploitive and non-exploitive alike, share the expanding sense of discomfiture abroad in the land, the slow slide into uncertainty. Not even *Risky Business*, which can think of nothing substantive to offer kids beyond the status of an exalted pimp, is an exception. Almost every one of the questions common to the form was addressed in the remarkable *Over the Edge*, completed in 1979. The picture, Dillon's first, was scheduled to arrive in the controversial wake of *The Warriors*. Instead, it was nervously pulled by the studio for two years and was belatedly greeted by good reviews and no business.

Directed by Kaplan at the age of thirty, *Over the Edge*—set in New Granada, a fictitious suburb of Denver—teetered dangerously between exploiting and romanticizing the antisocial behavior it depicted. But the *frisson* worked in its favor: it was a good, dangerous film, and it was good in part because it was dangerous. It put the viewers in touch with the kids' frustrations and let them feel the release an explosion can bring. The apocalypse at New Granada High School—the kids all but burn down the place—was a piece of commercial calculation, but the logic that led to it was propulsive; for the most part, *Over the Edge* caught dramatically the complexities of contemporary middle-class teenage lives. The problem, as the film defined it, is not parental absenteeism, self-centeredness, or hypocrisy, nor is it consumerism, lousy architecture, or an unconscionably delayed adulthood; it is not easy access to pharmaceuticals and alcohol, or an indifferent educational system; it is not video games, rock music, or excessively sugared chewing gum. The problem is none of those things in isolation, but it might be all of them in concert. *Over the Edge* had the depth to suggest that behavior is multidetermined, that responsibility is multiple. It combined bits of the thirties (blame the environment) and whiffs of the fifties (blame the family) with shards of the sixties (don't blame the kid). The film was as protean as the problem.

At the end, reform school beckoned. Four years later, *Bad Boys* got there. What *Over the Edge* accomplished on behalf of middle-class kids, *Bad Boys* (1983) undertakes on behalf of the underclasses. In the slums of Chicago, where the first half of the movie takes place, parents are seldom seen and never matter. The kids—black, white, Hispanic—are poor but not impoverished. They watch rich folks on Michigan Avenue. They ache to better themselves. They have no idea how. They do know they don't want to settle for what their parents have: next to nothing. Paco (Esai Morales), the Hispanic kid who will become the mortal enemy of Mick (Sean Penn), the white kid, tells his dad, "Look, I don't want a job, I want a business." The movie is sympathetic to that; these children, it says, have been promised. Who's going to pay up if the promises are not kept? Who's going to pay up if they are? There are no answers.

Sean Penn's performance is at one with the movie's claustrophobic, knife-edge naturalism. Penn, dubbed by director Rick Rosenthal "a baby De Niro," went into character for the entire shoot. He checked into hotels as Mick, spent hours talking to former and current delinquents, and even had a wolf's head tattooed permanently on his arm. His portrayal is tense, closed in; he does not explain the character, but seeks only to become him. When he looks at the camera, his reality is overpowering —but it is not a performance that earned him pages in teen magazines. Like De Niro at his best, Penn suggests a total human being, not an icon. Snuggling up to him is out of the question.

In *Bad Boys* none of the traditional verities apply. Change the environment, movies in the thirties advised. The environment in *Bad Boys* is verging on chaos, sinking into depression, apparently impossible to alter. Change the kid, movies in the fifties argued; punish him (conservative) or rehabilitate him (liberal). Punishing him, in *Bad Boys*, makes him worse. Rehabilitating him is seen as possible, if not likely: there are a few prison employees capable of helping the "students," the euphemism for delinquents, if the "students" cooperate. By his own admission, one counselor has reached four boys in nine years; a colleague tells him that reaching four is pretty good. But the movie does not posit a good job, two kids, and a car as the reward for an industrious ex-con. It posits a question mark. The kids who mature do so when they learn they are going to have to live with less—which is a supply-side moral, although the movie is uncomfortable with it. *Bad Boys* is an angry picture, but its anger is inchoate, locked in. Its own expections are low (and probably realistic); it hopes only for a marginal gain—one less murder, one less mugging, one less rape, one more life lived on the outside in what passes for freedom.

Rumble Fish came to the same dour non-conclusion. Shadows are stark, forbidding, and sometimes painted on buildings. Smokepots are everywhere: Tulsa is an estheticized garbage dump. Clouds scud across the sky in double-time (a technique Coppola borrowed from Godfrey Reggio's *Koyaanisqatsi*), afternoons pass in a blaze of sunlight, the hands of a clock twirl in silent testimony to an existence not only nasty, brutish, and mean, but short. Verbs are out of Lenny Bruce, violence out of Sam Peckinpah. Symbology is thick (the eponymous rumble fish are said "to kill themselves fighting their own reflection") but Dillon's Rusty-James is a devastatingly individualized portrayal of insecure machismo, Mickey Rourke's Motorcycle Boy is a chilling summation of a life burned to the bone, and Dennis Hopper's brief appearance as an alcoholic is a sobering reminder of what can happen when liquor turns out the lights. The film respects the socially maladaptive highs Rusty-James finds by doing things teenagers are not supposed to do, because it recognizes that forbidden highs are the only highs he can find. The picture leaves him stranded on a beach in Los Angeles, where he has gone to escape the carnage at home. As he stands silhouetted against the water, he's a lot older and a little wiser, and there's no place to go. What now? In the book, Rusty-James thought this about his future: "Even though nothing had worked so far, that didn't mean nothing ever would."

The Movie Factory:
Every Country's Cannes

Sodom-by-the-Sea is probably the fanciest sobriquet for the fattest and sassiest film festival of all, but it's not most accurate—the Cannes Film Festival is a circus, a sideshow, and a brothel, where everything from flesh to celluloid is for sale by the inch, but it's a capitalist sideshow, and it's about money, not decadence, and about marketing, not art. The only film artist who might have made cinematic sense of the glittering mess was Robert Altman in his heyday, and if you set the day-after-day, night-upon-night complexity of Cannes next to *Nashville*, with its twenty-odd characters, or *A Wedding*, with its forty-some neurotics, you make both of those movies sound like a concerto for a single violin. Hence this Altmanesque five-year panorama:

1979
Apocalypse Now and *The Tin Drum* share the top prize. Best actress: Sally Field, *Norma Rae*. Best actor: Jack Lemmon, *The China Syndrome*. Best director: Terence Malick, *Days of Heaven*.

No one can accuse her of not being an actress: At a *Norma Rae* press conference, Sally Field confesses to leftist European critics, "I'm not a political person. I have never been aware of unions or human conditions other than my own. That's a terrible thing to admit, but that's what I am."

Thank you, Dr. Freud: *Fast Company* distributor Danny Weinzweig says, "We're going to manufacture—I mean, produce—internationally accepted motion pictures."

Something new every day: Publicist Maureen O'Donnell moans, "I've got to figure out some way to get invitations to people whose yachts are not anchored in the harbor."

Best oral film review: Gene Moskowitz, *Variety*'s Paris correspondent, is asked what he thought the characters in *The Deer Hunter* were doing between 1968, when they all went to a wedding, and 1975, when Robert De Niro went back to Vietnam to find his buddy Christopher Walken. "They went to another wedding."

Speak of the devil: George Romero, director of *Dawn of the Dead:* "I don't know why these guys at Cannes keep slamming their heads against the sidewalk trying to make pictures. They ought to just sit on the beach and spread Vaseline on each other and forget it."

Rhetorical at best: A reporter confronts Roman Polanski: "Tell me, would you say you've had a hard life?"

Remake madness: Neil Diamond announces he will star in a new version of *The Jazz Singer*.

The devil made him do it: Barbra Streisand gave him the idea.

Listen to daddy: John Huston growls, "There is a willful lemming-like persistence in remaking past successes time after time. They can't make them as good as they are in our memories, but they go on doing them and each time it's a disaster. Why don't we remake some of our bad pictures— I'd like another crack at *Roots of Heaven*—and make them good?"

Gilding the snapdragon: Joan Collins, star of *The Bitch*, throws a party on a yacht called *My Charisma*.

Beyond Shirley's temple: A European child star by the name of Bobby appears in an Irish tearjerker by the name of *Teardrops* and sings, dances, and plays both sexes.

Believe it when you see it: Herbert Ross, director of *The Turning Point*, announces he will stitch the out-takes together for a dance movie.

Call him wild and crazy: Francis Coppola on *Apocalypse Now*: "I went into the jungle, whereupon this easy movie that I was going to knock off turned into a living nightmare for a year and a half. The crew working on the film were not following some cohesive idea that they knew or some logical script, they were following some madman's . . . I didn't have the heart to tell them I didn't know what I was doing."

Call him not responsible, Coppola II: "Why is it such a crime for me to spend money when they can spend it for a movie about a big gorilla or some jerk who flies around in the sky?"

Call him pleased as punch, Coppola III: "My film is not about Vietnam. It *is* Vietnam. It's what it was really like."

Only in America (or maybe Cannes): Joseph Wambaugh, the Los Angeles cop author of *The Blue Knight*, is sipping champagne in the lounge of a jumbo jet bound for Cannes, where he will show *The Onion Field*, when a woman introduces herself and says she's a good friend of Wambaugh's cousin, Mary. More champagne, more chatter. "Have you met Mary's husband?'' Wambaugh asks. "No , I don't believe so,'' the woman replies. "Is Mary a neighbor of yours?'' he asks. "Not exactly,'' the woman demurs. "Just what is your connection with Mary?'' he wonders. "Well, we're very close. Mary is our maid.'' Wambaugh: "Your maid?'' "Yes, and we'd really hate to lose her.''

No crystal balls for Colleen: In a Dr. Spock T-shirt, chubby Colleen McCullough discusses the planned telefilm of her best-seller *The Thorn Birds*. "Last I heard, believe it or not, they were going to shoot it in Kansas. They've talked about people like Robert Redford and Ryan O'Neal, fabulously inappropriate people, for the part of the priest. I would like to see it go to Terence Stamp or Richard Chamberlain, but that's wishful thinking; neither of them is box office.''

Who's on first? Peter Townsend, of The Who: "Music films tied into albums can actually engulf the whole globe. That's what I want to do, personally. The two promote each other. I know kids who went to see the *Tommy* film thirty times. I'm prone to exaggeration, but that's a true story. You see, we're on the brink of something new. It will be similar to the invention of the American musical in the thirties. There will be a conceptualized, musical-video product and everyone's waiting for the first *Sergeant Pepper*, if you like, on video-disc. The contemporary musical form is about to be discovered.''

Call me Ahab, Huston II: "*Wise Blood* was a very easy picture to make, with a small budget comparable to *Fat City*'s, and we filmed it in the wilds of Georgia. My God, I've never seen towns with so many pawn-brokers, loan offices, and opticians. They must go blind from reading the small print on their loan contracts.'' A photographer shouts, "You're a legend, Mr. Huston!'' The legend confides, "The only time I felt like a legend was last year when I was in the hospital and they were cutting on me. I felt quite legendary then. As soon as I got better, it stopped.''

Bred in the U.S.A., Romero II: "There's nothing left to celebrate in America except the fact that McDonald's exists.''

One hand claps: Irvin Kershner, director of the upcoming *Empire Strikes Back*, says the sequel to *Star Wars* will be "very zen.''

How Cannes is: In the magazine *Cinéma de France*, a picture of a seedy-looking young man talking to an equally seedy-looking young woman carries the caption, "*Parlez-vous d'argent?*''

1980
Kagemusha and *All That Jazz* share the top prize. Best actress: Anouk Aimée, *A Leap into the Void*. Best actor: Michel Piccoli, *A Leap into the Void*. Best director: Krzysztof Zanussi, *Constans*.

Honesty beyond the call of duty, part one: John McVicar, a British ex-con whose exploits form the basis of *McVicar*, a film starring Roger Daltrey of The Who, is asked one day if he liked the film. "It was OK. But let's not pretend: the movie is there because Roger wants to be a film star. I was Public Enemy Number One in Britain but I was only a mainstream robber; I never killed or maimed anyone. The year I was Public Enemy Number One was not a vintage year for crime."

One-man Hollywood: Rainer Werner Fassbinder announces plans to direct *Lili Marleen*, *Lola*, Pitigrill's *Cocaine*, and *Bent*, with Richard Gere.

Why Jean-Luc Godard, who brings Sauve qui peut (la vie) *to Cannes, is not well liked*: "Sometimes you can respect even a bad film. You can have more respect for a bad film from Fritz Lang than for a good film from Hal Ashby—if there were any good films from Hal Ashby, which there are not. I think there is less now that is good. Maybe later it will be better. I hope so. I like Martin Scorsese. When I saw *Alice Doesn't Live Here Anymore*, I thought, this is a movie that gives you the will to make movies. There are no critics anymore. For two or three years, Pauline Kael in New York, André Bazin here—they wanted to make criticism as badly as we wanted to make movies, and it was good. Now, they are not even as good as the sports critics, who at least have passion for basketball or tennis."

He earns an 11: Peter Sellers says, "I refused the Dudley Moore role in *10* many times. I didn't feel it was right for me."

Pourquoi pas? A French plastic surgeon comes to Cannes every year: "The women can simply point out to me the breasts on the beach they would like me to give them. Also, I like movies."

Modesty of the mighty: Asked to explain what a sequence in *Kagemusha* means, director Akira Kurosawa responds, "If you didn't understand what I was trying to show, then I made my film very badly. I'm sorry."

Suppose they gave a press conference and nobody came: Charlton Heston gives a press conference and nobody comes.

Overheard in the movies: "The wages of sin is higher wages" (Elisha

Cook, *Carny*). "Sorry is what fools feel" (Nina Hagen, *Cha Cha*). "He who has sex with nuns will later join the church" (The Clash, *Rude Boy*). "I've converted to blonde" (Deborah Harry bleaches her hair in *Union City*).

That's Miss, not Ms., to you: Linda McCartney is asked what she thinks of Cannes and says, "I don't like to talk, actually; I leave it to the man."

The man talks: Paul McCartney is asked what he would like to do other than music or movies and says, "What else is there?"

Another world: Filipino director Lino Brocka's slum melodrama *Jaguar* becomes the first movie from his country to be shown in competition at Cannes. It is banned in Manila. "Mrs. Marcos," Brocka declares, "does not want to have the world see the slums of Manila, which she herself does not see."

Don't Cry For Me, Filipinos: Brocka reports that for a time Mrs. Marcos banned *Evita*.

The apotheosis of little Ricky Schroeder: The ten-year-old, who charges $400,000 a flick and requires that an unlimited supply of pistachios appear on the set because Mummy likes them, hosts a party to celebrate the launch of *Little Lord Fauntleroy*. "Do you like making movies?" a woman in a big hat asks. "Oh, yes, making movies is fun." "Were you told to say that?" "Yes." The woman in the hat writes that down, then burbles: "So, you're a movie star, just like Shirley Temple." "Yes, ma'am!"

Je ne regrette rien: Hazel O'Connor is the punk star of *Breaking Glass*. She is drinking at the Majestic bar. "David Bowie, he's the first who ever cracked it sexually with both sexes—I like him. I like someone I can relate to sexually, like Iggy Pop, or like"—a black-rimmed eyeball rolls over the men at the bar—"well, I don't see anyone. Sure isn't much for me in this town that way. No crumpet for Hazel. I'm here because I want to be noticed, not like those stars who run round here saying they don't want to be seen. I want to last for years and years, like Edith Piaf."

Just another pretty whatsit: Harry (*Deep Throat*) Reems confesses, "I left porno because it has a stigma and I was getting older. I'm not sure I could go back now—I'm thirty-three—but I've kept fit. I enjoy getting older, getting kinkier and more perverse. So I'll sell cars if I have to. I know the breaks will come to this good Jewish boy from Westchester."

Origins of the unicorn: Marilyn Tenser, one of the tiaras at Crown International, is a bleached-blonde woman as forthright as a slap on the back.

(One of her major hits is *The Pom Pom Girls*.) "*Galaxina* is our biggest yet, but it's not so different from what we've been doing. We've had motorcycle gangs on earth in our pictures. Now we have a religious motorcycle gang in space. They worship the god Harley-Davidson. We appeal to the masses as well as the classes. I tested three hundred girls for Galaxina. The minute Dorothy Stratten walked in, I knew. She can act, she's nice, and she's bright, which she wouldn't have to be. Look at this photo: she's a hot lady. She has just the right quality for a woman of the twenty-eighth century, a woman created by men. Because that's what she is in our movie: a robot made by men."

John Carpenter on Sam Fuller: "I like Howard Hawks best, but I like Sam Fuller, too. He's nuts in his movies. I have a little craziness, but not that much."

Sam Fuller on John Carpenter: "So the kid likes Howard Hawks? I used to play poker with Howard Hawks."

Honest beyond the call of duty, part two, ex-con John McVicar: "I'm sitting on top of this dinky boat hired by some film producer to promote a film. I'm on a subsidized holiday. I've tried to talk to these film people, you see, but they're an unprepossessing lot. They're all insecure and trying to convince each other that they're biggies and, what's funnier, that they're artists. I wrote the movie because the money was good. I'd rather write a good book than a bad movie. If I can't get the money to write a good book, I'll take the bad movie. I know the difference, though this lot at Cannes doesn't. I was a robber but I see some of these people doing things I wouldn't stoop to."

✩

1981

Man of Iron wins the top prize. Best actress: Isabelle Adjani, *Possession* and *Quartet*. Best actor: Ugo Tognazzi, *Tragedy of a Ridiculous Man*.

Two crystal balls for Mr. Carradine: David Carradine says, "I knew when Marty Scorsese and I were making *Boxcar Bertha* we would become superstars."

You can take the boy out of college, but you can't take college . . . : Michael Mann, director of *Thief*, says of Frank, the James Caan character in his movie, "Doctrinaire Camus existentialism is something Frank comes upon by himself apodictically."

Truth in advertising, part one: An ad for Cannon Films declares, "With us, you laugh all the way to the bank."

Truth in advertising, part two: A hooker who hangs out on one of the side-streets has taken to sitting in her car wearing only a top because "there are so many transvestites, I must protect myself."

From the ridiculous to Divine: John Waters thinks Tab Hunter, one of the stars of *Polyester*, "is kind of conservative, you know, but he's not a Republican, or anything like that. He and Divine kiss. On the mouth. So you see, I haven't sold out to the Moral Majority."

From Divine to the ridiculous: John Waters will not reveal the name of the company responsible for the Smell-o-Vision cards for *Polyester* because "it's a very conservative company and they would be very upset if everyone knew they spent their time packaging the smell of farts."

Life beyond Divine: Waters has a dream: "I want to make *The Grace Metalious Story*. She wrote *Peyton Place*, became rich, bought Cadillacs, and killed herself. That's a great American story."

Synopses provided to the press in hopes scribes will look favorably upon the pictures thus described: "You can imagine what happens when three merry fellows have the mission of taking a stud bull to a cattle competition in Avignon and stop in St. Tropez" (*Three Lederhosen in St. Tropez*). "Carmen and Johnny have a traveling show. They have little to offer in comparison with modern showmen and romantic problems are added to their professional disappointments" (*Looping*). "Pierre searches for his mother, who disappears strangely from a train between Nevers and Paris. The search brings him near madness. His daughter comes along" (*Un étrange voyage*). "Angel, thirty, is a rock veteran. Lying on the seat of his old Ford Mustang, he reads in *Sounds* something about the times passing and changing, then goes off to the studio to record some rock" (*Asphaltnacht*). "Alice, a young woman, falls in love with a rabbit" (*The New Alice in Wonderland*). "Daily problems and conflicts in Iowa" (*Take This Job and Shove It*). "Victor Delcroix, a social climber with big ambitions and small talents, has always failed, but then the idea comes to him to commercialize sperm" (*Voulez-vous un bébé, Nobel?*).

Appreciated at last: Michael Cimino's *Heaven's Gate*—uncut version—is cheered by the European press. "The film is not an attempt to write history," he argues, "any more than *The Deer Hunter* was an attempt to write a history of the Vietnam war." Maureen Orth of *Rolling Stone* asks Cimino what *Heaven's Gate* "is about." The Europeans roll their eyes and laugh. Cimino refuses to answer: "I'm not that glib. I'm sorry." The Europeans applaud.

Not everyone claps: Gene Moskowitz, the Parisian *Variety* man, glee-fully translates a *Heaven's Gate* review by a French critic who writes, "This is a movie made by an American Claude Lelouch who thinks he's D.W. Griffith."

Clear as mud: Italian director Liliana Cavani provides a synopsis of her film *The Skin*, set in occupied Naples, which reads in toto: "All human or dog skin is the geographical map of the world."

Notre Dame de la Croisette: Swiss director Daniel Schmid summarizes his film about the Cannes festival: "Bulle Ogier plays a women whose card never gets her into the screening she wants to see. She finally watches the festival more and more on TV and when she runs by mistake into Jack Nicholson and he asks her what's wrong, she says she can't find her hotel key, never realizing she has met the star she came to Cannes to see."

Go ahead, try it: Sylvester Stallone reveals he will play the Marlon Brando role in *A Streetcar Named Desire*.

Apocalypse again: Martin Sheen says, "*Apocalypse Now* was probably the best thing that ever happened to me, even if I wasn't the star. Francis was the star, and that is as it should be on that picture. Everyone seemed to be consulted on the ending, but I was not. I had no say in the matter. I had no say in anything."

Some lives are just more interesting than others: In Andrzej Zulawski's *Possession*, a child drowns himself, Isabelle Adjani has sex with a slimy *Alien*-like creature, Sam Neill hits a man over the head and shoves his face into a toilet, and Adjani squats on a subway platform and excretes gallons of gunk from her vagina. "It is simply the story of a couple," the director maintains. "I took it from my own experience."

☆

1982

Yol and *Missing* share the top prize. Best actress: Jadwiga Jankouska-Cieslak, *Another Way*. Best actor: Jack Lemmon, *Missing*. Best director: Werner Herzog, *Fitzcarraldo*.

Gilding the lily: "I wanted to become a child to make this movie," grins *E.T.* director Steven Spielberg.

The Ellen Jamesians couldn't have put it better: The Greek film *My Guns Spit Flowers* is summed up by its press kit: "Young and of working-class origin, Linardos arrives in Athens closely followed by his sister Nanota, with whom he has a near-incestuous relationship. They live in the twilight area of town. Despite the junta, he argues in political terms about freedom. Therefore public opinion is with him and he becomes a popular hero. But he is condemned to twenty years in prison, which combined with torture, reduces him to silence, so he sews up his mouth with his own hands.''

Sorry we asked: Alan Bridges, director of *The Return of the Soldier*, answers a query as to Rebecca West's novel and his film of it: "There are two very different things, the book, which is an alive and beautiful animal, and the movie, which is another animal—you will have to tell me if it is alive and beautiful. There are not two different endings, there are two different animals. There is no doubt that the book's ending is alive. I hope the movie is alive. Your question is too esoteric, it's too deep a question. I think it's a good question—are the endings different? —but it's too difficult a question.''

German humor: Margarethe von Trotta has an English title she loves for her film about two German sisters, one of whom grows up to be a journalist while the other becomes a terrorist with the Baader-Meinhof Gang. "I want to call it *Leaden Times*,'' she bubbles. An unimpressed friend counters, "How about *One's Bad, the Other Baader*?''

All in a day's work: *Cinéma de France* cub reporter Bonnie Bruman is assigned to interview "the well-known Hungarian producer Buchholz Horst.''

All in the next day's work: The same editor assigns the same reporter to interview "the pert young English starlet Lindsay Anderson.''

Maybe, maybe: An Italian journalist asks if *E.T.* is about Elizabeth Taylor.

Thank God being from New York makes you tough: *New York Daily News* reviewer Rex Reed is the subject of an item reprinted in its entirety from *Screen International*: "Rex Reed had a bad day yesterday. He was told by director Terence Young that, for reasons of length, his scenes had been cut out of *Inchon*. And at the Brent Walker yacht luncheon for *The Return of the Soldier*, he queued for food and arrived at the buffet just as the crab salad had gone!''

It's good to hire the handicapped: Bodybuilder Lou Ferrigno is signed to play *Hercules*, and someone in his entourage dismisses his hearing problem. "He'll be great. Who says there's something weird about a Hercules with a hearing aid?''

You've come a long way, baby: Toronto Festival of Festivals publicist Helga Stephenson remembers her first job, at the National Arts Centre in Ottawa. "They told me to organize a press conference for the singer Elly Stone. I said, 'I only have two questions. What's a press conference and who's Elly Stone?' "

Christ stopped in Cannes: The ad slogan for the French product Jesus Jeans is, "He who follows me loves me."

Maybe they are: "These are film people," horror novelist Stephen King observes. "You never see them with Kurt Vonnegut or Stephen King. They are not readers."

Billy Wilder sums it up: "The other day I was sitting on the Carlton Terrace. I heard these two guys talking. 'I get Streisand and you get Redford,' one says, 'and we can get a major studio to come in for $34 million.' The waiter comes over to collect for the espresso. One guy starts to sign the check. The waiter says, '*Non, monsieur*, I check up on you, you do not stay here.' The other guy reaches into his pocket and can't come with the cash. That's Cannes—$34 million and too broke to buy a cup of coffee."   ☆

1983
The Ballad of Narayama receives the top prize. Best actress: Hanna Schygulla, *The Story of Piera*. Best actor: Gian Maria Volonté, *The Death of Mario Ricci*.

Dreamy at the bottom: On the terrace of a luxury hotel in Cap d'Antibes, Mary Steenburgen reminisces. "I always thought I would make it, but I didn't know what making it might mean. The dream that you put yourself to sleep with every night was always that someone would discover you and your secret magic. But you smiled even as you dreamed that, it was so impossible. The dream I smiled about at night was the one that happened."

Lonely at the top: "Then, I didn't know what to dream about any more. I lost most of my friends. No matter how hard they tried and I tried, it didn't work. I spent so much time trying to prove I was a decent human being. The year after I became famous was the loneliest year I ever spent in my life."

The moral: "I kept waiting for the clock to strike twelve. I was afraid it had been a whim of fate, but I learned to see that if I had been lucky, I had also been damn well prepared. And I hadn't hurt anybody to get there.

So what did I have to apologize for? My talent? My kid's diapers are just as grungy as anyone else's.''

Tender mercy: Robert Duvall accompanies a film he has directed about gypsies, *Angelo, My Love*, and reports, ''Francis Coppola liked it. He gave us some suggestions. Don't think we took them, though.''

Or Van Gogh when he cut off his ear: *Diva* director Jean-Jacques Beineix reacts to the boos that climax the screening of *The Moon in the Gutter*: ''They didn't understand Picasso when he painted *Guernica*, either.''

Aladdin's bane: Japanese pop singer and *Merry Christmas, Mr. Lawrence* star Ryuichi Sakamoto is asked if co-star David Bowie influenced his music: ''My major influence is the music of Claude Debussy.''

Have you? Festival translator Henri Béjart answers a question directed at *Merry Christmas, Mr. Lawrence*'s Nagisa Oshima—''Why did Mr. Sakamoto faint when kissed by Mr. Bowie?''—before Oshima has a chance to open his mouth: ''Obviously, you've never been kissed by David Bowie.''

Well, no wonder: While researching Rupert Pupkin, Robert De Niro says, ''I turned around and started asking autograph hunters for their addresses and phone numbers. I think they were surprised and a little suspicious.''

Well, no wonder, part two: LSD guru Timothy Leary and Watergate vet G. Gordon Liddy debate each other in the documentary *Return Engagement* and take the act to college campuses. Leary: ''We get paid less than a third-rate rock band.''

What passes for intellectual debate: Liddy says ''the purpose of society is mutual supplementation to achieve human existential ends.'' On hearing that definition, Leary says, ''Lawyers are intellectual hit men.''

Slipperier than an eel in oil: Asked if he has killed anybody, Liddy smirks, ''There's no statute of limitations on that kind of activity, but nice try. Judge John Sirica would be proud of you.''

One man's Cannes: Showbiz entrepreneur Dusty Cohl: ''I've seen no movies this year at Cannes. I'm a bit under par. I usually see one.''

Maybe you should, before 1997: *Boat People* director Ann Hui: ''I'm a totally apolitical person. We don't think about politics at all in Hong Kong.''

Vietnam had a habit of doing that: Hui continues, ''It is only after making this film about Vietnamese boat people that I can see that politics is a reality for people from other countries.''

Trivia pursued: "Nagisa Oshima is the best-dressed director I've ever worked with"—David Bowie.

Just like Peter Pan: Rex Reed explains he has programmed a great many movies about kids for a Toronto festival because, "I like movies about the problems of coming of age. I guess it's because I feel I've never grown up."

Tough at the top: *Cross Creek* producer Robert Radnitz, the film's press kit announces admiringly, begins "each day, whether winter or summer, with a plunge in the ocean, just steps away from his Malibu home."

1984

Paris, Texas receives the top prize. Best actress: Helen Mirren, *Cal*. Best actor: Alfredo Landa, Francisco Rabal, ex-aequeo, *Los Santos Innocentes*. Best director: Bertrand Tavernier, *A Sunday in the Country*.

Marianne Moore had the same idea: Werner Herzog says, "If I went into space, it would still be a German film. I think they should send poets into space. I think they should send me into space on the space shuttle. It is up to you press to convince them to do this."

An honest man: *Against All Odds* director Taylor Hackford, asked why he cast Debra Winger in *An Officer and a Gentleman*, replies, "I wanted someone who looked like a factory worker."

An honest woman: Actress Jane Greer responds to a critic who notes she was in the film *Where Love Has Gone* by smiling sweetly and saying, "What's it to you?"

There will always be an England: *Another Country* star Rupert Everett, himself a product of the kind of exclusive male boarding school depicted in the film: "They are deeply fascistic, mini-police states that haven't changed at all. Except the outfits people wear."

Two solitudes: In the Quebec film *Les années de rêve*, someone says, "He had two sons. One is dead. And the other works for the English in Alberta."

Laurels: *Under the Volcano* director John Huston says of star Albert Finney, "His knowledge of drunkenness is very profound."

Of course she does: Nastassja Kinski thinks the theme of *Paris, Texas* is "Sometimes you have to separate to really come together."

It's a nice white cane: "Sneak Previews" critic Roger Ebert asks *Once*

Upon a Time in America star Elizabeth McGovern to comment on the rape scene. A festival official points out that McGovern is not in the room; nor is she in Cannes.

No kidding: Christopher Reeve believes *Superman* is the most difficult role he has played because "you could make an ass of yourself playing Superman."

Depends on how you look at it: Reeve turned down *The Bounty* but is anxious to see it because "I want to see if I have to be jealous of Mel Gibson."

Political awakenings: "I was not brought up to think as I do now," Vanessa Redgrave whispers. "What happened? I suppose life happened."

Tough at the top: Producer Menahem Golan introduces Richard Chamberlain: "This is a very heavy job, just to fly in from Los Angeles. Believe me, I know, I did it sixteen times last year. I was sick a week each time I did it."

Another world: Filipino Lino Brocka brings *Bayan Ko* (My country), his *Man of Iron*, to Cannes: "I grew up movie-mad, and I sat there—a rather lonely little grown boy—and believed everything I saw, and mostly what I saw were American films. There was Jane Powell, always blonde and pretty and well-dressed, whose only problems were if the right boy would ask her to the prom. He always did. There was Esther Williams, always blonde and pretty and well-dressed, whose problems were which millionaire she should marry, and in addition she could stay underwater without needing air for ages. I believed all that literally and thought for a long time that Americans were super-human and that they really could stay underwater without air. I looked around me when I left the theaters and saw that everybody around me were as far from the people on screen as possible, and felt inferior, that something was wrong with us because we weren't all blonde and pretty and well-dressed and we had to worry about things uglier than who would ask us to the prom. I learned later those American films were fantasies that had nothing to do with anyone's life, and that even for Americans, they were sheer fantasies which touched none of the real problems of Americans' lives. When I saw them, they made me momentarily happy while I was in front of the screen, but ultimately they made me miserable with being me and with my life. *Nights of Cabiria* and the other Italian neo-realist films that amazed me—they amazed because the realities of Filipino society were reflected in them —made me miserable while I was watching them and I had to stay in my seat until everyone left because I had dissolved into tears, but ultimately they made me aware of the real world in which a real me lived a life that was not to be scorned, and that is part of the road to happiness.''

☆

1985
Father's Gone on a Business Trip wins the top prize. Norma Aleandro, *Official Version*, and Cher, *Mask*, share best actress. Best actor: William Hurt, *Kiss of the Spider Woman*. Best director: André Téchiné, *Rendez-vous*.

They call that the Cannes-can: A character played by Patti Love in the late Joseph Losey's final film, *Steaming*, says, ''I'd just like to lie there and have people pay to look at me.''

Ditto for all of us: A character played by Vanessa Redgrave in the same film says, ''I'd like to change, but I can't see what I'd change into.''

Leave the halo at home: *Colonel Redl* star Klaus Maria Brandauer says, ''I don't believe in angels. We are all devils in this world, some big, some little, some stupid, some intelligent. I am a brightly colored devil. An actor.''

A patriot for thee: In *Colonel Redl*, the repressed character played by the incandescent Brandauer says, ''Betrayal is a national virtue nowadays.''

Depends on how you look at it: Chicago Art Institute film programmer Richard Pena, asked for an opinion of *Joshua Then and Now*, answers: ''Horrid. Oh, I'm sorry, is that undiplomatic?''

Virginia, there is a Cinderella: One day on the beach, Cari Beauchamp, former press secretary to Jerry Brown, reports, ''I came for the sun this year. That's all. I'm not working. One day on the beach in Cannes several years ago, when I did have some work to do here, I found a ring. I thought it was glass. It wasn't. I took it home and insured it. Someone stole it. The insurance company paid off. And that's how I was able to leave Jerry Brown.''

Why that was a good idea: ''Jerry was neither hetero nor homosexual in his image, despite all the rumors. I always thought he had an asexual image. He encouraged that. All the women who worked for him had closets full of high-necked dresses. I said, 'Jerry, wouldn't it be cheaper to buy habits?' ''

Why he's not Jerry Brown: Actor Ed Harris, asked what he thought about the publicity that implied he would get John Glenn elected president by playing him in *The Right Stuff*, makes a hand gesture that's not nice at all.

Why Harris hurts: Ed Harris says, "Sam Shepard wrote *Fool for Love* for me and of course I did it in New York. Then Robert Altman called me and asked me how to get hold of Sam. I was glad Altman wanted to make the movie. Next thing I know, Altman is making the movie and Sam is playing my part."

Why Bill hurts: *Kiss of the Spider Woman* star William Hurt says of his portrayal of a screaming queen, "I walked the line. It's a tender line. It's like taking a hammer and forging a little gold needle or a feather."

Gotcha, but would you mind repeating that for posterity? William Hurt says, "The biggest decision in your work is to do the work."

Gray flannel by day: The writer of *Mask* says of the motorcycle gangs in the movie, "I didn't want them to be comic relief. But they weren't Hell's Angels in real life. They all had day jobs."

Blissed-out: A character in the Australian film *Bliss* says, "The whole of the Western world is built on things that cause cancer. My wife is dying of cancer. People come like ghouls to look at her. Her real friends stay away, of course."

And for Cordelia, Barbra Streisand? Jean-Luc Godard announces he will make *King Lear* for Cannon Films with—if everyone says yes—Marlon Brando as Lear and Woody Allen as the fool, from a script by Norman Mailer.

Maybe it'll wipe a mouth somewhere: Godard signs the contract on a cocktail napkin.

The Good Samaritan is alive and well in New Jersey: Peter Bogdanovich says of rock 'n' roll's top pessimist, Bruce Springsteen, "He sings songs of hope for people who have no hope."

A guy with a bent for the rhetorical when it comes to questions: *Mishima* director Paul Schrader poses with his child for the cameras, sits down to lunch and asks, "What kind of man would stoop to exploiting his sixteen-month-old daughter to promote a movie about death?"

Fresh from the frying pan: *Mishima* and *Kiss of the Spider Woman* screen-writer Leonard Schrader, brother to Paul, can't come to Cannes because he is at work on a screenplay for Volker Schlöndorff about modern-day Mormons, but he tells *Mishima* producer Tom Luddy, "If I can handle the Japanese right wing, I think I can handle the Mormons."

She got over it: *Mishima* set designer Eiko Ishioka remembers, "Once Paul didn't like one of my sets. I cried."

She didn't get over it: Mrs. Mishima, still violently opposed to the movie, has been paid in full, but producer Luddy reports, "The money is in escrow. She won't pick it up, and we won't take it back."

Nixonian, was he? Paul Schrader says of Mishima, "Those who knew him longest understood they knew him least."

Mister Mishima would approve: *Mishima* star Ken Ogata says, "After playing this role, my hair was completely gray and my eyes got very old."

Dunno: Ira Deutschman, the distributor of *Pumping Iron II, The Women*, picks up the muscle ladies at the airport and wonders, "Do you offer to carry the luggage of somebody who can bench-press you?"

That's what Cannes is for: British film seller Carole Myer says, "I do great business in Cannes. But I haven't seen a film here in three years."

Mother told you it would come in handy: *Joshua Then and Now* star James Woods says, "You have to be smart to play smart, I guess, and one of the things going for me is that I have an academic background."

Truer words: Told he has the reputation of having the highest IQ in Tinsel Town, Woods laughs, "That doesn't take much in Hollywood."

Mister Mishima felt the same way: Woods says of the filmmaking process, "It's extremely important to have a sense of life or death about what you do. It has to be perfect or nothing."

Next question? Asked how he could direct *First Blood, Uncommon Valor*, and also *Joshua*, Ted Kotcheff replies, "I guess I've become a restless person. I like to do different things. I grew up in a tough neigborhood so there's a streak in me that's interested in violence. On the other hand, my parents wanted me to be a concert violinist."

Bad trip: Gary Busey gazes at the glitter of the Carlton Hotel and hoots, "Whew, it'd be something to be on acid in here!"

Extenuating circumstances: An Amazon Indian in *The Emerald Forest* says to a white boy he has kidnapped, "Even though you are a Termite Child, I had not the heart to send you back to the Dead World."

Sounds like Times Square to me: *Emerald Forest* director John Boorman says, "If you go into the rain forest, there are various things to cut you, to prick you, to bite you, to eat you."

Honesty is the best policy: June Allyson appears in Cannes with Jimmy Stewart for a special screening of *The Glenn Miller Story* and says, "I was usually known as Miss Goody Two Shoes. The studio had previews of the movie and people said June Allyson would never stay mean, so we reshot the end of the film, which I think actually ruined the film, because it made me Miss Goody Two Shoes again."

Get the record straight: Jimmy Stewart says, "Mr. Hitchcock did not say actors are cattle. He said they should be treated like cattle. It's sort of like a cowboy steering all the cows and calves around. Mr. Hitchcock never had a lasso as far as I can remember."

Incitement to riot: *The Coca-Cola Kid* director Dusan Makavejev, informed that the old Palais of the festival is to be torn down for a Sheraton hotel, says, "Then the last day of the festival, let's blow it up."

The esthetics of anarchy: Makavejev bubbles happily, "In real life, we do not know who will be run over by a truck this afternoon; one of us could be dead this afternoon; we don't know who; that's the pleasure of life."

And he reads, too: Cannes festival translator Henri Béjart, taking refuge from the rain, shows up at Clint Eastwood's yacht with a shawl wrapped around his head. Asks the Man with No Name, "Are you in rehearsal for *Anna Karenina*?"

He reads, too, part two: Clint Eastwood tells Henri Béjart he would like to have filmed a book by Yukio Mishima, if Paul Schrader hadn't got there first.

He thinks, too: Explaining that one of his favorite films, *Honky Tonk Man*, will "open" in Australia on cassette without benefit of theatrical release, Clint Eastwood says, "We've done away with the middle man. The theater."

Cher shares: "It is no surprise to me Peter (Bogdanovich) would serve his interests before serving the interests of the film," the actress snaps of her director.

Turnabout with a vengeance: "I have to tell you I used every trick in the book to get that performance," the director of *Mask* snaps of his actress.

Annals of the suddenly famous: The other best-actress recipient, Norma Aleandro, arrives for the awards dinner, finds no table reserved for her, leaves, and later explains, "We did not stay, not because we were mad

—they would have made tables for us, finally—but I was hungry. We went out for pizza.''

Quote du jour, from Godard's Détective: ''Seeing is deceiving.''

Touché: Asked to discuss the Pope's negative reaction to *Hail Mary*, his modern retelling of a familiar story, and also asked about the narrative ''confusion'' of his recent films, Godard replies, ''The Pope certainly felt I could tell a story.''

Touché, part two: Pressed further on his opinion of the Pope's opinion of him, Godard smiles, ''I believe what Jesus said, but Jesus never said priests couldn't be fools.''

Why we can sleep tight: The character based on Marilyn Monroe in *Insignificance* says, ''Figure it out. All the same people with their fingers on the button are the people who own all the places that would get blown up.''

The last last word on Cannes, and maybe on the cosmos: *Insignificance* director Nicolas Roeg remarks, ''Insignificance, as a noun, is a state in which nothing is significant. It matters not that I'm a director and you're a plumber. Insignificance is . . . insignificance is the state of things.''

Reviews, 1978-1985

All of Me

When the spirit of Edwina Cutwater (Lily Tomlin), who's so rich she sneezes into pop-up disposable tissues made of Irish linen trimmed in lace, is transmigrated by mistake into the button-down body of attorney Roger Cobb (Steve Martin), who's such a nerd his idea of a good career move is to go out and buy a vest, androgynous chaos breaks loose. One side of Roger's body is controlled by Roger and it goes right on being macho and nerdlike and saying things like, "You're an energy vampire, you're gonna suck all the fun out of being a lawyer!" The other side of his body is controlled by Edwina, who's filthy rich but clean-minded (she's a phallophobe) and says things like, "I'm thinking of very old nuns," when Roger is ready to make out with a willing wench.

All of Me, directed by Carl Reiner and written by Phil Alden Robinson (with obvious assists from Tomlin), plays the premise for a fusillade of laughs—this is a screwball comedy for the eighties, a film that draws from but does not imitate the classics of the thirties. Only toward the end, when the insoluble situation demands a resolution, does the energy flag. But by then a good time has been had by all. Although Tomlin walks away with the audience's affection in a sumptuously garish characterization— she rides a wheelchair like a rodeo star; demands of her nurse, "Gas me!" when in need of oxygen; and orders an underling, "Zip it, Frank"— it is Martin who carries the movie and deserves an Oscar. (Did anybody ever think that anybody would ever think Steve Martin would deserve an Oscar?) His performance is a physicalized masterpiece, an encyclopedia of body language that ranks with the best of Buster Keaton and Charles Chaplin, and that will probably turn Marcel Marceau apple-green with envy.

From the second Edwina enters Roger and the body becomes a battle-ground, Martin is in total control of an apparently uncontrollable instru-ment. Roger goes to the bathroom and has to coax the Edwina hand to do its duty; Roger tries to drive a car and the Edwina foot floors it; Roger tries to greet a friend and the Edwina paw flops forward, limp as boiled asparagus. Reiner and his collaborators have tried to compensate for the inequity between the two roles—Tomlin is off screen a great deal—by hav-ing Edwina appear in the mirror every time Roger checks himself out, but good as she is, it's obvious that in agreeing to this movie Tomlin agreed to saw the second violin. Still, thank God she did. Who else could read the line, "I love it when you talk like a beer commercial," with the same combination of arch disgust and grudging affection? For once, a sequel should be encouraged, an *All of Me Too*, in which the roles are reversed and Edwina gets to strut her feminine stuff while distracted by the butch lusts of the beast within.   *(1984)*

All That Jazz

Near the beginning Cliff Gorman, playing a stand-up comic patterned after Lenny Bruce, sets up a litany: "Death is in," he sings, and he re-views Dr. Elisabeth Kübler-Ross's five stages of demise (anger, denial, bargaining, depression, and acceptance): "Sounds like a Jewish law firm." Near the end, he talks about death with dignity: "You know what death with dignity is? You don't drool." *All That Jazz* has been organized by Bob Fosse, himself a victim of a near-fatal heart attack (his collaborator on the script, Robert Alan Aurthur, died of heart disease before the film was completed), around the work of Dr. Kübler-Ross, whose *On Death and Dying* has gained acceptance as the definitive statement of the way we live when we die, and he has used the idiom of the Broadway musical to tap-dance the five stages into popular consciousness. There is even a neat numerical symmetry. As director-choreographer Joe Gideon, Fosse's alter-ego, lies dying, he hallucinates production numbers. Five stages, five numbers.

The film goes to the core of what West Coast poet Ted Rosenthal, dead at thirty-four of leukemia, meant when he wrote, "Life is grim, but not necessarily serious." *All That Jazz* has stirred up a lot of controversy and it's not hard to see why: as a view of death looked at from as close to the inside as someone still living can get, it is virtually unprecedented. Other worthy essays on the subject such as *All the Way Home*, *Cries and*

Whispers, and *The Seventh Seal* were serious and reverential; the most recent worthy American effort, *Promises in the Dark*, benefits from Dr. Kübler-Ross, but it , too, is a death-with-dignity picture of the no-drool school. Fosse's film is neither reverential nor serious; it is grim, but it sings; it is articulate, but it spits; it is heavy, but it dances; and although it is controlled by a master technician, it is embarrassingly confessional.

In *How Could I Not Be Among You?* Rosenthal reported that his terminal diagnosis allowed for "certain positive feelings and one was the total sympathy I would get from all people by making it a kind of grandstand play and announcing it. And it was almost a sadistic feeling. And everybody came over and kissed me and loved me and hugged me. But there was this undercurrent. . . . I was scared."

That sadistic, grandstanding component is part of *All That Jazz*; people may feel especially threatened by it because it utilizes big musical razzle-dazzle that has been associated exclusively with escapism. There is something repugnant and egregiously egocentric (also obnoxiously funny) about the hospital hallucination, when the ex-wife, girlfriend, and daughter exit atop a white hearse followed by chorus girls waving feather fans. What of an earlier sequence when actual footage of open-heart surgery is intercut with producers discussing the profit they could make from the director's death? And how is one meant to react as Gideon, wearing the rosy makeup of a corpse and a glittering Liberace jacket, sings in smiley close-up, "I think I'm gonna die"?

Roy Scheider, who plays Gideon, looks as much like the director of *Cabaret* and *Lenny* as the makeup department's considerable arts will allow. Every day starts with the same ritual: a shower, a squirt of Visine into each abused eye, a tablet of Dexedrine, a long look in the mirror, a vaudevillian lift of the hands, and the reiteration of the phrase, "It's showtime, folks." Every day is spent in editing films (Gorman plays Dustin Hoffman playing Bruce) or choreographing Broadway shows (Leland Palmer plays Fosse's ex-wife, Gwen Verdon, playing Roxie Hart in *Chicago*) or dealing with a daughter (Erzsebet Foldi plays Michelle, a stand-in for Fosse's child, Nicole), or soothing a new girlfriend (Ann Reinking plays Fosse's girlfriend, Ann Reinking). But one day, every day changes as Gideon falls victim to a heart attack, an ailment that leads to open-heart surgery and alters what remains of Gideon's life.

In the hospital, Gideon has the elongated facial planes, the tortured eyes, and the faintly persimmon complexion of Don Quixote as El Greco might have painted him. Gideon's surreal psychoanalytic conversations with Angelique (Jessica Lange)—representing his muse, sex, death, heaven, hell, you name it—turn from his romantic difficulties to his chances of survival. A man who has seen his entire life in terms of showbiz glitter and pelvic thrust finds that he is incapable of seeing his death in any other lexicon: he lies in bed, tubes violating a score of veins, and choreographs the biggest numbers of his life. His daughter sings "Some of These Days"; a chorus line waving fans the color of doves sings "Who's Sorry Now?" and his ex-wife bumps and grinds and belts "After You've Gone."

From a dance standpoint, the best work Fosse may ever do is in *All That Jazz*. One number—rejected by Gideon's producers—is the ultimate, orgiastic conclusion of most of Fosse's choreography. It begins with three couples—male/female, female/female, male/male—exploring their all-but-naked bodies and ends in a communal Kama Sutra that lays bare the erotic underpinnings of Broadway dance. It is the sexiest example of pop dance I have ever seen, and using the word pop to describe it may be too patronizing. In an utterly different key, Ann Reinking, whose thighs could sink ships, dances with Gideon's daughter to Peter Allen's "Everything Old Is New Again" and the two women have the improvisational freshness of the beginning of Judy Garland's living-room medley to James Mason in *A Star Is Born*.

Fosse's reactions to other people in the film are unfiltered—he is harder on himself vis-à-vis his women than Fellini was on himself in *8½*, but they share the same view of producers as buffoons and of collaborators as parasites. Fosse is a little less convinced of the primacy of his genius than Fellini was, however, and that's ironic, because at this juncture in his life I don't think Fellini could begin to compete with the technical virtuosity Fosse displays in *All That Jazz*. Few directors in any country could. This former dancer has brought to his cinematic autobiography a talent that nearly justifies his treatment of himself as the rakish Jesus Christ of Broadway, suffering self-crucifixion in his task to bring pleasure to the masses. He gives death a new lease on life.   *(1979)*

Amadeus

Amadeus, the Milos Forman film of Peter Shaffer's hit play, has as much to do with the historical Wolfgang Amadeus Mozart as Mika Waltari's novel *The Egyptian* had to do with real life along the Nile, but that doesn't stop it from being a smart and vastly enjoyable exercise in camp. *The Egyptian* was made into a thoroughly ridiculous and anachronistic but consummately entertaining 1954 costume drama with Edmund Purdom and Victor Mature. Something very similar has happened to Shaffer's play in Forman's film, which features a foul-mouthed Mozart who looks and sounds like Paul Simon on a bender, a perky Mrs. Mozart so West Coast she'll probably go back to windsurfing and coke-snorting in Santa Monica when her beloved "Wolfie" dies young, and an Emperor Franz Joseph who carries on as if he were the newly appointed chairman of the board of Austria, Inc. The movie is a parade of witty caricatures, deftly drawn on thin air.

Shaffer, a middle-brow playwright with a savvy commercial sense, specializes in "metaphysical" explanations of the inexplicable. *The Royal Hunt of the Sun* purported to explain why the Inca empire fell, and *Equus* went after the psychological roots of the idea of the holy. The press kit for *Amadeus* includes a modest comparison of Shaffer's "fantasia" on Mozart's life to George Bernard Shaw's *Saint Joan*; both plays are said to be rooted in the tradition of the Shavian "Theatre of Ideas." The "idea" in *Amadeus* is that God, for reasons known only to Him, has decided to make "an obscene child"—the scatalogically obsessed and sexually impish Mozart (Tom Hulce)—the "instrument" of His divine voice. Court composer Antonio Salieri, a good but not great Italian musician and (until the advent of what he calls "the creature") a good but not great man, is at first perplexed and then saddened and finally outraged by the perversity of Himself in allotting the ultimate talent in music to a rutting runt. In a line cut from the film, Salieri compared himself ruthlessly to Mozart: "From the ordinary he created legends, whilst I, from legends, created only the ordinary." (No wonder Shaffer sympathizes with Salieri.) In the theater, *Amadeus* strained to depict the tragedy of the second-rate; Forman has magically turned the material into a farce for the unfulfilled. The play's momentum was hampered by Shaffer's intellectualizing and by the fact that the villain, Salieri, was where the protagonist, Mozart, should have been—*Amadeus* was *Othello* told from Iago's point of view. Forman has given Mozart equal screen time and has refused to treat Shaffer's metaphysical mewlings regarding God's perversity as anything but a parody of a play of ideas. The film recognizes that, in the skewed scheme of things, implanting the immortality of genius in the mortal flesh of a horny hell-raiser is a pretty piddling example of divine mysteriousness next to, say, the slaughter of innocent babies in any war or natural disaster you'd care to mention.

Shot mostly in Czechoslovakia, decorated with a powdered-sugar sweetness and creamy lavishness unseen since the days of Josef von Sternberg, and performed by an eager to please, rootin'-tootin' American cast that would be comfortable in *Oklahoma!*, *Amadeus* is junk food par excellence. (There is nothing junky about the music, of course, and there is a lot of it.) In elderly makeup as the mildly senile Salieri, F. Murray Abraham is a courtly, rubbery old demon with a nose that wrinkles beneficently at the camera, like the faces of the Phase One cuddlies in *Gremlins*; the Mozart of Tom Hulce (pronounced Hulse) is a cackling, gleeful gargoyle, an ithyphallic cherub; and, in a small role as Salieri's opera-singing wife, Christine Ebersole is a rococo gum drop, all heaving pastel bosoms—Dolly Parton on a time-machine tour. Elizabeth Berridge is a Malibu you-hoo as the common-as-dirt Mrs. Mozart, however (too much method, too little madness), and Roy Dotrice, the composer's overbearing father, cuts a self-effacing hole in the screen.

Amadeus begins in a madhouse borrowed from Ken Russell circa *The Music Lovers* and *The Devils*, but Russell is merely one of the many directors Forman (*Hair*, *One Flew Over The Cuckoo's Nest*, *Ragtime*) sends up in his catalogue of cinematic excess—*Amadeus* ceases to be entertaining only on the occasions it forgets to be excessive. That's not often. People who bought Shaffer's line about a "Theatre of Ideas" will probably be affronted by this film, which offers one of the most astonishing internal critiques of its own mechanisms in the history of movies—it's as though Von Sternberg had been conscious of making twaddle when he was making *The Scarlet Empress*—but everyone else will no doubt be delighted. Speaking of the relationship between court composers and their rulers, Salieri said (in another line cut from the film), "We sacramentalized their mediocrity." Forman's sacrament is as enjoyable as its mediocrity is profound. (*1984*)

And The Ship Sails On

And The Ship Sails On, Federico Fellini's charming evocation of a different and vanished world, and a different and vanished style of movie-making, opens on a dock in July 1914. The images are at first silent, jerky, in black and white, and people keep ducking in front of the camera to make faces at it and fools of themselves. Slowly, almost imperceptibly, the images slow down and smooth out, the sound is turned up, and delicate color appears like the blush of apricot-tinted sunrays on cottony clouds at dawn; in no time at all, the ship is being boarded, the stevedores are lustily singing opera, and the voyage is in full Technicolor sail. Painter, set-designer, and opera aficionado David Hockney remarked recently that *And The Ship Sails On* is one of his favorite films, and there are a lot of people who are going to find themselves experiencing a rush of affection for Fellini they would not have thought possible after the tiresome indulgences and dreary repetitions of the moralistic-in-Babylon movies, beginning with *La Dolce Vita* (1960) and continuing through *City of Women* twenty years later. *And The Ship Sails On* belongs to the other and smaller tradition in Fellini, the playful and nostalgic Fellini who made *The Clowns* (1970) and the autobiographical *Amarcord* (1973), the latter co-written with Tonino Guerra, who collaborated on the ship-shape *Ship* script.

This *Ship* is a simon-simple allegory that makes *Ship of Fools* seem dense, but where the foolish ship was serious and heavy-handed, the Fellini ship is neither. Aboard a splendiferously phony ocean liner on a spectacularly stylized sea, a journalist (Freddie Jones) asks, "Where are all these beautiful people going?" and the answer is, of course, to hell and the First World War. But Fellini dosen't press the point; instead of the spangly anti-war statement you might expect, most of *And The Ship Sails On* is a gentle comedy that exults in its own artifice. Peering at a patently painted sunset, one woman chirps to another, "How beautiful! It looks painted!" Fellini is the granddaddy of effects that have been revived in *Diva* and *The Moon in the Gutter* by Jean-Jacques Beineix and in *One From the Heart* by Francis Coppola, and he brings them off with ease. Another film that actually set audiences to grinning at its endearing artificiality was Ingmar Bergman's opera masterpiece *The Magic Flute*, which *And The Ship Sails On* sometimes resembles: as Bergman gloried in the creaking mechanics of opera, Fellini glories in the klunky machinery of moviemaking.

Guerra co-wrote not only *Amarcord* for Fellini, he worked on *L'Avventura*, *La Notte*, *The Red Desert*, *Blow-Up*, and *Identification of a Woman* for Michelangelo Antonioni; *Sunflower* and *The Guest* for Vittorio De Sica; *The Mattei Affair*, *Lucky Luciano*, *Illustrious Corpses*, *Christ Stopped at Eboli* and *Three Brothers* for Francesco Rosi; and *The Night of the Shooting Stars* for the Taviani brothers. He has orchestrated Fellini's large cast, full of the "Fellini faces" audiences demand of cinema's most extravagant showman (the thinking man's DeMille), with a subtlety noticeably absent in most of Fellini's solo symphonies. And he hasn't worked out the First World War allegory so it's reductively obvious. True, Serbs are taken on by the ship as it sails to an island to conduct a memorial service for a great opera singer (played by Janet Suzman, seen solely in a silent movie carried on board by one of her admirers) and an action by a "Serbian terrorist" nearly unleashes an apocalypse, but as much time is spent on a comically perverse relationship between an impresario (Peter Cellier) who abases himself before his rapacious wife (Norma West) as on anything overtly allegorical or political. The hypnotizing of a chicken by a basso and the travails of a lovesick rhinoceros are also recorded with mock gravity. This is not, in sum, a *Ship of Fools*, and it's not *Fellini Marineland*, though there are elements of both those things; instead, it's a storybook *Ship of Twits*, Fellini's serene dream of a time that may have existed only in sleep.   (*1984*)

Apocalypse Now

When it was all over, when the audience had applauded desultorily, too devastated and perhaps too heartbroken and certainly too depressed to summon the bravos that were demanded, Francis Ford Coppola's $30-million Vietnam War movie, *Apocalypse Now*, would dissolve in the mind into one long, fluid camera movement, a movie fabricated from a single operatic take to a single operatic purpose, a movie commencing with the mundane and ending with the monstrous, a movie made with the swiftness, the silence, the subtlety—and the savagery—of a spear thrown home to the center of the heart.

Apocalypse Now is the Vietnam movie a lot of us were waiting for, but it turns out to be more than that: it turns out to be the *movie* a lot of us were waiting for. Movies have always been—at their most extravagantly appealing, sensually exciting and rationally disturbing—pieces of art with the power to bypass our defenses. A few times in the history of movies, one caught glimpses of a power that could turn the screen experience into a hallucinatory celebration of irrationality, of pure feeling, and even, perhaps, of insanity. *Apocalypse Now* goes further in that direction more successfully than any movie ever has: like its main character, a special-forces assassin named Willard (Martin Sheen), like the nation whose Southeast Asia involvement it excoriates, and like the times it talks of, it is larger than life and every bit as crazy. Filming Vietnam as the product of a madman's hallucination was—it now seems so obvious—the only way to film it, the only way to separate it from good wars, and the only way to re-create the experience so completely that questions of *Apocalypse Now*'s flaws (and it has them) sound like questions posed by an academic teetering on the edge of an abyss.

The first shot is of palm trees undulating in tropic heat. Jim Morrison sings "This is the end my friend" on the soundtrack and the palm trees explode into flames. Immediately, we are yanked into a naturalistic Saigon. Willard, the assassin, is given a mission: to travel up a river into Cambodia and put an end to the reign of a madman, an American officer named Kurtz (Marlon Brando) who has set up a kingdom among the Montagnards. "He's out there operating without any decent restraint," Willard is told, and we see without further assistance that Kurtz is the United States in Vietnam. Later we see, with a great deal of assistance, that he is also the dark side of all of us, the side of our face that avoids the sun—he is Mr. Hyde to Willard's Dr. Jekyll.

The plot will sound familiar: it is taken from Joseph Conrad's *Heart of Darkness*. *Apocalypse Now* flies into that pulsating black hole on the wings of a hawk, with compassion carried symbolically on the wings of a dove. The rest of the movie charts Willard's journey, and it is nothing less than a history of the American presence in Vietnam. Americans—the fun-loving, aggressive Americans of *The Deer Hunter*—water-ski on the Nung River and overturn sampans. Robert Duvall, as a Commander in a black cowboy hat, leads his troops to the beach and allows them to surf under enemy fire. Coppola himself appears as as network television reporter, exhorting soldiers to stop looking at his cameras and start looking at the village they are in the process of incinerating. A helicopter attack that destroys a hamlet is filmed ecstatically to Wagner: this movie hates war but it is strong enough to show you, and to make you feel, the giddy excitement and almost sexual gratification of devastation and danger. Then Playboy Playmates of the Month are dropped into the jungle and undulate like the palm trees for the benefit of our boys.

The film is going crazy. The boys on the boat take drugs—one of them drops acid at the Playboy concert. The atmosphere partakes of Carnival time—Tivoli Gardens at dusk or Disneyland at midnight. Willard's boat detains a vegetable-laden junk on the river—the soldiers are very young and very frightened and very nervous and for no reason at all massacre the Vietnamese going to market. They are just boys. Nice boys. A lot of people die.

Willard meets Kurtz. "Are my methods unsound?" the king with the glistening and hairless head asks. "I don't see any methods at all, sir," Willard responds. But he does. Kurtz is the United States in 1968—someone says of him "the man is clear in his mind but his soul is mad" —and the method of his madness is to appear utterly sane. *Apocalypse Now* ends the only way it can: there is a new order but nothing changes. Joseph Conrad will not soon go out of date.

The obvious comparison can be dispensed with summarily: esthetically, philosophically, historically, and psychologically, *Apocalypse Now* is to *The Deer Hunter* what James Joyce is to Ernest Hemingway. Coppola focuses on his Americans—the only Vietnamese characters in *Apocalypse* are victims and murderers seen peripherally—as sharply as Michael

Cimino did in *The Deer Hunter*—and he demonstrates their reasons for being in Vietnam even more succinctly than Cimino did. But *Apocalypse* is not filmed, as *The Deer Hunter* was, entirely from their point of view and it is not, therefore, a work of nascent fascism. And on a purely technical level, it makes *The Deer Hunter* look like something shot within the confines of a movie studio outhouse: the scope of *Apocalypse* is Shakespearean, its incidents (unlike the notorious Russian-roulette business in *Deer Hunter*) historically accurate, and its choreography magnificent.

Martin Sheen is on screen for the duration and gives a performance of amazing restraint. Brando does not appear until the end of the first two hours—he has little to do, but does it well. The film is narrated to words written by Michael Herr, author of *Dispatches*, and they are very good words, but I'm not sure they are necessary. Neither am I sure that Brando's jungle palace should resemble a pre-Columbian Tarzan temple—it's hallucinatory in the most banal fantasy-art way. But none of that is retained by the audience. What is retained is the fact that this film is a direct descendant of *The Birth of a Nation*, the fact that its importance would be difficult to overemphasize, the fact that it has made some sense of the senseless.   (*1979*)

Atlantic City

As Lou, an almost prissily natty numbers-runner certain that everything —even the ocean—has deteriorated, Burt Lancaster gives the performance of his life in Louis Malle's Canadian-financed film *Atlantic City*. It might be fairer to call the picture a John Guare film, for Malle has entered entirely into his gifted playwright's episodic, jazzy view of the universe—Guare's script for *Atlantic City* is a commodious comic masterpiece, but it's also a serious fable about the dangers of dreaming.

Everyone in the picture, placed affectionately in an evocative Atlantic City devolving from tasteful faded glory to tasteless refurbished glitter, dreams of getting ahead. (Is Atlantic City a metaphor for the filmmakers' America? Probably.) For the renegade sixties couple Dave (the talented Canadian actor Robert Joy) and Chrissie (Hollis McLaren, the schizo of *Outrageous!*), the boardwalk is a substitute for the San Francisco of 1966, buried as completely as Atlantis. The pregnant Chrissie wants to take LSD "so we can learn from the baby's wisdom" and Dave, a coke dealer, wants to dump his stash and his past. Sally (Susan Sarandon), who is both Chrissie's sister and Dave's estranged wife, shovels shrimp behind the counter of a casino oyster bar but meanwhile sees to *her* dream by attending dealers' school—"I gotta develop my blackjack; I'm gonna deal my way to Europe"—and, total woman that she is, works on improving her body with lemon juice and her soul with a cassette of Bellini's *Norma*. When she becomes romantically involved with Lou, she has one request: "Teach me stuff."

Near Sally's tattered domicile (Sally would use that word, rather than the mundane "apartment") Lou waits gallantly on Grace (Kate Reid), a former beauty queen and mobster's moll reduced by time and Lou's lack of discipline to a state of kitschy caterwaul. Lying in a bed strewn with ribbons and poodles and other fussy things, Grace bitches at and about Lou; if she were an inanimate object, she'd be a battered pink plastic lawn flamingo, but Lou, a romantic to the tips of his carefully ironed silk ties, cherishes the memory of what she was, while mildly grousing at the monstrous Baby Jane she is.

Lou's most notable characteristic is his tolerance: a man old enough to have "run numbers for the dinosaurs," a man who can say wistfully, "The Atlantic Ocean was *something* then"—this is not a man apt to be angry long at infirmity, senility, or even cruelty. Lou's dapper, chivalrous, compassionate existence informs the sensibility of *Atlantic City* with something very much like love; the movie's unpredictably explosive, joke-like tone can be inferred from the fact that Lou's splendid reviviscence is made possible by murder. *Atlantic City* is a cautionary comedy about a place where dreams can come true. Too true. (*1981*)

The Ballad of Narayama

The final forty minutes of Shohei Imamura's *The Ballad of Narayama*, winner of the Palme d'Or at the 1983 Cannes Film Festival, achieve greatness, the kind of clear-headed euphoria that comes only after the worst has been witnessed and resolved. People who have watched a loved one die a lingering but in the end calm and accepting death often talk of the experience as having been "beautiful," and it is that sort of beauty Imamura brings to the screen, a fatalistic, ferocious beauty that is a fitting conclusion to a fatalistic, ferocious film.

Narayama is a mountain in northern Japan where the elderly were once taken to die, regardless of their health, when they reached the age of seventy. Or so legend had it. *The Ballad of Narayama* is based on an anthropologically unverified mountain ballad that became a best-selling story in 1956 (the author was Shichiro Fukazawa) that in turn became, two years later, a popular, stylized, and sentimental black-and-white film by Keisuke Kinoshita. The new *Narayama*, in color, is neither stylized nor sentimental—to Western eyes, it is nearly terrifying in its repudiation of sentiment. But its presentation of earthy peasants unabashedly fighting and fornicating has proved equally popular in Japan, though perhaps not for the same reasons the film has been popular in the West. To Imamura, the story of the young man (the gifted Ken Ogata) and the sixty-nine-year-old grandmother Orin (Sumiko Sakamoto), who actively accepts her fate, believing as she does that her demise will allow the survival of new life in her starving village, is an affirmation of "primitive" wisdom and a critique of modern Japan. But the film works equally well when interpreted as a critique of inflexible tradition (Orin, in excellent health, is an asset to her people) and an affirmation of the value of the individual. It is no surprise that some Japanese critics were suspicious of the film *because* of its success in the West; they were probably right to be, in that Imamura's script is capable of speaking out of two sides of the same mouth.

In each case, the speech is eloquent. Whether the actions of the peasants are seen as Imamura sees them—"Enduring cruelty, following the laws of nature, adapting to its rules, this is the object of life, its most complete fulfillment"—or as the benighted and brutal activities of a people in need of "civilization," as they are likely to be viewed by Westerners, *The Ballad of Narayama* is an unforgettable and unique experience. The movie is full of low comedy and high visual poetry, and it's evident why William Shakespeare, another master at combining slapstick and poetry, is so popular in the East. But for Shakespeare death is usually tragedy, the result of character flaws and missteps and circumstance, while in *The Ballad of Narayama* it is the logical conclusion of a life lived well, an event to be greeted by the dying with stoicism and by the living with celebration.   (*1984*)

Betrayal

One of the first lines in the *très élégant* film version of Harold Pinter's play *Betrayal* is almost a parody of the famous Pinter Pause, the evocative ellipsis the British playwright has parlayed into a twenty-year career. Jerry (Jeremy Irons) has met Emma (Patricia Hodge), his ex-lover and the wife of his best friend and business associate Robert (Ben Kings-

ley), in a pub. Drinks. "Well (pause) cheers," Jerry says. Similar nice-
ties intersperse awkward glances framed by that ubiquitous (pause), and
then the conversation gains ground:

Emma: "Sarah's ten (pause) she must be."

Jerry: "She is (pause) she must be."

And:

Emma: (pause) "You think of me sometimes?"

Jerry: (pause) "I think of you sometimes."

We have met Jerry and Emma two years after their romance has ended;
the film goes on to track them backward through time to the point, nine
years earlier, at which their first tryst (one of the many "betrayals" of
the title) took place. For years, Jerry and Robert—Robert is a publisher,
Jerry a literary agent who supplies Robert with writers—have been friends;
for years, Jerry and Emma have met for what appear to be remarkably
passionless and iniquitously talkative couplings at a rented flat. On one
momentous occasion, they meet but do not mate; on another (the film's
finest sequence), Jerry and Robert discuss at lunch a trip to Italy during
which Robert discovered Emma had been getting it on with Jerry. The
food goes unnoticed, the waiter is berated by Robert, and feelings are
actually and emphatically expressed. That marks the scene as an oddity:
usually in *Betrayal* feelings are either betrayed or (at best) suggested.
Pinter is peerless at orchestrating the all but inaudible melodies of
innuendo.

There is little doubt that the film's schematic analysis of upper-crust
adulterous fall-out is clear, concise, and probably close to universal: the
troublesome triangle has earned its laurels as "eternal" for a reason.
Director David Jones choreographs the nonstop push and pull of speech
and silence with dexterity, and his cast is properly arch and imperious,
treating the lines as if they were stalks of celery to be snapped sharply in
half. Despite the extreme ingenuity of the concept, the craft in the direction, and the art in much of the acting, the end product has all the novelty
of divorce. Subtract time-travel and Pinter's expert manipulation of ambiguity and you are left as hapless witness to a gray-flannel affair (don't
people get enough of this in real life?). There is no law that fornication
must be fun, or even interesting, but this extramarital dalliance is enough
to restore monogamy's good name, which may be what producer Sam
Spiegel had in mind when he told *The New York Times* how "moral" he
felt the movie to be. The fear he hoped to implant in the audience's heart,
Spiegel said, was "There but for the grace of God . . . " Well, the thing to
fear is not wasting away from illicit love, or being trapped in tangled webs
of deceit; the bogeyman that gets you in *Betrayal* is boredom.   (*1983*)

The Big Chill

The last word on *The Big Chill* may belong to director Henry Jaglom (*Can She Bake a Cherry Pie?*) who dismissed it with: "Neil Simon does *The Return of the Secaucus Seven*." Writer-director Lawrence Kasdan's look at a reunion of survivors of the sixties is nostalgic and glib, it's funny and slick, it's acted to high heaven and directed at sitcom speed, but after you're out of the theater and after the chuckles have died down, you may try to figure out what it all meant and give up: *The Big Chill* is big, beautiful, and echoingly empty.

The funeral that brings the characters together amidst much cross-cutting indebted to Robert Altman's *Nashville* and *A Wedding* (alternate title for this one: *A Funeral*) is a device and nothing more; although the friend who died, a suicide, is discussed as the weekend wears on, we never learn much about him except that he was idealistic and had a young girl friend, Chloe (Meg Tilly), to whom he made love on the day he died. Losers are given little attention here; it is the well-groomed survivors and their plasticine problems that concern Kasdan:

⭐ Sam (Tom Berenger), rich, hunky TV star. Problem: no one takes him seriously;

⭐ Sarah (Glenn Close), physician, mother, moderate beauty. Problem: she's too perfect;

⭐ Harold (Kevin Kline), corporate executive, father, moderately handsome, husband to Sarah. Problem: he's too perfect;

⭐ Michael (Jeff Goldblum), *People* magazine reporter, egomaniac, comedian, lech. Problem: he's not rich enough;

⭐ Meg (Mary Kay Place), lawyer, wealthy, successful, unmarried. Problem: she wants a child;

⭐ Karen (JoBeth Williams), a beauty, wife of an older man, very rich. Problem: husband does not appreciate her;

⭐ Nick (William Hurt), Vietnam veteran, drug dealer. Problem: you name it.

This is not what you'd call a hard-luck group.

Each character, with the exception of the nymphet Chloe, who has one of the movie's few deeply felt moments when she says, "I haven't met very many happy people in my life; how do they act?", is a fast-talking quipster. The journalist: "I'm interviewing a fourteen-year-old blind baton-twirler." The liberal lady lawyer: "I didn't think my clients would be so *guilty*." The lady doctor: "Even fortune cookies are getting cynical." And Nick, the screwed-up veteran who can no longer make love (the movie never explains why), is a comic, too, despite his clinical depression: all these guys and gals are going to grow up to be Lawrence Kasdan, Hollywood screenwriter of *The Empire Strikes Back* and *Return of the Jedi*, Hollywood writer and director of *Body Heat*. Did *everybody* Lawrence Kasdan went to school with sound like Lawrence Kasdan? God knows it's to Kasdan's credit, and to the credit of his cast, that such questions are kept at bay by the cleverness of the picture—by the organ rendition of "You Can't Always Get What You Want" at the funeral; by Sarah's vast amusement when she decides her husband should give Meg a child; by the *People* scribe's horny Ichabod Crane come-on to Chloe; by TV star Sam's plaint, "I lost my idea of what I should be." When *The Bid Chill* is busy being funny, it's a great comedy, but when it goes for depth, it hits bottom an inch down.   (*1983*)

A Bigger Splash

British artist David Hockney, the subject of Jack Hazan's staged documentary *A Bigger Splash*, is a figurative painter whose works are deceptively simple, clear and sunny and clean, like the Southern California so many of them record. But underneath the muted Kodachrome colors of the still lifes, the portraits, and the groupings, there is frequently a core of silence so complete the paintings appear almost menacing, as though they were conceived in a sun-dappled corner of Forest Lawn. When people are present in these paintings, they are contemplative and frozen —self-involved to the point of catatonia. They do not communicate with each other. And one is not certain that they communicate with themselves.

A Bigger Splash, Hazan's first feature, follows the painter and his friends —who are also his subjects—through a period of several years, from Geneva to London to New York. The title, from one of Hockney's most famous pictures (a house, a pool, a diving board, and the wake left by a diver, conspicuous by his absence) refers to the splash he made in the media with his celebrity lifestyle, a combination of Andy Warhol and Truman Capote. It also underlines Hockney's breakup (which occurs during the film) with his longtime model and lover Peter Schlesinger, who vanishes from Hockney's life but leaves rings of ripples.

Some of the film is staged; some not. It is impossible to tell which is which, and I think it is irrelevant in any case. *A Bigger Splash* is not about Hockney's daily life, it is about his creative life, and the director is out to record the aspects of Hockney's existence that wind up on canvas. In this, Hazan is remarkably successful—you have only to compare *A*

Bigger Splash to reverential documentaries such as *Homage to Chagall* to see the difference. A subsidiary theme has to do with the impermanence of life, love, and good looks—symbolized in part by the breakup —and with the permanence of life, love, and good looks as captured in art. Throughout this fascinating, demanding film, Hockney's subjects confront themselves as Hockney sees them: they stand in front of his paintings and stare at themselves. The effect is goose-pimply: they realize that the only thing that will be remembered about them is one man's summation of them. In looking at their portraits, Hockney's subjects are looking at their own immortality. And at their own deaths.

In *David Hockney by David Hockney*, a collection of the artist's work, the painter says that when he first saw *A Bigger Splash*, "My impression of the film was that it was boring and long. . . . Then I thought, the photography was stunning. . . . In fairness to it, in many ways it's a remarkable film; I don't think it could be repeated, because to repeat it, you'd have to find innocent people." It is long, one hundred and five minutes, and much of it is boring. Hockney and his friends speak in ellipses, in the manner of a Pinter play, and although they travel, they go nowhere—jetage Chekhov. One of Hockney's friends realizes Hockney knows that "we're all incredibly critical and little fashion freaks." But Peter, the erstwhile lover who left Hockney (the movie never comes out and tells us that—it never comes out and tells us anything) may have more insight. In a dream sequence, which Hazan films as if it were Hockney's, Peter is swimming in California and emerges from the pool to stare fixedly at the heads of stuffed animals that appear in another Hockney painting. He seems to realize that for Hockney, and for posterity, he has become a stuffed head, a lasting but empty image of himself. Like the rest of the film, the dream sequence is filmed at a sleepwalker's pace and the sound is overamplified (the music belongs in a thriller), while the compositions are distinctly direct and, in their simplicity, evocative and . . . menacing.

What Hazan has done is to make a movie about a painter in that painter's style: Hockney had been at work on a painting of Peter, *Portrait of an Artist* (*Pool with Two Figures*), 1971, when the breakup took place; chronicling his efforts to complete the composition is as close to a narrative thread as the movie allows. Hockney tells a new lover he plans to sell all of his Peter pictures, and he snickers as he says it. The joke is on him: he is his own victim. For him, Peter may cease to exist, but not for anyone else. The only reality that counts in the long run, *A Bigger Splash* implies, is the reality of the artist's work. Art doesn't imitate life—it's all that is remembered of it.   (*1978*)

Body Heat

For almost an hour, the reason for the existence of *Body Heat* is elusive. Certainly, actor William Hurt, as hick Florida lawyer Ned Racine, a swinging single who gets involved with a rich and richly mysterious married woman, gives a bravura performance, but the plot is familiar to the point of implosion: lovers hotter than a hot tin roof and more nervous than the cat on it conspire to murder the woman's husband. *The Postman Always Rings Thrice.* But screenwriter Lawrence Kasdan (*Raiders of the Lost Ark*, *The Empire Strikes Back*), making his debut as a director of his own material, has merely embarked on one of the longest teasers in motion-picture history: the audience is meant to sink in seas of ennui, is meant to wonder why anyone would want to do a middle-class remake of *Postman* hot on the heated heels of the Jack Nicholson-Jessica Lange version. Kasdan sneaks up on you.

The themes of *Body Heat*—that fate delights in a bad joke; that wealth is a spurious goal; that only fools and dogs trust people—are no strangers to *Postman*, and Kasdan's plot is a respectable resurrection of classic suspense melodrama. *Body Heat* has been influenced not only by *Postman*, but also by *Double Indemnity* and *The Maltese Falcon*. The ostensible setting is Florida, but we are really at home in Movieville, on the street of broken and empty dreams called film noir. This is as movie-conscious a movie as *Blowout*, and Hurt has a grand time bringing Bogart to the eighties.

As a director Kasdan has an eager eye. His compositions are nice, and don't let you forget it, but as a dialogue-writer he has an ear just this side of tin. He has been to the Brian De Palma school of screenwriting but, unlike the De Palma of *Blowout*, he has not yet learned to satirize the conventions of clichéd movie lingo. When the mysterious rich bitch ("introducing" Kathleen Turner, icy and okay in a Lauren Bacall role) says, "No one must know," you know where that construction came from—"No one must know" is pure forties, as is the frequency with which the characters suck on cigarettes; there hasn't been so much smoke on the screen since Bette Davis last listed by.

The smoke is thematic. In the first scene, after a steamy bout of love-making with a stewardess, Ned looks across the Florida steppes at a huge fire and says sadly that an important building of his past is in flames. Repeatedly, the landscape is significantly obscured by fog in quantities capable of coating moors roamed by the hound of the Baskervilles, and Ned is forced to feel his way, significantly, through a terrain he thought he knew. Hurt is so good at capturing the charming and chilling Ned, by far the most complex character the star of *Eyewitness* and *Altered States* has been asked to play, that he almost makes up for the film's two primary weaknesses: Kasdan's inexperience (the plotting moves in on little cat's feet; the themes hop at you on phalanxes of frogs' legs) and a message significantly unpleasant. He cannot elevate the film to the ranks of the first-rate, but he does give it the glaze it needs to appear to be a shimmering objet d'art. Actors are said to be clay in the hands of their directors; if that is true, Hurt is a potter's best friend.   (*1981*)

The Bostonians

"Of course I like you too much," Olive Chancellor (Vanessa Redgrave), a dedicated feminist and repressed lesbian, tells the object of her affections, Verena Tarrant (Madeleine Potter). "When I like, I like too much." Olive is a plain woman, Verena is a beauty, and both are committed to improving the lot of their sex in the superficially civilized but still barbaric new American world of Boston and New York, 1875. *The Bostonians*, from the novel by Henry James, is the story of their relationship, one of the strangest in literature.

Unfortunately, that strangeness has survived the transfer to the screen less than intact, and satiric oddity has been replaced by romantic banality. James Ivory, an American director who regularly collaborates with British-born screenwriter Ruth Prawer Jhabvala, and who is renowned for the bloodless good taste of his literary adaptations, has organized a large and talented cast (also on hand: Linda Hunt and Jessica Tandy) as if envious of the pace and patina of "Masterpiece Theatre." Only a few scenes —one between Redgrave and Nancy Marchand (Mrs. Pynchon of "The Lou Grant Show") and several between Christopher Reeve and Potter —have anything approximating energy, and the swooning Reeve-Potter confrontations ironically owe more to Margaret Mitchell than to Henry James.

The Bostonians dramatizes James's fascination with and fear of feminism. In the person of Verena, limned far less satirically on film than in the novel, he constructs an unprecedented puppet, a gloriously gorgeous and sensual woman of uncertain sincerity who enters trancelike states to deliver feminist polemics to the wealthy. Her political mentor, Olive, is a tall, gangly, and melancholic reformer of depth and integrity who carries her sadness as Christ must have carried his cross—fatalistically, but secure in the ultimate vindication of her torture and her task. "I am awkward and dry," Olive says, *sans* self-pity or bitterness; asked why she does not become a more public spokesman for her cause, she asks in turn, "Do I look like the heroine of an occasion?" Redgrave's performance—red-eyed, quivering, opalescent—is peerless, the one incontrovertible reason to see the film.

Olive is engaged in a battle for Verena's soul—and for her body, though she is seldom frank enough to acknowledge to Verena or to herself the full nature of the spoils. Her nemesis is a rich and sexy southerner, Basil Ransom, a chauvinist who knows exactly what he is and what he wants. "My plan," he murmurs in honeyed tones to Verena, "is to keep you home and have a good time with you there." Because Reeve does this sorghum matinee idol schtick so well—James wouldn't recognize this Rhett Butler heartstopper as his somewhat scummy creation—few but the most politically astute are apt to see his invitation for the horror that it is. Other viewers, readers of romances by Harlequin and love stories by Cartland, are likely to think Verena a twit for not knowing a hunk when she sees one.   (*1984*)

The Bounty

Just as each theatrical generation sees a new face of *Hamlet*, maybe every movie era is going to get the *Mutiny on the Bounty* it deserves. The first major treatment of the tale, the 1935 version with Clark Gable as a dashing and uncomplicated Fletcher Christian and Charles Laughton as a slimy and sadistic Captain Bligh, was a perfect parable for a nation preparing to do righteous battle with the authoritarian evil of Adolf Hitler. The second edition, the 1962 adaptation with Marlon Brando as a smartass fop of a Christian who seemed to be repressing homosexuality and God knew what else, and with Trevor Howard as a corporate Bligh who would have presided quite cheerfully as chief of the House Committee on Un-American Activities, was equally apposite—the movie was about trying to keep all kinds of things clamped down, things that a few years later broke free with a vengeance.

And now there is the latest (and, speaking cinematically, the best) version, *The Bounty*, directed by New Zealand's Roger Donaldson (*Smash Palace*). This time Bligh, acted superlatively by Anthony Hopkins, is symbolic of imperialism with a human face—he's a basically decent xenophobe frightened by the loss of "civilization" that occurs when his crew begins cavorting with the natives in Tahiti; he's appalled, if you will, by the threat the easygoing Third World represents to imperialism. Christian, on the other hand, is callow and shallow, a twenty-two-year-old pretty boy not after much more than the best possible good time with the least possible effort. As Mel Gibson passively plays him, he's the Me Generation personified, and his rebellion against Bligh is initiated fundamentally because Bligh is an uptight old bloke (over thirty and therefore not to be trusted) who doesn't understand the hedonistic imperatives of the young. (Gibson's interpretation is intellectually consistent: when Fletcher Christian finally takes control of the *Bounty*, Gibson has him engage in what amounts to a temper tantrum, an extraordinary outburst of office-boy hysteria.) Bligh also doesn't understand—and here Robert Bolt's literate screenplay is expressively poignant and disarmingly political —that his punkish sailors have little reason to want to return to England. Donaldson has cast the crew with actors in their late teens and early twenties, and has dressed them in reasonable facsimiles of the duds worn by audiences at Van Halen concerts. These Dickensian toughs are presented as uncouth and uncultured proles living in a land with no exit, in a time with no future. They are analogues for the thousands of kids out of pocket in Mrs. Thatcher's England, and once they reach the film's idealized Tahiti, with its bare-breasted women and bulging breadfruit, they get high on the first unqualified pleasures of their lives.

The picture is slightly too long, there are some special effects (especially during a storm at sea) that don't come off, and Vangelis's electronic moans on the soundtrack are sporadically anachronistic, but *The Bounty* is otherwise a spectacularly sustained piece of epic filmmaking. Possibly because Donaldson is a New Zealander and is therefore analyzing the weaknesses of British society at a distance, and perhaps because he is withal a product of British culture and cares passionately about the abuses of its virtues, and certainly because he is a cinematic technician of the first rank, *The Bounty* joins the short list of memorable movie epics: this is an epic with heart, an adventure in intelligence.   (*1984*)

Breaker Morant

Harry Harbord Morant—a horse-breaker nicknamed ''Breaker,'' a poet nicknamed ''The Tennyson of the Transvaal''—was the Lt. Calley of the Boer War, the ritual sacrifice by a beleaguered establishment to the tin gods of good behavior and fair play. The solidly entertaining and thoughtful

Australian film *Breaker Morant*, which tells the story of Morant's court martial with smooth efficiency, allows Morant to see the reasons for his suffering with a surety granted few men: "They want to apologize for their damn war. They're trying to end it now, so we're scapegoats."

The facts, as the script by Jonathan Hardy, David Stevens, and director Bruce Beresford (working from a stage play by Kenneth Ross), sees them, are these: the Boer War, in which the Australians joined the British battling the Boers (mostly Dutch settlers), was the first modern war, a war in which the "rules" of warfare became obsolete because the Boers engaged in what we now recognize as guerrilla tactics. "It's a new war for a new century," Morant (Edward Woodward) says in 1901. Morant's mistake is to believe that Lord Kitchener and the rest of the British ruling class will back the Aussie regiments when the Aussies—acting with sub rosa British approval—fight the war the way it must be fought: dirty.

"It is customary during a war to kill as many of the enemy as possible," Morant, paradoxically a great warrior and a concerned humanist (a combination Hemingway would understand), observes after he and two subordinates are put on trial for killing prisoners. The Australians maintain correctly that Kitchener let it be known POWs were not to be taken; in sending an aide to the trial to lie for him, Kitchener notes privately that the lives of the soldiers are a small price to pay for ensuring that a projected peace conference will take place—the deaths of the three colonials are planned as a gesture of British goodwill! Although its sympathies are apparent, the script is rigorously analytical, a conflict of not-so-good good guys against not-so-bad bad guys—the British bad guys are well-meaning puppets sincerely convinced of their superiority, and the ostensible Aussie good guys almost deserve what they get, in that they should never have been there in the first place. When Morant says dourly, "Well, gentleman, this is what comes of empire-building," one wonders why he didn't stay home with his horses. But who would have thought, as the defense puts it, that soldiers would be "held up as murderers for obeying rules"? Morant sourly recognizes what has happened in a toast: "To the Bushveldt Carabineers, best fighters in a bad cause . . . these days it's so very easy to be on the wrong side."   (*1981*)

Broadway Danny Rose

The persona Woody Allen developed in his early movies and perfected in *Annie Hall*—the sexually aggressive, emotionally insecure, upwardly mobile intellectual schnook—became a seriously alienated figure in *Manhattan*, a misanthrope in *Stardust Memories*, and an irrelevancy in *A Midsummer Night's Sex Comedy*. There seemed to be no place for Allen to take his beloved nebbish, and last year he adroitly sidestepped the dilemma: *Zelig* was a movie about a man with no identity at all, and while it was Allen's best effort since *Annie Hall*, it was a picture without a pedigree, a brilliantly sustained joke closed to repetition, elaboration, or evolution. Now, in *Broadway Danny Rose*, Allen faces the dilemma head-on and stares it down. The title character, a marginal theatrical agent who represents ventriloquists, paunchy crooners, and a parrot who sings "I gotta be me," combines parts of the old persona with a fully realized, independent creation, an itchily ambitious loser with too few smarts and too much heart, a man who tells the unsentimental truth when he wails, "I never did anything and I still feel guilty."

The will-o'-the-wisp plot, simple as a silent movie, pairs Danny Rose with a bimbo interior decorator, Tina, a tall, gum-chewin' gal in shades and a sixties beehive. In what may be the most shocking physical transformation since Christine Jorgensen went to Scandinavia, she is played by that erstwhile waif Mia Farrow as a tough, voluptuous, no-nonsense variation on Judy Holliday. Tina is the girlfriend of Danny Rose's most valuable client, Lou Canova (Nick Apollo Forte), a chubby middle-aged singer with velvety Tony Bennett pipes, and she is also the girlfriend of an Italian "poet"—a pathetic, mother-dominated man—whose relatives decide to take action when they mistakenly assume she is having an affair with Rose.

Running from this misshapen Mob (they make the crooks in *The Godfather* look like the Nelson family) gives Allen the chance to stage some old-fashioned *Take the Money and Run* high jinks—there is a great sequence in a helium factory—but the comic turns are in context, and the chuckles Allen plucks from the audience like spring flowers have been organically grown. "He's got integrity; he cheats with one person at a time," is a vintage Woody Allen remark, the kind of quip that might appear in one of his satires for *The New Yorker*, but when Danny Rose says it of Lou Canova he is not trying to be funny (and is therefore a riot). In his too-large suits, his hair pasted to his scalp like pasta splayed across a paper plate, Danny Rose is a thorough product of New York show business, an ideal vehicle for Allen—the whole shtick of the stand-up comic (the timing, the eagerness to please, the sleazy manipulation) can be exploited and explored at the same time. Splendidly viewed through Gordon Willis's gleaming black-and-white cinematography, the story of Danny Rose, narrated by a group of aged comics reminiscing at the Carnegie Deli, becomes a bittersweet examination of dreams that don't come true. *Stardust Memories*, Allen's nightmarish film about a filmmaker, was his hate letter to celebrity; *Broadway Danny Rose* nostalgically considers the alternative and finds it to be preferable. Almost. In Allen's performance of Danny there is an unconscious yearning for klutzy anonymity that is both endearing and a little sad.   (*1984*)

Bye Bye Brazil

Lord Gypsy, also known as The King of Dreams and Time, and his companion-counselor-concubine Salome, a.k.a. The Rhumba Queen, travel a recently liberated, recently industrialized Brazil in a painted pickup truck with a carnival tent bouncing in the back. The Gypsy Lord does magic tricks and reads minds; The Rhumba Queen dances under hot red lights and does a little hooking (not of rugs) on the side. They are in showbiz.

They are the entrancing heroes of Carlos Diegues's effervescent musical parable *Bye Bye Brazil*, one of the few Latin American movies to rank with and reflect the dazzling explosion that is taking place in Latin American literature, In common with the works of Borges, Cortázar, Márquez, Puig, Souza, and all the rest, *Bye Bye Brazil* stirs every esthetic spice from the sensual to the sarcastic in a stew that is an invigorating concoction of fable, elegy, political observation, and simmering sexuality. It could only be served up by Latin hands, and the temperate optimism with which it is brought to the table may be feasible only in Brazil, emerging from a police state into the troublesome but preferable chaos of contemporary democracy. *Bye Bye Brazil* is dedicated by the writer-director to "Brazilians of the twenty-first century." How many serious, politically oriented artists (Diegues was one of the original founders of the leftist *Cinema Novo* movement in the sixties) in other climes would be comfortable with presuming the existence of a twenty-first century? The astute Third World optimism—psychological, political, economic—that bubbles through *Bye Bye Brazil* is unthinkable in North America or Europe right now, and it's a tonic.

With his leather wrist-band and androgynous eye makeup, Lord Gypsy (José Wilker, remembered as the first of Dona Flor's two husbands) is a macho, beneficent Joel Grey from *Cabaret*—he thinks he's seen it all. Miz Salome (Betty Faria), whom the Gypsy introduces as the former "mistress of the President of the United States," has adopted her tacky, regal manner from Ann Miller and Susan Hayward movies—what she hasn't seen, she thinks she can imagine. They ply their respective and mutually supportive trades in some of the most exotic regions of the country, Altamira and Belem along the Amazon, Brasília on the central plateau, and Entremontes in the poorest sector of the nation, the northeast. Their itinerant life (orchestrated with echoes—and no more than echoes—of Fellini's *La Strada*) is threatened by "fishbones," as they call television antennae. Everywhere, in the smallest hamlet, the poor gather in front of flickering tubes to marvel at sitcoms and disco-dancing; on reaching Altamira, which he believed to be a primitive village aching for his kind of entertainment, the Gypsy is disgusted: "This joint's busier than Rio and São Paolo combined."

There is nostalgia for a way of life that is dying, certainly, but Diegues, who has been accused by some of his hard-line leftist associates of abandoning "the revolution" with this movie, has no nostalgia for the poverty which industrialization is ameliorating, and he has an almost boundless faith in the ability of his people to adapt to the new order. (When an Indian woman sips her first drops of Coca-Cola, the approving presentation of the incident is as sweet as the liquid traveling up the baby-blue straw.) "One must say goodbye to a Brazil that no longer exists, and stop reasoning about it like a romantic intellectual of the last century," Diegues has written. "We have to believe in the possibility of a new tropical civilization, and live the adventure of this dream without plans or prejudices, on our way to the twenty-first century." This movie about change maintains, via the sexual melodrama of a subplot in which a backwoods accordionist and his pregnant wife are educated in the ways of the world by the Gypsy and his woman, that some things never change: that innocence will always be corrupted, that the corruption will always be painful, and that the upshot of innocence's loss may surprise both the corrupter and the corrupted.　　*(1980)*

Cal

Cal is a forceful film about an unexceptional boy trying to make the best of abysmal circumstances. Cal (John Lynch) is a nineteen-year-old working-class Catholic who lives in a Protestant neighborhood in Northern Ireland, and his problems make the pitfalls faced by middle-class North American teenagers look pretty paltry. Growing up is never easy, but growing up in Beirut, say, or in the South Bronx, throws up obstacles higher and wider than anything you'll find in *Risky Business* or *Fast Times at Ridgemont High* or even in *Rumble Fish*, the only so-called youth film that *Cal* remotely resembles. But *Cal* is not set, as *Rumble Fish* was, in some mythological, movie-drenched Southwest Expressionist time-warp. *Cal*, sensitively directed by Pat O'Connor, has the grit of documentary and the depth of art; the film is designed to go behind the headlines, to give a human face to the barbarism and bigotry of the mess in Northern Ireland that the evening news has made so contemptible in its familiarity. It does what it sets out to do superbly: in unfolding the events that occur in a short season to its somewhat callow hero, *Cal* brings more under-standing and certainly more sympathy to the knotted lives of Catholics and Protestants in Northern Ireland than a library of magazine articles or a festival of documentaries.

Shamie (Donal McCann), Cal's father, works in a slaughterhouse and Cal can have a job there, but it's the only job he *can* have and he doesn't want it. The thin, introverted boy with the sharp, sad face wants some-thing better, even if he can't imagine what better might be. His only exit from the drabness of his surroundings, the poverty of his people, and the pallidness of his life is the romantic schoolboy crush he develops for an enigmatic, middle-aged librarian, Marcella (Helen Mirren), who is con-nected to him in ways that could destroy him. Marcella is Italian by blood and Catholic by religion, but her Protestant husband was murdered by IRA terrorists and she has been forced to live on a farm with her Protes-tant in-laws. Possibly as the result of his association with his son's widow, Marcella's father-in-law, who employs Cal to do odd jobs, has relaxed his hatred of the other side, the papist Antichrist. "I haven't got anything against Catholics," he tells Cal, "it's their religion I can't stand." And when Cal's house is firebombed by Protestant extremists, he is support-ive: "There's bad bastards on both sides."

Marcella has been forced by "the troubles" to make certain conces-sions, and so has Cal, but his concessions have been far more destructive— he has been drafted against his will into an IRA terrorist cell from which there is no escape. The film's analysis of the methods used by the IRA to "persuade" the reluctant to join the cause is chilling, but as with every-thing else surveyed in the movie, care has been taken to stress that the inexcusable devastation has been set in motion by people, not monsters —the audience understands the reason for the existence of the IRA even as it condemns it. At one point, Cal is being lectured by an IRA operative who works as a teacher by day. "Not to act is to act," the teacher pontifi-cates, and it takes no imagination to see just how attractive an offer to act can be to teenaged boys with no work and no hope. *Cal* argues that if

Northern Ireland's agonies have been engendered by religion, they have been exacerbated by economics and the presence of the British, whose troops constantly hover backstage, ready to mount the stage at the slightest provocation.

As the film moves toward its inevitable conclusion, aided by the extraordinarily subtle performances of Lynch and Mirren, there is barely time to appreciate the carefully composed but never arty photography of Jerzy Zielinski or the haunting music (whistles and Irish pipes) of Mark Knopfler. But there is time, later, to reflect on *Cal*'s predominant concern and major message, a call for compromise and compassion. The film is a brief on behalf of the human.   (*1984*)

Carmen

Francesco Rosi's *Carmen*, photographed for the sixty-three-year-old Italian director (*Eboli*, *Three Brothers*) by Pasqualino De Santis, looks like no other film. Shot on location in Andalusia, the images are dusty and spacious, and superficially journalistic, but stylized in odd ways, rather like Picasso's *torero* drawings. The opening is the key not only to the imagery, but to the opera itself, and to Rosi's attitudes. A matador faces a bull in an ochre ring. This is Escamillo (Ruggero Raimondi), the macho man the gypsy girl Carmen (Julia Migenes-Johnson) will choose over the solid Corporal Don José (Placido Domingo), who loves her with a passion that plummets into the pathological. On the soundtrack, crowd noises and what could be an orchestra tuning up. On the screen, an all too real bullfight, recorded in slow motion, is in progress (Rosi directed the wonderful 1965 bullfighting film, *The Moment of Truth*). A tight shot of the already dying bull's face fills the frame: the eyes, black and bulging and shiny, like glistening ripe plums, are unfathomably sad, inexpressibly painful—and shockingly stupid. A close-up of the implacable, murderous expression of the matador is the prelude to the revelation of the sword, to the moment the metal is inserted, cleanly, up to the hilt in the animal's hide. Instantly, the *Carmen* overture, with its familiar cheery march, blasts ironically into the auditorium.

In that one scene, Rosi has told the tale, but who is the bull? The conventional interpretation is that big, dumb Don José, who becomes Carmen's lover only to be reviled by her, is the doomed plaything. But as Rosi sees the Prosper Mérimée novel used by librettists Henri Meilhac and Ludovic Halévy and scored by Bizet, the lovers dance on both sides of the cape: Rosi's background is in detailed, socially critical filmmaking, and he is not about to leave complexity behind in this story of a twisted love.

On the contrary. The masterly director invests *Carmen*'s Andalusia with all the historically accurate socioeconomic commentary at his command, and he does so not to surmount the opera but to serve it. "I want to show," he has said, "that there is at once the reality and the interpretation of reality, which leads at certain moments to lyrical romanticism. This has always been my preoccupation." When Carmen, a carnal cartoon who warns men she's trouble and then is true to her word, first meets Don José, he finds her swaggering lack of inhibition vulgar. (New York singer Julia Migenes-Johnson gives the hottest and most uninhibited operatic performance ever put on film; it's stylized, all right, but it's stylized steam.) She is in turn tickled and then outraged by the goody-two-shoes aspect of Don José's personality, his readiness to repress his desires, and she makes fun of him for it. (Of Placido Domingo's peerless singing nothing need be said; of his ability as an actor, it is enough to say that his weaknesses—the man's a stick on screen—have been incorporated into the cloddish character.) As Don José becomes progressively enchanted by Carmen, she becomes progressively disenchanted with him; when he murders her, almost against his will in a haze of petulant jealousy, she has already murdered his love, swiftly and surgically and wilfully, in her mind. In her campaign for independence, she can be seen as a feminist prototype, a woman who in trying to be true to her nature runs afoul of society. Rosi does not view her, as she has been viewed by others, as a flawed and fickle creature who embraces tragedy as a just punishment for a sullied past. "I was always skeptical, when I saw Carmen on stage, about the idea of fate. According to me, on the contrary, Carmen fights not to die, but when she understands that in order not to die, she will have to lie, to deny her love for another man, then she accepts death; otherwise she would lose her dignity." That Rosi allows her. It is her only compensation for so much she never had.   (*1985*)

The Chant of Jimmie Blacksmith

The first words spoken in Fred Schepisi's *The Chant of Jimmie Blacksmith* —one of the key films of the seventies—are "Blast blacks." The blacks in question are aborigines; the speaker is a white, turn-of-the-century Australian who, like the rest of the whites in Schepisi's monumental dissection of race relations, is convinced of his own rectitude and lack of bigotry. He's a monster, but he's not a bad man. The picture bulges with that sort of paradox. Basically a record of the fitful and finally unsuccessful (or perhaps too successful) acculturation of a half-breed aborigine, *The Chant of Jimmie Blacksmith* offers no sweeping generalizations and no surcease from the pain of prejudice; it charts the course of conflict between two cultures and shows how both are dehumanized, with an objectivity that is occasionally terrifying. Visually—the ultimate stylistic paradox—it is formed from a pearly succession of images that recall Vermeer and David, but that are of awesome antediluvian landscapes and primordial aboriginal camps, images unique to Australia.

The half-breed Jimmie (Tommy Lewis) is not at home in his own culture (when he makes love to an aborigine woman he calls her a "black bitch") but he is accepted by whites solely when it suits their purposes; he proves a handy husband for a promiscuous and slightly retarded woman impregnated by a white man. Throughout the first part of the film, Jimmie goes from one situation to another in which he is treated poorly (and sometimes worse) by the dominant culture, but we are never sure exactly how he is reacting to his abasement—he plays Uncle Tom to the whites and to the camera—and we can see that the Australians who are humiliating him mean him no real harm. They simply cannot believe that he is fully human, and consequently treat him with the same mixture of contempt and affection experienced by unpredictable children. We can also see that his white ambitions (he is proud that his wife knows where to put the soup spoon when she sets the table, for example) are bewildering to his aboriginal brothers.

The preamble is necessary if the tragedy that follows is to make sense. When Jimmie rebels against his oppressors, he does so randomly and irrationally, explosively and self-destructively. He gets revenge, but against the innocent as well as the guilty (Schepisi has made it clear that the concepts are meaningless: everyone contributes to Jimmie's desperation, but no one is responsible for it), and your feelings about him and about the film will probably be decided during the scene in which he takes the top of a small boy's head off with a hatchet. Schepisi, who both wrote and directed the movie, is not interested in understatement: he is interested in showing what genocide does to both sides, and one of his conclusions is that revenge in the form of terrorism results in the total dehumanization of those once victimized. By the time he has become a fugitive, the half-breed is as racist as any of the whites for whom his existence, until he began his killing spree, was so trivial. *The Chant of Jimmie Blacksmith* is a dirge for the casualties of colliding cultures. (*1980*)

Chariots of Fire

The Paris Olympics, 1924. Two British runners are in white-hot competition. Eric Liddell (Ian Charleson), a red-headed Christian Scotsman, is running for God and country, in that order. Harold Abrahams (Ben Cross), a swarthy Jewish outcast, is running for revenge. "I am what you call semi-deprived," Abrahams informs his girlfriend. "It means they lead me to water but they don't let me drink." An apt description of *Chariots of Fire*, the British film in which the competition takes place: directed by Hugh Hudson and featuring in bit parts most of the great men of the English stage (John Gielgud, Ian Holm, Lindsay Anderson), this film is all shiny inspirational veneer. It leads you to issues but it won't let you think.

"The values I was given as a youngster were real values," producer David Puttnam has said, and so the bloated and pictorial *Chariots of Fire* —David Lean in running shoes—is like spending two hours in a particularly patriotic and ethnocentric Sunday school. It may be good for you, but it's not entertainment. And it may not be good for you: lurking at the edge of the film's sunny celebration of brotherhood is the faint but unmistakable shadow of anti-Semitism.

Harold Abrahams is not allowed to run uncomplicatedly for his God; he must run against the Christians. His race—the script cleverly twists the plot so the Christian and Jew need not face each other—comes first, leaving the real race, the Christian's race, to climax the picture. An American contestant (Brad Davis) says of the Christian contestant, "He's got something to prove. Something personal. Something guys like Coach will never understand in a million years." The Christian knows exactly what he's about: he's got God and the Prince of Wales on his side. The Jewish runner says of himself, "I'm forever in pursuit and I don't even know what I'm chasing." He may have been chasing Jesus Christ: the movie ends with an epilogue, circa 1978, in a Christian church. Adidas for Jesus.

The filmmakers would no doubt argue that *Chariots of Fire* deals with but does not condone anti-Semitism. Yes and no. While clearly castigating obvious outbreaks of bigotry, the movie structurally (and, I've no doubt, unconsciously) partakes of that which it would criticize. Why else would a scriptwriter imagine that the only reason a Jew could have for wanting to excel would be to get back at Christians? (Nor is Abrahams allowed to avenge his race; he avenges only himself.) In toto, the picture is less a period piece than a piece of a period past—it harks back to the days when the Empire never questioned its superiority.

Splendidly shot, lethargically edited, and performed by an excellent cast positively a-shimmer with technique, the kind of technique that quickly sops up any messy real feeling, *Chariots of Fire* is a hymn to discredited verities. The races, underscored by a terrific but inappropriate electronic score, are ritualistic affirmations of once-common values and are therefore fatally lacking in suspense. How can there be suspense? How can God—or England—lose? At the Olympics, the only other country whose contestants we see are the Americans, and they are around so the Brits will have someone to beat. The theme of *Chariots of Fire* is that He will never allow the sun to set on His chosen children (who are not necessarily Jews). The secondary theme—a neat corollary—is that He will never allow the sun to set on the you-know-what.   (*1981*)

Choose Me

The credits are hard-candy neon, pink and blue. In the bar called Eve's, where most of the movie takes place—Eve's is a singles' bar, an Eden gone wrong, a Paradise Kaput—there is a sign that says, "Blue on the sax, Rose on the piano." Pink and blue. Alan Rudolph's comedy *Choose Me*,which won the International Critics' Prize at Toronto's Festival of Festivals, is pink and blue with a backdrop of black, an absurdist's look at love that has a real *look*. To Rudolph, the look of love is too funny and too sunny to be *film noir*. It's more like *film rose*. And *film bleu*. It's more like terrific. In contrast to Rudolph's previous explorations of California angst via *Remember My Name* and *Welcome to L.A.*, there is no doubt that the comedy in *Choose Me* is planned. Rudolph heard Teddy Pendergrass's pastel soul song "Choose Me" and thought he could base a movie on it. And did.

Send in the clowns. Mickey (Keith Carradine) is a wild and crazy guy who really is wild and crazy ("You don't want to know what I think; I just escaped from a mental hospital"). Dr. Nancy Love (Genevieve Bujold) proffers advice to the lovelorn and love-starved and love-stuffed on the radio waves but doesn't practice what she preaches ("I have never loved anyone; I don't think I can"). And Eve (Lesley Ann Warren), well, Eve's got it all and can't keep any of it ("I wrote the book on sex; I'm a prisoner of it").

Mickey comes to Eve's bar and meets Pearl (Rae Dawn Chong).
Pearl is the wife of Zack (Patrick Bauchau), a lover of Eve's.
Pearl will become a lover of Mickey's.
Mickey will become a lover of Eve's.

Pearl: "Ever been married?"

Mickey: "Yeah."

Pearl: "What happened?"

Mickey: "Which time?"

A bartender comes over and asks Mickey if he's new in town. "No, I'm the same. Town's different."

Dr. Nancy Love comes in, but nobody knows who she is, and she keeps it that way.

Dr. Love moves in with Eve. She will become a lover of Mickey's.

Dr. Love: "I don't have much success with men."

Eve: "I have too much."

Mickey goes over to Eve's house and meets Dr. Love. Mickey has already said to Eve: "Your name reminds me of a time when I was a lot happier."

You can imagine what Dr. Love's name does to him.

You can imagine what they all do to each other, in their decorated-to-the-plucked-eyebrows environments—Rudolph (this is a compliment) doesn't so much direct his movies as design them, and he allows his actors (this is a compliment) to act up hurricanes. Genevieve Bujold's Dr. Love, for instance, is an expansive, stops-out comic performance unlike anything she has ever done. And Lesley Ann Warren's Eve, well, Eve sums up the sores of the whole ever-loving world when she tells the little white lie that tells the truth all about Eve. "All my men," Eve says, when she's asked when she's gonna settle down, "are the right man." (*1984*)

Cutter's Way &
The French Lieutenant's Woman

Two great beginnings:

Cutter's Way, the Ivan Passer film of Newton Thornburg's novel *Cutter and Bone*, opens with a parade in Santa Barbara, California. In slow motion and black-and-white, flamenco dancers approach, gaining speed and color as they come.

The French Lieutenant's Woman, the Karel Reisz film of John Fowles's novel, opens with a clapper board calling our attention to the fact that a scene from a film is about to be shot. The scene is the novel's most famous: a lone woman in Victorian England stands "motionless, staring out to sea, more like a living memorial to the drowned, a figure from myth, than any proper fragment of the petty provincial day."

The novels that gave birth to these movies are very good novels with an all but identical theme, a theme elucidated by the narrator of *Cutter and Bone*: "One could spend all his life climbing onto crosses to save people from themselves, and nothing would change. For human beings finally were each as alone as dead stars and no amount of toil or love or litany could alter by a centimeter the terrible precision of their journeys."

In *Cutter's Way*, in modern Santa Barbara, Richard Bone (Jeff Bridges), a good-natured but gone-slightly-to-seed blond hustler, and his friend, Alex Cutter (John Heard), a nasty-tempered, one-eyed, one-legged drunk, attempt to save themselves and, metaphorically, modern idealism when they discover that a rich man has committed a murder. In *The French Lieutenant's Woman*, in Victorian England, Charles Smithson (Jeremy Irons), a gentleman born and bred, and Sarah (Meryl Streep), a provocative woman who walks alone, attempt to save themselves and, metaphorically, modern romance when they discover that Sarah's obsessional feelings for a long-absent French lieutenant have been transferred to Charles. These are two movies about friendship, love, and the limits of Good Samaritanism.

☆

These are two movies about the limits of cinematic adaptation.

1. Because Fowles's novel was not only set in Victorian England but was *about* a novel set in Victorian England—was *about* the process of creating a novel about Victorian England—director Reisz and his illustrious screenwriter, playwright Harold Pinter, have decided to make *The French Lieutenant's Woman* a movie about making a movie of *The French Lieutenant's Woman*. American star Meryl Streep plays an American star playing the French lieutenant's woman—the two stories, of her romance in Victorian England and of her romance with the modern actor playing her Victorian lover, are intercut throughout the film and come together at the end, when one story collapses into the other. But there is a problem: Streep plays a fictitious American actress by the name of Anna having an affair with a fictitious British actor by the name of Mike—Streep and Jeremy Irons, as real people, do not figure in this conceit. When John Fowles spoke to us in the novel as John Fowles, it was the *real* novelist speaking: the parallel Pinter has invented for Fowles's voice is false and reductive. The effect is irritating. The film invites us to consider how closely related we are to the Victorians. We get the point. It invites us to revel in the process of artistic creation—*Day for Night* and *The Stunt Man* go on literary location. But each time the Victorian tale becomes interesting, we are wrenched away to the modern drama. (People who count this sort of thing report that this takes place fourteen times.) The modern drama never does become interesting; being wrenched away

from it is a matter of being returned to the lesser of two evils.

2. *Cutter and Bone* was one of the toughest and grimmest American novels imaginable. *Cutter's Way* is grim, but not grim enough: it's *lyrically* grim. The novel has been Hollywoodized, and has become a black farce with what in these troubled times amounts to a happy (and asinine, and farfetched) ending, rather than a black comedy with a direly pessimistic (and organic, and shattering) conclusion. Cutter's wife Maureen (Lisa Eichhorn) has been sentimentalized into a romantically doomed Tennessee Williams dipsomaniac; in the novel, she was a junkie who neglected her baby son. John Heard's performance as the terrifyingly witty Vietvet Cutter proffers the cutest stylized gutter-bum since Ratso Rizzo: Tom Waits meets Chester. Eichhorn gives every evidence of wanting to become Gloria Grahame. Only Jeff Bridges's Bone is true to the bitter, decaying, sun-smooched culture that Thornburg brought to blistered life.

The performances in *Cutter's Way* are devastated by the script; the performances in *The French Lieutenant's Woman* are the result of perverse casting. In her first lead, Streep, an actress with an aura no more mysterious than that of a Pop Tart, has been asked to play a woman whose mysteriousness approximates that of Garbo—or of Vanessa Redgrave (who should have had the role) in *Blow Up*. Not since Barbra Streisand donned a precarious British accent in *On a Clear Day You Can See Forever* has an American actress fallen so short of bridging the Atlantic. Streep is not mediocre: her failure is of a flamboyance that is its own kind of achievement. During her *pièce de résistance* monologue— "I have set myself beyond the pale, I am nothing, I am hardly human any more, I am the French lieutenant's woman"—you can easily become distracted by her carroty pre-Raphaelite hair or the grainy cinematography. She reads one of the most extraordinary speeches in the English language as if deciphering the Rosetta Stone. Fowles used as an epigraph to the final chapter of *The French Lieutenant's Woman* a Matthew Arnold aphorism that is especially applicable: "True piety is *acting what one knows*." But there is one good thing to be said of the interminable close-ups of Streep: they keep her co-star, Jeremy Irons, out of the frame. As the romantic hero Charles, a man as crazy in his own way as the French lieutenant's woman is in hers, Irons is an asexual epicene nonentity. His accent is, however, impeccable.

Bastardized film versions of great or good novels are said to be helpful —they are said to make people want to read. Do they? Will anyone pick up *Cutter and Bone* or *The French Lieutenant's Woman* after sitting through these visual aids? We are told that the novel as a form is dying. When a work of fiction does show signs of life, it is quickly clubbed into the oblivion of false fame by a filmic "treatment." Charles Darwin, whom Fowles quotes in *The French Lieutenant's Woman*, could have been talking about novels and movies, and about their relationship each to the other, when he wrote in *The Origin of Species*: "I think it inevitably follows, that as new species in the course of time are formed through natural selection, others will become rarer and rarer, and finally extinct. The forms which stand in closest competition with those undergoing modification and improvement will naturally suffer." (*1981*)

Days of Heaven

Terence Malick, the writer-director of *Days of Heaven*, was once a professor of English and once worked for *The New Yorker*, filing material from South America. We have the right, then, to presume that *Days of Heaven* will be literate, if not literary, and we also have the right to presume that it will be distanced, if not cool, in the manner of *The New Yorker*'s prose. It is, and it is. But no presumption is preparation for the lushly extravagant, painterly images, which draw on the best in American art. *Days of Heaven* is so unapologetically beautiful, so calculatingly gorgeous, it is certain to arouse resentment in the minds of those who find visual hedonism a sin in movies, and to arouse suspicion, if not outrage, in those who require that movies have heart.

It begins in black and white, with photographs recalling the Depression work of Walker Evans and Dorothea Lange (though set in the Texas panhandle prior to the First World War, the sensibility is postwar and the actual locale is Alberta). Those famous, classic photos—clichés of Photog 101 by now—are used as a departure point by Malick, who has read his Ezra Pound ("Beauty is a brief gasp between clichés"). This poverty-pummelled Texas weds the Panavision of *Giant* to the dusty sensuality of *Bound for Glory* (Haskell Wexler, who photographed *Bound for Glory*, worked with Nestor Almendros on *Days of Heaven*). There are endless vistas of undulating wheat, of chocolate bison standing motionless in the waving bread, of blue-black nighttime campfires that are as elegiac and nostalgic as anything by Remington. There is no wrath to be found: the grapes are sweet and ripe.

The beauty—the inordinately romantic style of the photography and of Ennio Morricone's music—is played against a minimal plot. Richard Gere, Brooke Adams, and Linda Manz constitute a penny-poor trio from Chicago who happen onto a good thing, a rich, laconic rancher (avant-garde playwright Sam Shepard) who is dying and who marries Adams while keeping Gere, posing as Adams's brother, and Manz, who narrates the film in the uninflected, desiccated style Malick used in *Badlands*, about the place, much against his will. These are the *Days of Heaven*. The nights of hell arrive in the form of locusts and jealousy; before dawn the idyll is over, ending in death. But unlike *Bonnie and Clyde*, or even *Thieves Like Us*, *Days of Heaven* treats its tragedy unemotionally, as having no more significance than a wheat fire or a sunset. Everyone, Malick is saying, is at one with nature, but he means the statement neither romantically nor cynically. We don't like or dislike the characters. Ultimately, we don't care about them, in the same way we don't care about people whose lives brush ours coincidentally and ephemerally. The rancher (Shepard looks like an encapsulization of the good-guy greenhorn American immortalized by Norman Rockwell) is a type one would normally care for, but Malick makes his naiveté seem a form of self-indulgence. He doesn't deserve his fate, but neither does he deserve anything else: *Days of Heaven* is formally, clinically, intentionally amoral.

Many people do not like this movie—and it does not ask to be liked, any more than *The New Yorker*'s short stories request applause—but it does ask to be appreciated with the partially objective, partially self-conscious response one brings to abstract painting: the senses and the intellect are addressed, the emotions ignored.   (*1978*)

The Deer Hunter

Some years ago, Dick Cavett asked the poet James Dickey what his first novel, *Deliverance*, was about. Dickey smiled and in a low voice dripping with molasses replied, "It's about why decent men kill." *The Deer Hunter* is constructed symphonically, in three movements—it lasts three hours—with a recurring motif that never quite becomes a theme; but it, too, is about why decent men kill.

It is late in the day late in the decade—1968—in a steel-mill town, Clairton, Pennsylvania. Three buddies, Michael (Robert De Niro), Steve (John Savage), and Nick (Christopher Walken), are preparing to ship out to Vietnam. Steve, the youngest, will marry before leaving. The extended, allusive first movement of *The Deer Hunter* takes us through the Russian Orthodox wedding, the reception, an early-morning hunting trip organized by Michael, and the hunt's drunken aftermath. The milieu is sub-culturally specific, but the emotional dynamics are not: director Michael Cimino, who once worked as a medic with a Green Beret training unit in Texas, draws the outlines of American machismo. He does not try to explain what he sees—I don't think he understands intellectually what he's doing—but he is able to make us feel the synergic relationship between patriotism and religion common in the white working class of the time. As a sign at the reception reads: Serving God and Country Proudly. We also feel the frustrations of the three bonded males. The night is one long beer bust. The three men and their two friends, Stan (the late John Cazale, who was dying of cancer when the movie was shot) and Axel (Chuck Aspergren) are constantly diddling danger and coming on to violence. Their high spirits are sexual and aggressive. Linda (Meryl Streep), a woman attracted to both Michael and Nick, is beaten by her father. He drinks and stares out of his window. The buddies drink and careen from macho cliché to cliché. Cimino shoots Michael's deer hunt mystically, with a Russian choir in the background. One feels that the boredom in Clairton is profound.

Vietnam explodes on the screen. In the first few seconds, heaving helicopters descend, a Viet Cong soldier throws a grenade into a bomb shelter full of women and children, Michael immolates the soldier with a flame-thrower, and pigs tear the corpses apart. Although Michael acts chivalrously, one easily imagines turned tables; My Lai hovers like a phantom helicopter over these scenes. The second movement ends when Michael goes home. Earlier, the three buddies were reunited in a Viet Cong prison camp where they were forced to play Russian roulette—the recurring motif—in a sequence so well edited the technique is assaultive. Nick vanishes in Saigon and Michael finds Steve, crippled and withdrawn, in a stateside hospital. Linda expends energy controlling her hysteria. "I get along," she says. "Just." Michael is unable to comfort her: he is an ascetic enigma, to her and to himself. When his two friends recommence their good ol' boy byplay, he is enraged and forces one of them into Russian roulette.

The third movement takes Michael back to Vietnam in search of Nick, who is found in the pits of Saigon during the city's fall. He is on drugs and plays Russian roulette for money in a casino. The return to Pennsylvania is a coda; Michael and his friends sing "God Bless America" in a bar.

One of the catch phrases of the sixties was, "If you're not part of the solution, you're part of the problem." Cimino's film is part of the problem.

Other Vietnam movies have looked at the war from the outside in, from a pacifist perspective. *The Deer Hunter* is conceptually apolitical and emotionally conservative—it sees from the inside out. Its lack of a coherent point of view, its romanticism, its indifference to the Vietnamese, and its fumbling attempts to characterize women are its great esthetic weaknesses —and its great sociological strengths. It's one-sided, but you get to know that one side as you never have. The Russian-roulette motif refers not only to the suicidal behavior of the United States, but to the internalization of violence that ensued in many recruits and also to war's ability to provide what the existentialists call authenticity—an authenticity neither Michael nor Nick could locate in Clairton.

The writing has been criticized as superficial. And yet, most of the people I knew who went to Vietnam went without knowing why and came back without knowing how to articulate what they had been through or what it meant to them. The war may already have been explained (politically in *The Best and The Brightest*, psychologically in *A Rumor of War* and *Winners and Losers*) in print as completely as it can be. In comparison, *The Deer Hunter* is circumscribed, fabricated not by the Ivy League mentality that planned the war, nor by the movement that opposed it, but by the sensibility that executed it.

Cimino wants us to reconsider those people: look, he says, they were not demons. They should be granted compassion for their situation and respect for their grief. Without detracting from the performances of De Niro and Walken, which are exceptional, Cimino could have saved himself a lot of grief if the actors playing Michael and Nick had been draft-age; their hell-raising would appear less indulgent, their shallowness more natural, and their ordeal even more harrowing.

To judge *The Deer Hunter* solely as a movie is to judge it an honorable failure with redemptive sequences of great power. But to judge it as part of a cultural process is quite another matter. As I watched the "God Bless America" conclusion, feeling slightly sickened by Cimino's avoidance of a moral statement, I remembered a high-school friend who left home the same time I did. I went to college. He went to Vietnam. We were friends, but we had argued—I enthusiastically, he reluctantly—about the war. I came home at Christmas in a jet. He came home in a box. Hank was serious in his support of what we called the U.S. involvement. He has been dead for ten years. Now, a movie is weeping for him and for thousands like him. It weeps in a way he, and they, would understand. One does not have to agree with *The Deer Hunter* to sympathize. One does not have to like it to recognize its value.   (*1979*)

Diner

When *Diner*, a serio-comic cavalcade of six buddies coming of age in Baltimore, was previewed in St. Louis and Phoenix, the results were catastrophic: the teenaged audience, on the prowl for what had been advertised as a hell-raisin' rock 'n' roll movie, all but ate the seats. Weeks later, when the same movie opened in New York, reviews were ecstatic and audiences enthusiastic. The seats were safe.

Diner's writer and director, Barry Levinson, a man who had every reason to crow, didn't. He pointed out, mildly, that pitching *On Golden Pond* to a teenaged audience as the story of a "young boy's journey to meet his grandfather" wouldn't have been very bright, either. "*Diner* could always have turned a very handsome profit for the studio," argued Levinson, whose credits include . . . *And Justice For All*, "The Carol Burnett Show" and the forthcoming *Best Friends* (Goldie Hawn and Burt Reynolds). "It only cost $5 million. It was probably the least expensive studio film done last year." Then what did United Artists have against it? Why can Levinson say with justification, "*Diner* was as close to being put away as you can get"? The theory is that the studio didn't know what to make of a movie of young adults (not teenagers) watching their dreams dribble away, a movie punctuated with music of the period (1959), à la *American Graffiti*, but a movie that was never subservient to its soundtrack, and a movie that instead of celebrating sexual high jinks explored a bumpier psychosexual road—one of the major themes is that only in sex do men and women bridge the gender barrier. Levinson's autobiographical feature was a serious and funny and subtle work—a work of art—that was easy to confuse with exploitation teeny-bopper quickies because it did what the quickies had tried to do. But *Diner* did it right.

Had it not been for the support of several New York critics, who saw the picture privately and warned the studio they would review it even if there were no movie to review, it might have died.

Diner commences in Baltimore on Christmas night, 1959, and we meet its primary sextet in short order. Boogie (Mickey Rourke, the arsonist-for-hire of *Body Heat*) works in a beauty parlor, is a compulsive gambler, and would have adored Bruce Springsteen had Springsteen existed; Fenwick (Kevin Bacon) is rich, cute, incipiently alcoholic, and given to bestowing approval by saying, "It's a smile"; Billy (Timothy Daly) is concerned with doing the right thing, which at the moment means marrying a career woman he has made pregnant—a woman who does not want to marry him; Modell (Paul Reiser), the most passive member of the group, all but apologizes for his existence with every gravy-drenched french fry he bums; Eddie (Steve Guttenberg) is about to be married, but not before his fiancée passes a lengthy test to prove she is worthy of becoming his wife—the test is devoted to the football team the Baltimore Colts, to which Eddie is devoted beyond reason; the final buddy of the bunch is the one male already married, Shrevie (Daniel Stern), whose wife Beth (Ellen Barkin) is beginning to realize that nail polish and a Patti Page hairdo are insufficient to ensure happiness.

"I always had the idea of *Diner* in my head," Levinson recalled. "But it never made sense to me, what we did in those days and why. Then one day it occurred to me: it was that we really didn't know how to communicate with girls. By upbringing, boys play with boys. At about twelve, you realize, 'Oh, there are girls!' So then you have a date and run back to the boys. Then, at some point, you're supposed to get married and not run back to the boys. But where's the preparation for spending your whole life with a woman? I took this idea to Mel Brooks and he said, 'It's a good first film. Do it alone.' "

In *Diner*, the bonds between the boys are breaking but there is nothing to replace them. Shrevie's dissection of his marriage is disheartening. Remembering that his courtship was consumed by talking about doing it, arranging a place to do it, and then actually doing it, he says, "All that sex-planning talk is over with and so is the wedding-planning talk, because you're already married. We got nothin' to talk about." Eddie differs: "If you want to talk, you always got the guys at the diner. You don't need a girl to talk." But Eddie's insistence on a test for his fiancée proves that he has his own doubts, doubts he confides to Boogie: "I keep thinkin' I'm gonna be missin' out on things." Boogie is philosophical: "Yeah, but that's what marriage is all about."

That is what marriage is all about in *Diner*; the film analyzes the chemistry of the divorce explosion of the sixties and seventies. "The divorce rate is based on years and years of no one relating to one another," Levinson said, "except that we didn't even have the words, then—we didn't say 'relate.' Now we do. I wonder how much else has changed." Modell may be speaking for Levinson when he observes, "The whole thing with girls is painful and it seems to be getting more painful."

Levinson's emphasis in interviews on the male-female dichotomy is slightly misleading—although the communication gulf is its major theme, *Diner* deals with many other aspects of leaving youth for adulthood and, although the middle-aged characters, the mothers and fathers and uncles, are by necessity sketched on the run, they are sketched strongly.

Diner has been mentioned in the same breath with Fellini's *I Vitelloni*, George Lucas's *American Graffiti*, and Arthur Penn's *Four Friends* and, while it is true that this whole area has been given the cinematic once-over more often than Shirley Bassey has sung "Goldfinger," nothing in *Diner* feels rehearsed or rehashed. "That may be due to the fact that I'm a terrible student," Levinson laughs. "There are directors I like but, when I go to the movies, I keep getting involved in what I'm watching at the time. Later, people say to me, 'Didn't you love it when he did this or that with the camera?' and I don't remember a thing."

Rhythmically, *Diner* is uneven. The strong opening gives way to a somewhat lassitudinous half hour, but when the pace does pick up, it never wobbles—the film works slowly, but surely. Visually, the use of blues and grays recalls the infinitely inferior *Four Friends*; the environment is dark, dense, and almost gloomy, with the texture of a dream that could at any moment become a nightmare. Not until there is a sunny countryside break (one of two) does one realize how fully Levinson has borrowed from the palette of the Ashcan School.

"Conceptually, there were certain things I wanted when I began *Diner*," he said. "I wanted to bury the camera—I didn't want it to be doing pretty things. I didn't want any primary colors in the movie, except when you get the color of the Colts football team at the end. I planned to have rehearsal time for the actors and the six guys spent a week together, but I didn't rehearse actual scenes. I used the week so the guys could just be together, to understand what I wanted. What I tried basically to go for, throughout, was great simplicity. I wanted *Diner* to be very clean." (*1982*)

Diva

"He's in his cool phase," says a Vietnamese thief (Thuy An Luu) in *Diva*. She is explaining her choice of shoplifted music—the man for whom she has snitched the records, Mr. Cool, is her boyfriend. When we meet the boyfriend, we discover that she was speaking literally: his apartment is painted blue, he is at work on a jigsaw puzzle of the sea, and kinetic sculptures strewn about the loft wobble water back and forth. The boyfriend lives in a New Wave Arctic womb.

Diva, more sheer fun than any work of movie art since *The Stunt Man*, is rich with symbolic statements that later turn out to be literal and vice-versa. Critic David Overbey has defined the plot to wit: "*Diva* is based on a Delacorta novel which recounts the adventures of Gorodish, an eccentric who drives a white Citroën and practices the Zen method of buttering bread (Gorodish is Mr. Cool). Into his carefully arranged private world falls Jules, a young postman who has made private recordings of his idol, the American soprano Cynthia Hawkins. Jules has accidentally come into possession of an incriminating tape made by a dead prostitute.''

The film, a first effort from Jean-Jacques Beineix (pronounced Ben-ex), can be said to be about police work—if *The Stunt Man* can be said to be about stunt work. It is as much about the joy of making movies and the delight of finding beautiful images (there are tableaux right out of Magritte) as anything else. There is also, in the performance of American opera singer Wilhelmenia Wiggins-Fernandez, a celebration of the tacky. Wiggins-Fernandez, whose French is as bad as her singing is good, and whose acting talent is as tiny as her beauty is awesome, is the diva of the title, the star Cynthia Hawkins, the woman worshipped by Jules, the postman. Like so many opera stars, she's the ridiculous and the sublime in one glittering but by no means gutter-free package. When Jules (Fédéric Andrei) steals her gown and tapes her voice—and inadvertently becomes the carrier of another tape, the tape left by the dead prostitute—he sets in motion a crazed plot that results in a moped race through the Paris Metro that is one of the funniest (and one of the longest) chases yet committed to celluloid.

The sensibility behind *Diva* illustrates what has become of humanism in the modern world—it is at once cynical, bemused, and benign. There is a fair amount of violence and death in this thriller, but because the right people get it, we don't mind, and when the wrong people occasionally do get it, the movie zips past their demises with a *c'est la vie* shrug implying that the kindest thing is not to dwell on the inevitable. (A Hollywood movie would either mourn the deaths or make us cheer for them.) *Diva* has looked around at the technologically adept, design-oriented, physically resplendent but still corrupt-as-all-hell capsule that is Western civilization, and has made of it a comic carnival. This is the most impressive debut from a French director since Godard's *Breathless*, twenty-one years ago.   (*1981*)

Dressed to Kill

With *Dressed to Kill*, Brian De Palma, who once remade *Vertigo* and called it *Obsession*, expands his adoration of Alfred Hitchcock by remaking *Psycho*. Hailed at one time as the logical successor to the master, De Palma has proved to be less a successor than a disciple, and he now appears to be a disciple in danger of becoming a chic geek of cinema, an entertainer who survives by swallowing whole the movies of another man. Adoration by way of imitation is an activity most artists outgrow by the age of thirty, but De Palma, who will be forty next year, and whose talent (he also directed *Carrie* and *The Fury*) is undeniable, has progressed mightily as a craftsman and minimally as an artist.

In horror-film terms, *Dressed to Kill* is a better buy—it is at least sporadically discomfiting—than *The Shining*, and the Hitchcock references are exquisitely accomplished (though the net effect, as often occurs while watching a slavish impersonator at work, may be a hankering to see the real thing). When Angie Dickinson visits an art gallery, for example, the editing is as elegant as a composition by Satie, and De Palma utilizes silence nearly as capably as Satie did. The first murder, despite a preponderance of blood that is an unfortunate shade of magenta, is precise and achieves the desired emotional reaction, a queasy combination of revulsion and pity. Yet another set piece, this time in a subway station, uses the arc formed by the girders supporting the roof as a spooky catacomb—a hapless hooker, fleeing from a murderer, is accosted by a gang of black kids and escapes them only to be assaulted by the indifference of a cop. There is a suggestion here that the real villain of *Dressed to Kill* may be New York City (or Society), but it is only a suggestion; the script toys with it, à la *Eyes of Laura Mars*, then drops it and returns to *Psycho*.

The advantage of doing a remake is the opportunity to edit whatever failed the first time, so it's a shock to find that De Palma has retained the worst in *Psycho* as well as the best. *Dressed to Kill*'s update of Anthony Perkins's Oedipally obsessed maniac (vagueness is mandatory here if the plot is to be kept a nominal secret) may be the last word in seventies chic, but the explanation of the homicides by a psychiatrist (exactly as in *Psycho*) seems as silly now as that sequence in *Psycho* came to seem once the pop Freud of the fifties had passed away. Angie Dickinson, Nancy Allen, and Michael Caine have all been directed poorly; one is made to think again and again of Hitchcock's lack of dexterity with actors, a lack that did not heretofore afflict De Palma. What has been added to Hitchcock? Explicit violence and verbiage, explicit sexual encounters —all necessary to give the movie a chance with a contemporary audience. But didn't De Palma calculate as part of his commercial equation the fact that *Psycho* was a popular success because it was full of perverse twists of fate? The selfsame "surprises" are back in *Dressed to Kill*; De Palma adds his own goodies, to be sure, but they are not especially ingenious, and the big one is recycled from *Carrie*. (When he isn't paying tribute to Hitchcock, De Palma pays tribute to himself.) The technical packaging of his picture is terrific—high-tech Manhattan, split screens, and slow motion—but the goods inside are shoddily second-hand.   (*1980*)

Ernesto

Ernesto, a sensual 1979 Italian comedy, arrives belatedly in the wake of a *Village Voice* hurrah that claims the picture harmonizes the legacies of three directors: Pasolini, Fassbinder, and Renoir. *Ernesto* is by no means equal to the best work of the three gents, but it does share in various degrees the concerns of all three, and it is a breakthrough in the cinematic treatment of homosexuality. That breakthrough consists of the fact that its gays are treated with the same evenhanded mixture of analysis and sympathy accorded the rest of its characters. In form, *Ernesto* is a sophisticated comedy of manners, specifically of Italian manners in Trieste in 1911. That director Salvatore Samperi rarely strays, tonally or temperamentally, from the period is one of the movie's more impressive achievements.

Ernesto (Martin Halm) is a callow, seventeen-year-old Jewish boy comfortably simmering in the juices of a self-important adolescence. His mother (Virna Lisi), a Jew, was deserted by his father, a Christian, when Ernesto was a baby, and the two have since depended on the largesse of Ernesto's aunt and uncle, a tiresome bourgeois pair who incessantly remind Ernesto's mother of her "disgrace." As the film opens, Ernesto has taken a job with a contractor, which Ernesto's mother sees as a ticket to independence and Ernesto sees as a dead end—for him, the future is to be found in a great career as a concert violinist. There *is* a little artist in Ernesto, but there's a lot more Duddy Kravitz.

While working for the contractor, the boy is put in charge of a group of workers, one of whom, a swarthy laborer with come-hither eyes (Michele Placido, awarded the best-actor prize at Berlin in 1979 for this performance), befriends him. "Do you know," the worker asks as he takes Ernesto's slim white hand into his own callused palm, "what it means to be the friend of a man like me?" Ernesto has an idea of what it might mean and is eager to put his fantasy to the reality test. In a series of sexual trysts at once tender and combative, trysts distinguished technically by the director's ability to suggest everything while showing nothing, Ernesto gives in to lust. The worker gives in to love. Trieste's class structure and the means homosexuality employs to surmount it (if only briefly) are outlined in a fashion reminiscent of Fassbinder's *Fox and His Friends*, and Samperi's unapologetic eroticism and critique of bourgeois values recall the cinema of Pasolini, but the romance with the worker is by no means the totality of the movie. When Ernesto grows narcissistically bored with the man—and frightened by the depth of the worker's mature passion—he resolves to practice his newly acquired talents on a malleable fifteen-year-old boy he meets at a concert. The boy, Ilio, is also ready to experiment sexually, but he has a surprise in store for the grateful Ernesto: he is a package deal. Just as Ilio and Ernesto are about to consummate their attraction, Ilio's ravishingly beautiful, identical twin sister, Rachele (both siblings are played by the same actress, Lara Wendel), bursts into the room. She has erotic abilities of her own and she is equally anxious to put them to use.

Actually photographed in a ripe and sun-drenched Spain, *Ernesto* is performed by an unimpeachable cast, and the intelligence of the script is rigorous, but there are a few drawbacks. Samperi's camera is irritatingly "fluid" (there are times when you want to slap it, to make it sit still), and the conventionally "haunting" musical score is trundled out whenever sentiment is summoned. But Samperi concludes the picture with a bravura stroke—in a series of crisply edited takes at a party, he magnificently sums up the society of the time and, in the process, reminds us of the personal aspirations and institutionalized prejudices of its people. Then, without stopping for the smallest of breaths, he gracefully and precisely places a sweet and sour period at the end of Ernesto's story. That it can end at the age of seventeen is expressive of Samperi's serious intent, softened though it may be by laughter: this is a pastel study of the snares set by propriety to trap the freedom of the unwary.   (*1984*)

Falling in Love

Any movie that reaches its peak when a man plays tic-tac-toe with a chicken is not a movie you need to see. *Falling in Love*, directed by Ulu Grosbard and written by Michael Cristofer, stars Meryl Streep and Robert De Niro as commuters who meet but do not mate on a train. They meet and do not mate for most of the movie's two-hour running time: this must be the longest brief encounter on rails. Meryl, doing Diane Keaton, and Bob, doing his usual, but turned down, are strangers on a train. (Does Bob, usually semi-psychotic on screen, seem believable as an ordinary guy? Who knows? If anything around the writing was believable, you might be able to tell.) Bob is happily married and so is Meryl. They get their Christmas gifts accidentally mixed up in a bookshop and Meryl gives her husband *Gardens For All Seasons* at about the time Bob's wife is opening *The Big Book of Sailing*. It is worth pointing out that the actress playing the wife is Jane Kaczmarek and the actor playing the husband is David Glennon, and they both play second fiddle honorably. But back to Meryl and Bob. And to the script by Cristofer, who once won a Pulitzer Prize (*The Shadow Box*) and is lucky there's no such thing as a recount: in this case, he's incapable of coming up to the level of Neil Simon. If it were on stage, the script would be about doors opening and closing. On film it's about trains coming and going. And about not doing It, which the script equates with romance. (Some might call it frustration.) So what happens if nothing happens? Meryl meets Bob on the train. They make a date. She tries on clothes in the mirror (*donnez-moi un* break—who does Meryl think she is, Barbra Streisand?). Then Meryl meets Bob. Then she gets cold feet. At the one-hour, ten-minute mark, you find her moaning: "I'm sorry, I can't." A few minutes later they're trying again, in a borrowed apartment, but since the camera is practically sitting on their wedding rings, you know morality will out. Nothing is wrong with not doing It, of course, but there is something wrong with not dramatizing not doing It. Beckett dramatized boredom and made it look interesting, but Cristofer, trying to make fidelity appear to be the best thing, or the right thing, or some thing, makes it look like a wake in a waxworks.

Postscript. Bob plays tic-tac-toe with a chicken in a video arcade. The chicken wins.   (*1984*)

Fanny and Alexander

Fanny and Alexander, which the sixty-five year-old Ingmar Bergman has said will be his last film, has been designed as a summing up of everything that has intrigued the dour Swede during the forty years he has spent making more than fifty movies. That staggering output includes an equally staggering number of masterpieces—*The Seventh Seal* (1957), *Wild Strawberries* (1957), *The Virgin Spring* (1960), *Persona* (1966), *Shame* (1968), *Cries and Whispers* (1973), *Scenes From a Marriage* (1973), *The Magic Flute* (1975)—that would instantly find space in any serious inventory of the century's enduring artistic achievements.

So: *Bergman's Greatest Hits*. But if *Fanny and Alexander* is a catalogue of familiar Bergmanesque feelings and forms, it is also a profound departure for the master of cinematic modernism—the balmy, self-actualized, compassionate sense of life that informs the fantasy from beginning to end is closer to the work of the late Jean Renoir than to anything filmgoers have come to expect of the unsparing analyst from Uppsala. In the past, Bergman movies have been deliberately puzzled (and puzzling); *Fanny and Alexander* puts the pieces together. Set in a provincial Swedish town in 1907, the movie is structured in opposing lifestyles. On one side is what might be called progressive liberal humanism, personified by the moderately wealthy, mildly hedonistic, marginally intellectual Ekdahl family, owners of the town's theater and inhabitors of a marzipan mansion, all pink and white rococo curves. On the other: rigid, repressive, religious authoritarianism in the form of the monastic Vergérus family, denizens of a rough-hewn, almost literally black and white wood structure.

The Ekdahls are led by a matriarch, Helena (Gunn Wallgren), who has found peace in much the way Bergman may have achieved it: "I don't care," she says, "if nothing makes sense." The Vergérus family is helmed by the town's Bishop (Jan Malmsjö), a cheerlessly exacting inquisitor worthy of *The Crucible*, a black shadow of a man who in due course marries the lusty widow Emilie Ekdahl (Ewa Fröling), mother of eight-year-old Fanny (Pernilla Allwin) and ten-year-old Alexander (Bertil Guve). That somewhat unbelievable mating allows Bergman to contrast his actual upbringing (he was the son of a dictatorial Swedish Lutheran parson) with the artful existence he adopted later on. As befits a life lived in, and perhaps for, art, Bergman draws on innumerable sources, not only Dickens and George Eliot, but Shakespeare and Sophocles, Ibsen and Strindberg (the latter provides the movie's rationale: "Anything can happen, anything is possible and likely, time and space do not exist, on a flimsy ground of reality imagination spins out and weaves new patterns") and, most of all, Bergman. The movie's charming opening sequence, in which the Ekdahls present a Christmas play, recalls the delight in rickety stagecraft Bergman brought to his brilliant transcription of *The Magic Flute*, and later sequences re-explore questions of identity posed in *Persona*, questions of resignation raised in *Wild Strawberries*, and questions of suffering and redemption considered in *Cries and Whispers*. Throughout, the aim is to soothe, to console, to remove from death its sting and from the grave—if not its victory—then at least its morbidity.

Working with his nonpareil cinematographer, Sven Nykvist, Bergman has achieved an elegance of image that is both sumptuous and spare—the interior of the Ekdahl home may be overdecorated, but the lighting leavens the excess. The lens that looks fondly on the Ekdahls is rose-colored; the lens that records the activities of the Vergérus clan is unmercifully microscopic. The striking visual assurance extends to the performances but not to the structure. *Fanny and Alexander* is neither more nor less than the sum of its parts: it is composed, like *That's Entertainment*, of virtuoso bits that sometimes seem to have as much and as little to do with each other as two strangers on the same park bench. The first hour is unnecessarily protracted and at the end, when Bergman is straining for transcendent reassurance, the enumeration by one of his heroes of the aspects of existence that give life meaning (waltzes, trees in bloom) threatens to climax in a chorus of "My Favorite Things." *Fanny and Alexander* is a trillingly pleasant experience, a magnificent medley, and a tuneful swan song. The thing it's not is a great movie.   (*1984*)

Fitzcarraldo

When the so-called conceptual and performance artists of the late sixties and early seventies were doing their dramatic thing—Chris Burdon crawling across broken glass, Christo draping a Colorado canyon in orange cloth—they immortalized their ephemeral activities with what they termed "documentation." The art work itself ceased to exist—Burdon got up off the glass and applied iodine, the winds tore Christo's curtain apart —but the notes and drawings that led to the art, and the photographs and films that were shot while it was taking place, would go on tour: you didn't see the art, but you did see its leftovers, its leavings.

Fitzcarraldo is the first mainstream movie in that tradition. *Fitzcarraldo* may not be a movie at all—it may be the "documentation" for an entirely separate work of art, a work of art that was the sum of the interaction between *Fitzcarraldo*'s director, Werner Herzog, and the South American jungles in which the movie is shot. Les Blank's documentary on the making of *Fitzcarraldo, Burden of Dreams*, tells the story: Herzog, the Hermann Hesse figure of the New German Cinema, sets off to Peru to do a follow-up to his classic up-the-river picture *Aguirre, The Wrath of God*. Jason Robards is to play Brian Sweeney Fitzgerald (called Fitzcarraldo by the natives because they cannot pronounce his surname properly) and Mick Jagger is to play his assistant. Problems. The natives are not easy to control. Robards contracts amoebic dysentery and drops out. Jagger must return for a concert tour and drops out. Years pass. Klaus Kinski takes over from Robards. Extras are killed. Filming continues. Werner Herzog tells journalist Michael Goodwin, "If I believed in the devil, I would say that the devil was right here, and is still right here. But I have no choice; I have to do this work. I live my life or I end my life with this project." The only question that remains in the mind when the two hours and forty minutes of Fitzcarraldo finally crawl to their ludicrous conclusion is: why? Why did this story of a man of indecipherable motives, referred to in the film as "the conquistador of the useless," have to be told? Why was it considered essential for us to follow the interminable folly of a man who wants to build an opera house in the jungle? Why was it necessary to rewrite history in order to give the man a secondary obsession—the desire to cart a huge steamship over a mountain? Why was Herzog committed to using a real steamship and real labor instead of allowing the special-effects people to take over? And why, if a real ship had to be employed, did he film the sequence in such a way as to give it the appearance of a special effect?

The movie does have its moments, but there's nothing in it to equal for comedy, grandeur, tragedy, or absurdity either Les Blank's documentary on the Peruvian filming, or any interview Herzog has given in the last year. Herzog has always been attracted to existentialism—his *The Enigma of Kaspar Hauser* is virtually an explication of Sartre—and it is easy to see that Fitzcarraldo's big boat is a grandiose extension of the rock that Sisyphus kept pushing up that hill. It is also easy to see that Fitzcarraldo and his improbable dreams (dreams that are magically realized) is a stand-in for Werner Herzog and other visionary artists. In *Burden of Dreams*, Herzog addresses the camera with one of the most astonishingly condescending statements ever made by a major movie maker—he tells us that he's no better than we are, but that because he can articulate his dreams and we cannot, he is an artist and we are not. Herzog doesn't deign, then, to create a character for Klaus Kinski in *Fitzcarraldo*: he's The Artist. He's Werner Herzog, the Boy Scout guru. Fitzcarraldo gets his opera in the jungle and Werner Herzog gets his movie (and an award for best director at the Cannes Film Festival) and that's somehow supposed to make us feel better about every little thing—like the universe.

If *Fitzcarraldo* were a book, it would be called *How I Made My Movie*, by Werner Herzog, and it could be filed next to *How I Built My Pyramid*, by Cheops. The difference is that Cheops' accomplishment was actually more interesting and awe-inspiring than its "documentation." Herzog's filmmaking odyssey, as recorded by Blank, is both interesting and awe-inspiring, but the film itself inspires something in the vicinity of revulsion. There is so much waste in *Fitzcarraldo*—Claudia Cardinale, who

plays Fitz's girlfriend, is restricted to brief smiles and waves and voluptuous displays of lace underwear—that the picture eventually seems to
be little more than an inventory of an act of ecological insanity.   (*1982*)

The Fourth Man

At the age of thirty-five, Dutch novelist Gerard Reve was baptized a
Catholic, but the theology he publicly embraced was obviously an idio-
syncratic vision of the writ of Rome. Reve continued to maintain an active (and unapologetic) gay sex life, and he continued to publish books
that outraged the more conservative elements of his picturesque little
country. One of them was *The Fourth Man*, an experiment in Mariolatry
(worship of the Virgin Mary) that has been brought to the screen by Dutch
director Paul Verhoeven with all its macabre humor and autobiographical candor intact.

The film's hero, one Gerard Reve (Jeroen Krabbé), is a "lightly alcoholic" homosexual novelist in his thirties who sets out to deliver a lecture in a provincial town, Vlissingen, at the invitation of the local literary
society. But first he has to get there. On awakening in Amsterdam, he is
victimized by the shakes so severely he is unable to shave, fantasizes
murdering his roommate, and then, in the train station, obsessively chases
a young tough who has caught his fancy. Once safely on the train, he is
anything but safe: a beatific blonde woman dressed in blue (Geert de Jong)
makes a halo for her baby out of an apple peel, engendering in Gerard's
briny brain a bloody Mary fantasy in which the Blessed Virgin leads him
to a hotel where the walls literally have eyes. Gerard snaps out of his
nightmarish reverie in time to be met at the train station by a hearse carrying a casket he fears is his own. Safely in town, he is in true peril: he is
introduced to a bourgeois beautician, Christine (the delectable Renée
Soutendijk), who dresses in red and is more than she seems. (The name
of her salon is Sphinx, but two neon letters in the sign have burned out,
leaving "Spin," the Dutch word for spider; under the credits, a female
spider kills and consumes her mate.) Christine serves Gerard a Bloody
Mary. Eventually she takes him home, where he finds that her boyfriend
(Thom Hoffman) is the hunk he saw in the train station. He also finds that
she has had three previous husbands, all dead. He is the fourth man.

Because he wants to bed the boyfriend, he ignores the warnings prof-
fered by Mary and stays with Christine; meanwhile, the past and future
develop a nasty habit of obscuring (and sometimes replacing) the present

as his hallucinations, nightmares, and episodes of precognition multiply. Symbol piles on symbol and allegory on allegory (example: the Virgin comes to the beauty salon and is picked up by her husband and infant in a van with the legend "Joseph's" on the side), but *The Fourth Man* is never enigmatic: Verhoeven's staging is precise and his tone—deadpan farce—is sure. The surface, courtesy of cinematographer Jan de Bont, is burnished to an incredibly sensual salmon sheen. Not once does the picture resort to naturalism or to anything so crassly conventional as "believability." During Gerard's lecture to the literary burghers, he reveals the movie's method when he says, "If I tell a story often enough, I'll believe it myself. I lie the truth. What you make of reality is far more interesting than reality itself."

The Fourth Man is an eschatological sex comedy (is this a first?) masquerading as surrealism—there is nothing automatic, random, or "godlessly" psychoanalytic about its interlocking symbols, though it is stiff with enough psychoanalytic starch to send even the hardiest of shrinks into diabetic coma. The picture is both shamelessly titillating and resolutely spiritual, a combination that (despite the Vatican's professed distaste for the erotic) has found a secure and not always subliminal home in the art of Rome. *The Fourth Man* is a fabulously executed oddity, a metaphysical farce that sings the body religious.   (*1984*)

Gandhi

At more than three hours, Richard Attenborough's *Gandhi*, a biography of the diminutive Hindu who levelled an empire, is a triumph of compression—John Briley's script packs events tightly into a wide-screen, standing-room-only teaching machine. The story of Mohandas Karamchand Gandhi (uncannily impersonated by Ben Kingsley) is also, of course, the story of the liberation of India, a nation whose autonomy was the product of the most exciting revolutionary technique—non-violent resistance—to emerge in the twentieth century. It is dispiriting, then, to have to report that the ideological aspect of Gandhi's development receives short shrift in Attenborough's epic; the great man's ideas appear to have been knocked whole-hog into his head when he was tossed off a South African train in 1893. The movie's shorthand is not exactly inaccurate—Gandhi's political philosophy was fomented during his South African stay, and he considered his mistreatment by porters in a whites-only carriage to be formative—but the ideas the incident eventually fostered (of *swaraj*, self-rule for India; of *satyagraha*, a complicated Gandhi neologism embodying non-violent resistance; of *hartal*, a mass cooperative closing of businesses to make a political point (a technique adopted by Poland's Solidarity) are neither explained nor explored by the movie. *Gandhi* is a thoughtful epic paradoxically parsimonious with thought. Attenborough, whose credits as a director (*Oh What a Lovely War!*, *Young Winston*, *A Bridge Too Far*, *Magic*) are notable for soporific good taste, dreamed of bringing Gandhi to the screen for decades, and he has done so with discretion and decorum. Good taste. The violence that followed the partitioning of Pakistan, violence of nearly unimaginable horror, is left nearly unimagined by the director, who settles for smoky, sketchy suggestion. Good taste. The British slaughtered hundreds of unarmed Indian men, women, and children at Amritsar, an event generally credited as the single most influential factor in loosening Britain's grip on India; the slaughter is included, but it is filmed academically, at a distance, with no more than one quick, classic cut to an orphaned child in tears. Good taste. Many, many famous figures (Trevor Howard, Candice Bergen, Martin Sheen, John Gielgud, John Mills) come and go, playing other, equally famous figures, and not once does a famous face seem out of place—not once does one groan at the ghastly inappropriateness of having, say, Shelley Winters turn up as Mary Magdalene. Good taste.

Good taste, and a lack of feeling that verges on the fatal. The sweeping panoramas are invariably composed statically, with no thought to pictorial drama. The editing is equally pedestrian. Never, as in the Odessa Steps sequence of *Potemkin*, or in portions of *Bonnie and Clyde*, or in the operatic conflict of *Lawrence of Arabia*, is the terror of what Gandhi spent a lifetime battling—the murderous potentiality of the human heart —presented with an immediacy that is more than mildly uncomfortable. Does that matter? I think so. By removing much of the sting of India's history, the film removes a fair share of Gandhi's glory. *Lawrence of Arabia* was an epic, too, but it was exciting in cinematic terms. *Gandhi* is not: call it radio for the eyes. The story itself guarantees our interest, but Attenborough's plodding technique never expands the telling beyond the respectable and ecumenically meritorious.

This is a monument that should be visited, but it is a monument of importance *only* as a reminder of the thing it seeks to memorialize. *Gandhi* may not be a hagiographic embarrassment to its subject, but it's a waxworks movie, a victory for British reserve. (Under the circumstances, that is a Pyrrhic victory.) The film has a great future in high-school auditoriums.   (*1982*)

The Green Room

In *The Story of Adèle H.*, François Truffaut studied a woman for whom a romantic obsession became a way of life—and a religion. His fine film, *The Green Room*, a companion piece to *The Story of Adèle H.*, depicts a man for whom an obsession has also become a way of life (and a religion), but in this case the obsession is death—the contours of the hero's life are defined by the shapes of shades he has known, the Dear Departed. His devotion to the deceased is Egyptian in scope, Oriental in outline.

We are between the wars. Julien Davenne (Truffaut), a journalist whose speciality is obituaries, is a veteran. "Most of my friends died in the war," he tells Cécilia (Nathalie Baye), an acquaintance who comes to share his obsession. No one has replaced them. His wife is also dead; consequently, on the upper floor of his home, in a green room, he has erected a shrine to her memory. "The dead belong to us, once we belong to them." In this universe, even the gods are dead, incapable of providing succor to those maimed by modern life. *The Green Room* begins with a funeral at which a priest attempts to console a bereaved husband. Davenne throws the cleric out while advising his widower friend that the only way to conquer his grief is to keep the memory of his wife alive. Slowly, and brilliantly, *The Green Room* (based in part on Henry James, although the Gothic emotionalism of the plot is close to that of Poe's "Annabel Lee") develops its theme, which has to do with the role played by the fear of death in the expression of the religious impulse: Truffaut diagrams the creation of a new belief. Davenne's religion is very close to ancestor worship. At first, his devotion to photographs of his wife seems morbid but understandable. Then the devotion deepens: he approaches a priest and secures the right to renovate an unused chapel on cemetery grounds. In that chapel, he places pictures of his Dead—the subtitles have begun capitalizing the word—and lights votive candles to Them. (Truffaut here jokes with his own Dead—the photos are of Renoir, Vigo, Cocteau, Oskar Werner, Wilde, James.) "Now that I have this chapel, I feel my Dead protect me," Davenne announces. There has been an earlier shot of the interior of the abandoned chapel, a broken Pietà upturned in the rubble; when Davenne has completed his work, Maurice Jarre's music swells and Nestor Almendros's cinematography bathes the screen in flickering light. Truffaut's intent is clear: for Davenne, the place has become a sanctuary, a concrete representation of what Rudolf Otto called the idea of the holy. This religion, Davenne's religion, lives.

Robert Graves tells us that agnostic Greek philosophy, having conquered Roman thought, left the masses without a workable religion; hence the pragmatic necessity—and political wisdom—of deifying Roman emperors in an age when to the common man the gods were at best remote intellectual constructs: Augustus became a deity because there had to be something to worship. *The Green Room* takes place in a cultural climate not far removed from Graves's Rome: for many people the period between the wars was a time of intellectual liberation, but for many others, and Davenne is one of them, it was a time of destructive temple-bashing. *The Green Room* is a pensive study of the ways and means of finding comfort and a sense of worth—Davenne's worship of his Dead brands him a spiritual cousin to the Moonies and born-again Christians of a later era. (Truffaut's attitude toward Davenne is embodied in his performance of the character—we understand him, but we do not sympathize with him in any conventional regard. This is a careful, questioning film.) In a spiritual vacuum, Truffaut maintains, the worship of almost anything (the dead, the stars, a fat Korean, a new diet, Miss Piggy, or Bob Dylan) is possible. And maybe better—that is, more therapeutic —than the worship of nothing at all. And maybe worse—Truffaut is scrupulous, and undecided; his ending is ambiguous, but humanely, perhaps profoundly ambiguous. In trying to make life bearable through worship, Davenne worships himself into oblivion. This is a film about a Catch-22 of the spirit.   (*1979*)

The Hunger

The Hunger, a designer-jean vampire picture with a new-wave throb, is everything the horror film fan could ask for: the stars are of the first magnitude, the direction is sharp as a scalpel, the premise (vampirism *sans* fangs, garlic, and other Transylvanian paraphernalia) is only semi-silly, and the visuals are suitable for exhibition in a gallery specializing in high gloss S/M. Last year, Paul Schrader released a deplorable attempt to modernize Val Lewton's classic *Cat People*; *The Hunger* is the movie he was trying to make, a film so effective at granting the age-old request—"Scare me!"—it's enough to make you wish you hadn't asked.

Age-old request, age-old fear: the fear of old age is the film's animating force. Miriam (Catherine Deneuve) is a wondrously vapid, chic woman married to John (David Bowie), an equally chic but slightly less vapid man. Boy, have they got a secret. It seems they've discovered a way to arrest the aging process, but there are certain side effects, most of which will be familiar to readers of Bram Stoker and to fans of Hammer horror films. The audience is introduced to John and Miriam as they stalk human quarry in a gleaming ebony disco, an obsidian cavern shiny with malice. When they return home with their chosen victims, we make the acquaintance, via cross-cutting, of the other major character, Sarah Roberts (Susan Sarandon), a research physician who is tracking the secret that John and Miriam have found. As John and Miriam slit their victims open, the film cuts to Sarah, watching one of her research primates rip his mate to bloody shreds. The events are not unrelated: it takes no seer to see that three paths will cross.

From there on—everything so far described takes place in the first five minutes—*The Hunger* is relentless in its pursuit of a disorienting, clammy creepiness that recalls Nicolas Roeg's *Don't Look Now*. Deneuve's alien, overripe beauty is put to canny use, David Bowie's celebrated androgyny creates an unexpected pathos, and Sarandon proves once again that for loose-limbed, all-American charm, even in the most unlikely circumstances, she has few peers. An already famous love scene between the two female stars lives up to its billing as an erotic tour de force, but it is something more than that—it's a rather cagey comment on the collision of two sensibilities and two acting styles. (The winner, in every sense of the word, is Sarandon.) Toward the end, *The Hunger* gets a bit famished for effects—any movie that includes a scene, no matter how brief, in Ancient Egypt, has got trouble—but the damage to the audience's nerve endings has already been done. Not even a ludicrous denouement can expunge the feeling expertly engineered by this film, the feeling that, no matter what, things will *not* be all right. Not as long as time and mirrors coexist.   (*1983*)

Kagemusha

Nineteen minutes are missing from the "international edition" of Akira Kurosawa's contemplative historical panorama, *Kagemusha,* but they are minutes removed by the master himself and their excision has rendered the film, which in its three-hour version shared the top prize at the Cannes Film Festival with *All That Jazz*, that much more accessible to an Occidental audience; the snipping may even have rendered *Kagemusha* a better movie by any standards. Despite the judicious trimming, the twenty-seventh picture by Japan's greatest director remains to Western eyes the somewhat alien but invariably beautiful behemoth it was at Cannes. (For different reasons, it is a behemoth in some Oriental eyes as well. The Far Eastern reviews were by no means uniformly positive, and the Philippines' most respected film critic was brutal: "Kurosawa has lost his touch.")

At a final cost of between $6 million and $7.5 million, this is the most expensive movie in the history of Japan, completed only after the executive producers of the international edition, Francis Ford Coppola and George Lucas, persuaded Twentieth Century-Fox to join Toho Studios in a financial arrangement. Regardless of the comparatively generous budget— many of the battle scenes were shot at night against Kurosawa's wishes because fewer extras were required—it is not at all clear that *Kagemusha*, a heavily Buddhistic saga of late sixteenth-century clan wars, is everything the seventy-year-old director wanted it to be. The literal translation of the title, "the shadow of the warrior," is lumpier but more expressive of the film's premise than the Lucas-Coppola subtitle, *The Shadow Warrior*. The warrior is Shingen Takeda, the brilliant but ailing chief of the Takeda clan, who orders his entourage to avoid revealing his death for three years; the shadow is a Doppelgänger, a common thief who replaces the chief and who rules adequately until he becomes dangerously confident of his abilities. (Both roles are played exquisitely by Tatsuya Nakadai.) The double is banished and the Takeda clan commits what amounts to mass suicide on the battlefield. (To a Japanese audience, the Takeda clan's demise is of signal historical import: Shingen Takeda's strongest rival, Ieyasu Tokugawa, was to become shogun of all Japan in 1603, thereby inaugurating the Edo era, which would not end until 1867, fourteen years after Admiral Perry opened the country to the West.)

The final battlefield sequence is an apocalyptic slow-motion masterpiece in which the thief watches with horror as his society throws itself resolutely into stylized suicide. What Kurosawa has sought to do is visualize the Japanese feudal attitude toward heroism. Because death, under the proper circumstances, was to be embraced, even the blood on this corpse-covered terrain has become beautiful—instead of realistic clots of crimson, men are daubed with entirely unreal splatters of mauve that might have been placed for maximum esthetic effect by an abstract expressionist. But *Kagemusha*, directed by a man who has himself attempted suicide, is not celebrating self-destruction: that which is visualized is also criticized. The orgy of immolation—it should be noted that we see only the aftermath of the slaughter—is designed to question a trait common in Japanese culture, a trait Kurosawa has derided as the worship of the "esthetic of death," exempified by the kamikaze of the Second World

War and the hara-kiri of Mishima. While the soldiers manfully expire out of camera range, we stay with the thief, whose horror is our own; but being, in the last analysis, a child of his culture, he follows the only course of action open to him, and his final decision brings into play the full pathos and power of *Kagemusha*.

If the patience one must bring to this epic pays off in the end—and it does—that doesn't mean the journey is consistently rewarding. There are times in this costume drama when the only drama is the costumes; when the acting alternates between realism and silent-movie gesticulation; when the pageantry is mesmerizingly soporific. However, at other times the welcome presence of rambunctious low comedy reminds one of Kurosawa's continuing admiration for Shakespeare, and at no time is there a composition in the film unsuitable for sale in a signed, limited edition. Unwieldy but moving, simultaneously grandiose yet unadorned (like a Japanese tea ceremony), distanced but compassionate, *Kagemusha* is less a movie than a monumental frieze—it's Kurosawa's *Ivan the Terrible*, animated by the socially outraged, sentimental heart of Mark Twain's *The Prince and the Pauper*.   (*1980*)

The Killing Fields

The "killing fields" were near the village of Siem Reap in Cambodia, and one day, Dith Pran—a translator and journalist who had worked for *New York Times* correspondent Sydney Schanberg when the Lon Nol Government fell to the Khmer Rouge revolutionaries—went to see them. "In the water wells, the bodies were like soup bones in broth," he told Schanberg, who later used the material in a *New York Times Magazine* article, "The Death and Life of Dith Pran." "And you could always tell the killing grounds because the grass grew taller and greener where the bodies were buried." There were two fields near Siem Reap, and Pran estimated that each held about five thousand bodies—a small number, really, when compared to the uncounted Cambodians, between one and three million, who died between 1973 and 1980. *The Killing Fields*, produced by *Chariots of Fire*'s David Puttnam and directed by the astonishingly gifted Roland Joffé (known until now only as a theater director), dramatizes Dith Pran's visit to those fields, and much else besides. This is a full-scale and almost totally successful treatment of war and cultural upheaval as seen through the eyes of the people who, in the words of Schanberg, "paid the price and took the beating."

Though focused primarily on the years between 1975 and 1979, the film opens with a prologue on August 7, 1973. As part of their coverage of the covert war in Cambodia, Schanberg (Sam Waterston) and Pran (Dr. Haing S. Ngor, himself a Cambodian refugee) hasten by hook and crook to the scene of an accidental American bombing. At the site, executions are conducted casually while children scream, reporters report, and a soldier's radio incongruously blares Paul McCartney's "Band on the Run." Held captive by a Cambodian with a twitchy trigger-finger, Schanberg is adamant about his rights as a reporter—he displays the Big Apple arrogance that is used by scriptwriter Bruce Robinson, adapting Schanberg's own article, as a partial metaphor for the American presence in the East. "All right, I've had enough of this bullshit, I've got a story to get to New York!" Schanberg roars, barely aware that he values the story more than the people in it. He comes to feel otherwise. If *Apocalypse Now* was a movie about men who go to war and the reasons they love it, *The Killing Fields* is about the bodies those men crawl over; if *Apocalypse Now* is about the ghoulish glory of combat, *The Killing Fields* records as never before the hallucinatory hell of trying to stay alive. The difference between *The Killing Fields* and its predecessors (one of the many differences) is that even the greatest of anti-war movies have usually been suffused with the romantic ethos of the warrior. *The Killing fields* is not; because it views war and revolution through the perceptions of professional observers, it is concerned exclusively with consequences. We know what the Nixon Doctrine was; this is what it meant.

Schanberg returned to the United States in 1975, not long after the Khmer Rouge began the holocaust that was to continue until the Vietnamese ousted the Pol Pot regime four years later, but he was forced to leave Dith Pran behind. As the film follows Schanberg to New York, where he is resolute in his efforts to secure Pran's release (and wins a Pulitzer for his Cambodian reportage), it also trails Pran into the heart of darkness, into Khmer Rouge camps where twelve-year-old children in red scarves do as they are told—and what they are told to do, often enough for it to seem routine, is to kill people. The Cambodian countryside is photographed in *The Killing Fields* as a dreamlike landscape of lime, lavender, and yellow-green, and the camps are no exception; rarely has a nightmare been enacted in a setting of such sumptuous beauty. Rarely has a nightmare been so convincing. From the beginning, Joffé orchestrates natural noises unnaturally, and washes Mike Oldfield's pedestrian music over the dialogue. The result is a stylized score that comes to the listener from a distance, as if underwater. Even the images—helicopters photographed through the blades of other helicopters, Phnom Penh exploding into blood-streaked balls of fire—are apprehended languidly, at a distance, as if they, too, had been photographed underwater, through goggles. The eruption of random violence works unsettlingly in this context to pull the audience out of the reverie the film itself has induced, to persistently destroy the illusion that the dream can be forgotten or denied when the dreamer wakes up. Goya said the sleep of reason produces monsters. *The Killing Fields* is about what happens when the sleeper awakens with total recall.   (*1984*)

King David

"It is good to be the king," says Mel Brooks. Bet Richard Gere doesn't think so. Gere is the star of *King David*, a très serious retelling of the Old Testament tale that has audiences across the country and around the world laughing in unkind ridicule at the spectacle of one of the modern cinema's most famous sex symbols, the hard-working son of an insurance salesman from Philadelphia, prancing through Jerusalem in his undies as the King of Israel. You see, when David is crowned King, the Holy Ghost—or something else with a mean streak—moves him to celebrate by shaking his royal tail: *King David*; or, *Shabbas Night Fever*.

The movie, directed by Australia's Bruce Beresford (*Tender Mercies*, *Puberty Blues*, *The Getting of Wisdom*, *Breaker Morant*), who must have felt the need to do something ineffably ridiculous just once in his career, never recovers from David's display of bum-bobbing. (The picture's best line: the woman who confronts the King after his B.C. video and says, "I saw no King. I saw only a dancing man.") Before long, the unsympathetic audience is singing "Just a Gigolo" at the actor who starred in *American Gigolo* in happier days and roaring with helpless laughter as he squints his eyes at the spotlights and does his best to give the shaking of his gilded earrings dramatic momentum.

Gere isn't all that's wrong with *King David*; not even close. There's the Old Testament itself, which, treated literally, appears savage, primitive and unforgiving. It doesn't help that Beresford has used as his model for the battle scenes the work of Kurosawa—the Israelites are depicted as bloodthirsty Semitic samurai. In the film's nastiest sequence, they also become repulsively racist. King Saul orders his soldiers to kill a passle of priests, and at first the soldiers refuse. Eventually, one of them, a light-complected man, comes to the fore and sends a spear into the chest of a holy man. "It takes a gentile to obey," says Saul approvingly. The God of these Chosen People is no more attractive than his followers. When David experiences major lust for Bathsheba (Alice Krige) and has her husband Uriah (James Lister) sent to the front to get him out of the way, God gets angry and punishes David in various ways. One of them, the narrator tells us, is to smite the first-born son of the duo after only seven days of life. You can't help wondering: what did the *kid* do wrong? The next baby finds "favor" and is allowed to grow up to be Solomon, of temple fame.

In addition to Kurosawa, Beresford has studied Zeffirelli (*Jesus of Nazareth*) and Pasolini, whose *The Gospel According to St. Matthew* remains the single convincing Biblical epic. Beresford has said he wanted to stress authenticity and verisimilitude, and there are a couple of admirable performances in this context, especially from Edward Woodward as the deteriorating King Saul and Jack Klaff as his loyal son, Jonathan. The weirdly stylized Gere aside, realism is paramount: there are no miracles in the movie and even Goliath has been slapped down to size. When the young David (Ian Sears) goes out to do battle with the monster (Luigi Montefiori), he finds nothing more than a big ugly guy. Having already dispatched the bruiser with one of his five smooth stones, David hacks his head off, thus displaying the generosity of spirit endemic in this film. It can't be coincidence that the preface to the press kit consists of this quote from Ecclesiastes: "Who knows the meaning of anything? God has so ordered the world that man cannot find the answer. However hard a man may try, he will not find the answer. . . . Emptiness, emptiness! all is emptiness and a striving after wind." *King David*; or, *Nihilism Goes to the Promised Land.* (1985)

The King of Comedy

The King of Comedy is so smart—acerbic, astute, and appallingly amusing —it's breathtaking. It goes without saying that Martin Scorsese's tragicomedy is daring (a picture that uses Jerry Lewis as Robert De Niro's *straight man* is a picture that takes to chance as a duck takes to water) but what may need saying, in light of the negative response the movie is going to kick up in some quarters, is that it is deeply subversive: this is a show-biz movie that debunks one of the industry's sacrosanct myths, the notion that celebrities, by virtue of their gifts, deserve every perk they get or grab. Lenny Bruce indicated the road taken by Scorsese and his screenwriter, former *Newsweek* film critic Paul D. Zimmerman, when Bruce charged it was "obscene" for performers like Sammy Davis and Sophie Tucker to earn more in one week than a teacher could make in a lifetime, but Scorsese and Zimmerman go Bruce one better: they argue that the teacher, under the right circumstances, might *become* Sammy Davis or Sophie Tucker. (I recently asked Meryl Streep, in connection with the release of *Sophie's Choice*, if she ever experienced "survivor guilt" over her good fortune. She laughed and said she had. I then wondered how she had learned to deal with the knowledge that there were other people who could do what she had done—and I used myself as an example, explaining that I knew, and I thought every journalist or artist knew, that although he or she might be unique, replacement was clearly possible. Streep cut me short: she firmly believed, she said, that she was the only woman in the world who could do Sophie.)

Scorsese and Zimmerman maintain otherwise—their thesis is that although everyone may be unique, no one is irreplaceable. But in its first hour, when *The King of Comedy* follows the campaign of one Rupert Pupkin (De Niro), a would-be comedian and full-time nobody, to become a colleague and friend of talk-show host Jerry Langford (Lewis), it does seem to hold to the Meryl Streep line. Pupkin is presented as a creepy guy in loud clothes (checked jackets, white shoes) who is thirty-four years old and probably has no talent. He is pushiness incarnate: there is nothing he will not do to get his shot at the big one, including, it turns out, the crime of kidnapping. When a demonstration tape of his comedic routine— "My whole life," he calls it—is rejected, he turns ugly and snatches Langford. "Friendship is a two-way street," Pupkin tells Langford, "and you couldn't care less about me." The stories of Jodie Foster and other celebrities who have been tortured by the over-enthusiastic are evoked, along with Scorsese's own *Taxi Driver*, of which *The King of Comedy* is both elaboration and partial rebuttal.

The "friendship" Pupkin mentions is the ersatz intimacy fostered by television: both Pupkin and his partner in crime, a wealthy groupie named Masha (Sandra Bernhard), feel their loyalty to Langford's televised persona entitles them to certain rights, Pupkin to a guest shot on the show that has defined his life and Masha to Langford's amorous attentions, attentions she attempts to excite during a hilarious and poignant sequence at her townhouse, the site of Langford's farcical incarceration. Masha croons "Come Rain or Come Shine" to Langford, tells him she wants him to take her on the dining-room table and then says simply, "I love you." The poor creature means it.

Zimmerman's script, shot by Scorsese with evident craft but without the supercharged style of *Taxi Driver*, *Raging Bull*, or *Mean Streets* (the flat, two-dimensional look suggests television; Pupkin's fantasy sequences are always seen as videotapes), has provided De Niro with a continuation of characters he has earlier essayed: Pupkin is a (relatively) benign, dreamy version of Travis Bickle in *Taxi Driver*, except that Scorsese may well see Bickle, with his holy crusade to clean up the "sewer" of New York, as the more morally responsive of the two. Pupkin's goal, to "be king for a night" rather than "a schmuck for a lifetime," is less maladaptive, socially speaking, but it is more vapid; the vapidity of what passes for goals in America is one of the film's touchstones, and Jerry Lewis's Langford (the performance is grave, and spectacular in its assurance) is the symbol: Langford, the funniest man in the world, is a lonely, irascible figure for whom success of a nearly unimaginable magnitude has become an occupation like any other. It is his *job* to walk down the street and receive adoration. It is his *job* to feign interest in endlessly interchangeable guests on the order of Dr. Joyce Brothers. It is his *job* to be rich and famous, to inspire envy, and perhaps even to suffer guys like Pupkin. Behind *The King of Comedy*'s intricate insight is Andy Warhol's fatuous statement that everyone will become famous for fifteen minutes. The film's thesis is that Warhol was wrong, that only a few will find themselves in the limelight, but that many might qualify, if things were different, if the pie were big enough. This is a movie about the size of the pie, and about the kinds of people who eat it.   (*1983*)

The Last Metro

François Truffaut's *The Last Metro*, in which a theater company strives photogenically to survive the German Occupation (time: 1942; place: Paris), is cautious, nostalgic, tiny perfect moviemaking—an egg-tempera miniature, jewel-like in its peach-colored cinematography, eminently civilized in its whimsically humanist attitudes. That the film, written by Truffaut, Suzanne Schiffman, and Jean-Claude Grumberg, is set against the horrors of Nazism, anti-Semitism, collaboration, and the Resistance, is as irrelevant as the fact that *West Side Story* was supposed to have something to do with race war; *The Last Metro* is a comic musical that has mislaid its music.

There are three heroes: Jewish director Lucas Steiner (Heinz Bennent), evading the Nazis by living in the cellar of his theater; his wife Marion Steiner (Catherine Deneuve), a film star whose flawless ice-sculpture face packs the house; and Bernard Granger (Gérard Depardieu), a potato-pussed satyr hired to play opposite Mme Steiner in the theater's newest play, which will be directed by Steiner from the cellar. In its examination of the way a production is put together, there is a little of Truffaut's *Day for Night*, his movie about moviemaking (we are made privy to back-stage rivalries, lesbian *scandale*, homosexual flirtation), and in the tri-angulated relationship there is a little of *Jules and Jim*, but there is a great deal more of the director Jean Renoir, and especially of Renoir's final film, *Le Petit Théâtre* (1970), which utilized a café set that Truffaut has either copied or resurrected.

Renoir's *Grand Illusion* (1937) is, of course, the great French romantic anti-war film; next to it, *The Last Metro* is a precious, bloodless, sweetly spiritless essay on similar themes. Truffaut never raises his voice, never points a finger, never calls our attention to anything messy or ugly or even vulgar (this is an extremely peculiar war—the same war that was fought in so many idealized Hollywood films of the *Since You Went Away* ilk). The anti-Semites are silly, impossible to take seriously, and the goon-show collaborators, including an obnoxious Nazi drama critic, get what's coming to them with a justice rarely found in the real world (the drama critic is a creep, pure and simple; there is none of the psychological in-sight that Bernardo Bertolucci brought to the analysis of his collaborator in *The Conformist*). But this is not, Truffaut would remind us, the real world. The one detail missing that would allow the film to function memo-rably as a fantasy is *frisson*. Deneuve is as lovely to look at as ever, and her ivory bones take very well to the makeup and clothing of the period, but we know no more about her than what the script tells us: she walks, albeit beautifully, through the role. Depardieu, the apotheosis of raunchy peasantry in *1900*, *Get Out Your Handkerchiefs*, *Going Places*, and the brilliant *Loulou*, is a good actor but he's not able to act one: his miscast-ing as the worldly Bernard is woeful, and he and Deneuve play together with no more sexual magnetism, and with much less ability, than Wayne and Shuster. Their exploits are, moreover, inordinately confusing at times; but, Truffaut would remind us, the times were confusing. And, if these heroes seem, under the circumstances, to be inordinately content on oc-casion, we would be reminded again that Jean-Paul Sartre himself asked, "Will I be understood if I say both that the Occupation was intolerable and that we managed to adapt to it rather well?" *The Last Metro* illus-trates expertly, if at indefensible length, the question's second clause; the first is discarded, an unsightly sliver of a shattered reality that has no place in a pretty picture.   (*1981*)

A Love in Germany

When shopkeeper Kropp (Dieter Kirchlechner) leaves the small town of Brombach to do his duty for the Third Reich, his middle-aged and comely wife, Paulina (Hanna Schygulla), promptly falls into the strong young arms of a Polish prisoner of war, Stani (Piotr Lysak). The union is forbidden in Hitler's Germany, of course, but that doesn't stop Paulina and Stani from consummating their passion greedily and recklessly, heedless of the good and loyal citizens who will be forced to take action against this love in Germany. One of the most interesting aspects of Polish director Andrzej Wajda's unfailingly interesting adaption of Rolf Hochhuth's novel *A Love in Germany* is that the victims are *not* dragged kicking and screaming to their destinies. Quite the reverse: it is the victimizers who have to push themselves, kicking and screaming, to do their duty. Paulina's best friend Elsbeth (Elisabeth Trissenaar, once *The Station Master's Wife*) warns her to end the romance before tragedy ends it for her, and with the single exception of Maria (Marie-Christine Barrault in a rambunctiously over-stressed performance), a neighbor anxiously coveting Paulina's shop, the majority of the residents of Brombach are scandalized. Mainly, they wish Paulina would come to her senses. Even Lt. Mayer (Armin Mueller-Stahl, the star of *Lola*), the SS officer assigned to the case, tries to get the lovers off the hook—he gives Paulina an out when he pleads with her to renounce Stani, and he allows Stani a new lease on life when he suggests the proud Pole accept "Germanization." (The offer follows an absurdist sequence, comic and horrible, in which Stani's right to be considered Aryan is confirmed by a physical examination that involves the application of calipers and other devices.) Neither Wajda nor Hochhuth is arguing that this behavior is anything but appalling, regardless of the reluctance with which it is embraced, but as a politically committed and compassionate Polish filmmaker, Wajda understands all too well how ordinary people can be coerced into cooperating with a system they might otherwise resist. The film removes the mystery from fascism: *A Love in Germany* is a pellucid depiction of how atrocities get carried out by good people.

Piotr Lysak, the Edmonton actor and Polish exile who plays Stani, has reported that in Europe it is the sociological analysis, the depiction of Brombach as a village of decent people who countenance the indecent, that receives favorable comment—the love story is perceived as window dressing. He has been surprised, and not pleasantly, to find the reverse in

North America. "In New York, where the movie has been very success-ful, it is the love affair critics like. In Europe, the convention of 'the impossible love' is a spent convention." If so, it is not the fault of the actors. Schygulla, in her warmest and most expansive performance to date, is astonishingly unpredictable but never mannered or theatrical. When she buys condoms in a pharmacy and emerges into the light and shakes her face with her tongue out, she gives a concrete, unique expres-sion to the release of tension. Her Paulina is an irresponsible sensualist carried away by a passion she envisions as grand, but when the time comes she lives up to her vision; Stani is at first no more than a horny kid, but when his fate is sealed by his refusal to disavow his Polish patri-otism, he too attains the grandeur reserved for the tragic—his final scenes are as starkly heartrending as Goya's *Disasters of War*.

Like Wajda's previous films (*Danton*, *Man of Marble*, *Man of Iron*), the style of *A Love in Germany* is energetic and kinetic, fast and furious, and because the operatic is intermittently allowed, the ridiculous is occa-sionally approved. In addition to Barrault's embarrassing performance, there is one other punishing flaw: the film is framed by sequences in which a man and his son travel to Brombach in 1983 to investigate the events dramatized in the film. The technique served Orson Welles in *Citizen Kane* and it served Wajda in *Man of Marble*. In *A Love in Germany* it serves to underline the obvious.   (*1985*)

The Lonely Lady

In Harold Robbins's *The Lonely Lady*, a movie about Hollywood, Pia Zadora, the stacked Munchkin with the rich husband, reads Sylvia Plath's *The Bell Jar*, loses her virginity to a garden hose, is rescued by a rich screenwriter in a Rolls-Royce, is made pregnant by a matinee idol, gets the brush-off, gets an abortion, is romanced by an Italian nightclub owner, is turned over to a Sapphic woman who likes to smooch and a fat man who likes to watch, has a best friend who's gay, gets hooked on drugs and booze and wicked sex, has a nervous breakdown, is sent to a mental institution, gets out, sells a script, is turned over by her gay friend to a lesbian who likes hot tubs, wins an Oscar—for screenwriting—and in her acceptance speech says, "I don't suppose I'm the only one who had to fuck her way to the top."

Well, shucks, it could happen to any girl.   (*1983*)

Man of Flowers

The titillation twins, Ken Russell's *Crimes of Passion* and Brian De Palma's *Body Double*, have been defensively hailed by the majority of male reviewers for bringing sex back to the cinema and the cinema back to adulthood. But the movie that really does those things, and does them with artistry and integrity and intelligence, is a low-budget Australian film, a zesty profile of a dear old man dotty for art. Paul Cox's *Man of Flowers* is a minor masterpiece of sexual eccentricity, a singular comedy that finds fun in fetishism and love in lovelessness, and has more to say about the problems people face in trying to connect with each other, spiritually and physically, than *Body Double* and *Crimes of Passion* put together.

Norman Kaye, the actor who plays Charles, the "man of flowers" of the title, was the star of Cox's previous film, *Lonely Hearts*, and his performance here is every bit as miraculous. Charles's mother has died, but he still writes to her ("You were right, Mother, flowers have hearts; I shouldn't say what they remind me of") and offers gratitude to her ghost for the freedom her death has made possible. Mother's wealth permits Charles to indulge three interrelated loves—art, elaborate floral arrangements, and naked women. His taste in art tends toward the flowery, his taste in flowers toward the artistic, and his taste in women toward . . . well, he sees them as living blossoms, as paintings in motion, and once a week, on Wednesdays, he pays an artist's model, Lisa (Alyson Best), to come to his home and strip to the strains of a Donizetti duet.

Charles's unwillingness to touch Lisa or any other woman is, it turns out, Oedipal in origin (the roots are unearthed in lyric flashback) and harmless in practice: Charles cannot or will not distinguish between art and life, between the art object and the sex object. When Charles gives money to Lisa and orders her to "spend the check on something useful —buy some orchids," he is not posing as Oscar Wilde, nor is he joking when he tells her cretinous artist boyfriend David (Chris Haywood), "I'm not sure a man who can't paint flowers can paint at all." The existence of David and his mistreatment of Lisa brings a crisis to Charles's life that must be resolved with a crime of passion, a crime whose commission is out of Poe. But even at its most baroque, *Man of Flowers* never loses sight of its own lambent reality, and never fails to find in Charles's predicament a metaphor, and never fails to find in the metaphor a joke—in Cox's world, every character is a person and every person is a character. This, for example, is what a postman (Barry Dickins) has to say about the cosmos: "It has been estimated that Queen Elizabeth the Second has made a pertinent comment about the weather on 245,015 separate occasions to perfect strangers, all of whom remembered the exact comment all their lives . . . if a random and arguably inaccurate estimate of the impending climate by one overpaid human being in a flower hat can bring a large part of remembered joy to one underpaid human being in a flower hat, well, the sources of happiness on this planet are almost inexhaustible, aren't they?" Paul Cox is a comic genius: Jean Renoir with a giggle, Krafft-Ebing with a sense of humor. (*1984*)

Manhattan

"Morality is expediency in a long white dress," says Quentin Crisp. "I worry that I tend to moralize, as opposed to being moral," says Woody Allen. His worry has usually saved him—when he makes movies, the moralistic tone of his interviews vanishes and his perspective shifts into relative. At his best, he is the most modern of the moderns. *Manhattan* is midway in style and achievement between *Annie Hall* and *Interiors*—more serious than the former, less serious than the latter, not as funny as the former, much funnier than the latter. It's not as good a movie as *Annie Hall*, but it is very close to being as good, and in a different, much higher and harder-to-attain key. Never before has Allen been able to integrate comedy and pathos as deftly as he does in *Manhattan*. In one scene, where his alter ego, Isaac, tells Tracy, the seventeen-year-old high-school student (Mariel Hemingway) with whom he is having an affair, that he doesn't want to see her, the laughs catch in the throat, break free, and are captured again within the same sentence; the writing of *Manhattan*, by Allen and Marshall Brickman, is a thing of beauty.

The plot is defined by a *Ronde* of sexual and emotional attachments. Isaac is dating a girl who does homework. His best friend, Yale (Michael Murphy), is having a fling with Mary (Diane Keaton), an intellectual from Philadelphia who relishes making pronouncements on the order of "It has a marvelous negative capability" when viewing modern art and who, with Yale, has erected an Academy of the Overrated (F. Scott Fitzgerald, Ingmar Bergman). Isaac's second wife (Meryl Streep) has custody of their child, is living with another woman, and is writing a non-fiction account of her heterosexual years. Perturbed at the prospect, Isaac moans, "It's not that I have anything to hide, but there are a few disgusting moments." More than a few. Isaac has a surprisingly choleric streak ("When it comes to relationships with women, I'm the winner of the August Strindberg Award," he cracks), but that doesn't deter him from being attracted to Mary (winner of the Zelda Fitzgerald Emotional Maturity Award) against his will. He waits to make his move until Yale has grown weary of the emotional toll taken by the affair and shoots Mary like a squash ball to his best friend. Isaac and Mary—unmarried, bright, witty—should be an ideal couple, and they know it.

"This is shaping up to be a Noel Coward play," Isaac says when he learns Mary is seeing Yale again. He's right: *Manhattan* is in part an update of *Private Lives*, that frothy but profound statement of the peculiar perversity of sexual attraction—except that *Manhattan* seeks to be profound on purpose, instead of by accident. It nearly makes it. In the twenties, Coward would not have been able to get away with teaming one of his protagonists with a seventeen-year-old girl, but Allen can, and Hemingway's resonant, squeaky-voiced performance ("You sound like the mouse in the Tom and Jerry cartoon," Isaac tells her) rides over the idealized conception of her character.

Allen has played Isaac many times before, of course, but in *Manhattan* he has courageously darkened the nebbish. He still jokes compulsively and still masks insecurity with sexual braggadocio ("I want you to enjoy me," he instructs Tracy, "my wry sense of humor and astonishing sexual technique") but Isaac can also be cruel (as he is to Tracy) and inconsiderate (as he is to his best friend, who accuses him of playing God). Isaac rests close to Woody Allen's bone: he's an angst-ridden moralist.

That aspect of the artist leads to a discussion of Manhattan's shortcomings. Allen conceives of New York (visually in black and white, aurally to the often ironic accompaniment of Gershwin) as a metaphor for the effects of a deteriorating civilization on individual relationships. We know otherwise from Coward, from Flaubert, from Euripides: men and women have always had these problems. When Allen films a scene of himself and Keaton (there is no trace of Annie Hall) in a planetarium, trying to connect on a mock-up moon, it's as if John Cassavetes had taken over—you're bulldozed by symbolic evocation. Allen's moral rigidity may also explain why Meryl Streep's tell-all character is treated as a one-dimensional bitch. To Allen, publicity-seeking is abhorrent, and he allows his prejudice to corrode the compassion that elsewhere gives *Manhattan* the rich sympathy of *Grand Illusion*, Isaac's favorite movie. For, despite a rather silly monologue in which Allen declares that people create for themselves unnecessary neurotic problems that keep them from dealing with the more terrifying unsolvable problems about the universe, *Manhattan* is at last a humorous and sad glimpse of the ways we work against ourselves to keep ourselves from achieving peace. What made *Annie Hall* so haunting also gives *Manhattan* its silent, deeply cutting edge: we can't help it.   (*1979*)

Marianne & Juliane

Marianne & Juliane, which won first prize at the Venice Film Festival in 1981 under the original German title, *Die Bleierne Zeit* (*Leaden Times*), and first prize later the same year at the Chicago Film Festival under the title *The German Sisters*, is, whatever it chooses to call itself, a near masterpiece. The passage of three years has diminished its stature not an iota; what seemed merely timely in 1981 now seems in 1984 not only timely, but prescient. For example: long before Germaine Greer got there, writer-director Margarethe von Trotta was wondering where childbearing and maternal responsibility fitted into the women's movement, and where the women's movement fitted into the task of improving everything for everyone.

Von Trotta's framework for a hundred thoughts and a thousand questions is the sad but instructive real-life story of the Ensslin sisters, a story inexorably enlarged into a metaphor for postwar Germany and its "leaden times," its refusal, in the director's words, "to admit feelings of guilt at all." The methodology is Proustian: Von Trotta cuts with effortless clarity back and forth through the sisters' lives, from scenes of childhood (air raids under Hitler) and adolescence (a chilling vignette when the girls come face to face with the death camps in the form of a documentary screened in the classroom) to sequences in modern West Germany (where feminism and family are at first viewed as mutually exclusive).

Christiane, to whom *Marianne & Juliane* is dedicated, was and is the elder Ensslin sister, and for a time worked at a progressive women's magazine, *Emma*. Gudrun, the younger sister, was rounded up with the Baader-Meinhof terrorist group, three of whose members, including Gudrun, died mysteriously in prison. Gudrun becomes Marianne in the movie and is played with a perfection that must be seen to be believed by Barbara Sukowa, who undergoes a complete psychic transformation, from dutiful daughter of a Protestant minister to haughty, intransigent terrorist. Sukowa was the star of Rainer Werner Fassbinder's *Lola* and the doomed, innocent Mieze in his *Berlin Alexanderplatz*. Here, although she looks like the same actress, she acts not at all like her: her own transformation is as total as her character's. Equally arresting is Jutta Lampe as Juliane, the fictional name assigned to Christiane, the liberal journalist whose sibling rivalry with Marianne assumes political and philosophical dimensions as the sisters grow older. The film's fulcrum is the ambivalent relationship between the two, dramatized with extraordinary immediacy in the confrontations that take place in the visiting rooms of the two prisons where Marianne is incarcerated. Marianne argues that in becoming a terrorist and in having given up all pretense of bourgeois existence, including the care of her son, Jan, she has expunged her past and has discharged a social responsibility higher than slavish adherence to corrupt codes of conduct; she is confident that history will justify her. Juliane, while admitting the justice of many of Marianne's criticisms, maintains that both sisters are trapped in their personal and national histories, and that no positive steps to freedom can be taken until the size of their cell has been surveyed.

Von Trotta sympathizes with both. She passionately communicates Marianne's outrage at the way things are, but she shares Juliane's concern with understanding the past so as to illuminate the present. (And to avoid the excesses of self-righteousness: when Juliane screams that thirty years earlier Marianne might have been a Nazi, Von Trotta does nothing to signal disagreement.) *Marianne & Juliane* is a document that struggles to come to terms with an impossible past in a barely feasible present, and its director appears to realize that her film, like its heroines, is trapped by history, which is why she avoids pretending to be definitive—either about the sisters, or about the agonies of the nation she has presumed to concretize in their story. "I'll tell you all I know," Juliane says to Marianne's son when he asks about his mom, "but it's not everything." *Marianne & Juliane* is not everything, either, but it's more than any reasonable filmgoer might expect. If Von Trotta finds few causes for optimism, she must know that the existence of her own movie is one of them. *(1984)*

Modern Romance

Robert Cole (Albert Brooks), who edits movies, and Mary Harvard (Kathryn Harrold), who works in a bank, are having a modern romance: at the beginning of *Modern Romance* they split up. Robert tells Mary he doesn't want to see her. "Okay," Mary responds, "it's over again." Robert reveals his reasoning: "You've heard of a no-win situation, haven't you? Vietnam. This." But Robert doesn't really want to leave Mary: Robert wants to have her and beat her too.

Brooks, the frenetic force behind a virtually unseen 1979 parody of cinéma vérité, *Real Life*, once appeared as a stand-up comic on "The Tonight Show" with a routine that continued for five agonizing minutes without a single titter. At the end of the five minutes, he apologized for the lack of laughs by explaining that he had been working as comedian for five years and had run out of material. Johnny Carson swears that the hilarity following this set-up, one of the longest in the history of stand-up comedy, lasted a full minute; Brooks is a comedian who takes chances, a humorist who wagers on the intelligence of his audience. In *Modern Romance* (Brooks is the star, the director, and, with Monica Johnson, the co-scriptwriter) the bet is that the audience will accept a satirical study of sexual possessiveness that never gets sentimental, a study that rescores for the cadences of comedy one of the dissonant melodies of *Raging Bull*. The first thing that should be said about *Modern Romance* is that it is very funny; the second is that it is too true to be as funny as it is. The critical animosity Brooks has engendered in some quarters with this picture may be based on the inevitable but untrustworthy comparison to Woody Allen. Unlike Allen, Brooks is not afraid to be disliked. His Robert Cole is a greedily possessive, self-dramatizing California schnook who uses his "love" for Mary Harvard as an instrument of blackmail. (Brooks has begun his film career with the psychological sophistication Allen did not develop until *Annie Hall*.) Cole is not Jake LaMotta—not quite—but neither is he that simpering little intellectual goon in hornrims, that adolescently sex-obsessed nebbish Allen purveyed to several grateful generations. Allen was a classic clown, an alter ego you could laugh at because he exaggerated your worst fears about yourself and dispelled them (no matter how bad off you were, you were better off than Woody Allen). Brooks wants to be the audience's *ego*—he has no interest in dispelling fears, only in reflecting them, in getting us to laugh at the messes he believes love makes us.

With thorough Me Generation self-indulgence, Robert lives through his post-separation trauma: he drops Quaaludes; chews vitamins; jogs; tells himself, "Alone's kind of a nice place to be, one *isn't* the loneliest number." "How difficult can it be to find one perfect person?" he wails. When he plays the radio, he hears "Love Hurts"; he switches the station and hears, "God Only Knows (Where I'd Be Without You)"; yet another twirl and, "Along Comes Mary." In the throes of loneliness, radios are minefields, telephones torture racks. Robert's relationship to Mary echoes early Woody Allen in one respect: the woman's half of the equation is stinted. We don't know why Mary puts up with Robert when he comes crawling back to her (in real life, Mary probably wouldn't know either) and her character resembles Diane Keaton's women in the window-dressing phase of Keaton's career. Even so, *Modern Romance* captures with the immediacy of journalism the difficulties of working it out in an age when making it is so much easier than keeping it.   (*1981*)

Mommie Dearest

On paper, *Mommie Dearest*, Christina Crawford's gloves-off memoir of life with monster mum, the redoubtable Joan Crawford, was a pathetic tale told by a badly bruised child who had grown into a wounded and understandably vengeful adult. On screen, with Faye Dunaway giving the performance of several lifetimes as the broad-shouldered, self-styled Queen of Hollywood, *Mommie Dearest* is the story of a madcap mother who beats her adopted daughter who in turn grows up and finds the happy ending by selling the glass slipper. It's the first full-scale comedy about child abuse: *Auntie Maim*.

That couldn't have been what director Frank Perry and three other scriptwriters had in mind, or could it? *Mommie Dearest* is such a mess it's difficult to be sure. What appears to be one of the worst movies this year—it was hissed at an invitational screening—might be a consciously subversive satire of hype, the American dream, the nuclear family, gossip-mongering, and the movies themselves (no one ever goes out a door without pausing at the threshold to make a curtain speech), all filmed in the style of a Joan Crawford vehicle. Then again, it might be a hoot 'n' holler stinker, more dirty fun than mud-wrestling. Whatever it is—the truth lies somewhere in between—it's a terrific movie for audience back-talk. When the aged Joan Crawford moaned, "I'm scared, Christina, what will I do?" someone hollered, "Go to work." Laughter during Joan's beatings of her children was constant, capped by applause when the tiny blond "Tina," having lived through another onslaught of mummerly love, rolled her eyes and said, "Jesus Christ."

The opening image is the best: an Art Deco alarm clock rings and a gloved hand emerges from satin sheets to silence it. Perry keeps the camera away from The Face throughout the credits; when we do finally see the bushy eyebrows and the red lips, the incarnation is eerie, as advertised. The Face is *her* face, the mannerisms are *her* mannerisms and Dunaway manages magnificently to depict a woman whose acting off screen is no better than her acting on. But Joan Crawford was never particularly sympathetic and the movie—what with Mommie Dearest covered in cold cream and rolling her eyes like a demented Kabuki creature while demanding that little Christina scour the bathroom floor and submit to coat-hanger beatings at 4:00 A.M. —makes her less so. Dunaway has been quoted as saying she feels for Joan. Feels what?

Perry and his writers obviously do not believe Christina's account of life with Auntie Fame and they have therefore turned the volume into one long, lushly appointed joke. (This movie is physically and maybe philosophically what Fassbinder was after in *Lili Marleen*.) We are given a Joan out of *Whatever Happened to Baby Jane?* maniacally pruning rose bushes in the middle of the night with garden shears (a great line here: "Tina, bring me the axe!") and in Tina we are given a child victim whose poise and calculation are authentically creepy. So many alternate titles suggest themselves that it's hard to choose, but one has to be *Christina, The Omen IV*. The movie implies that Christina *made* mummy do it. Auntie Blame.

There's nothing to sympathize with but the sets, which get far too many drinks spilled on them. Well, not quite: there is a good supporting performance from the costumes, which also get too many drinks spilled on them. Both sets and costumes are sadly required to witness entirely too much empty hysteria from their unappreciative owners. Because Perry, et al., have taken Christina's account with a salt lick, they have eschewed excesses that would have been wonderful in the movie's trash-forties context. Christina reports that her mother died in the presence of a Christian Science practitioner: "The woman, realizing there was nothing more she could do, began praying. . . . My mother raised her head. The last coherent words from her mouth were, 'Damn it . . . don't you dare ask God to help me!' " Why is that scene missing? And why aren't we told of the birthday and graduation present Joan sent her daughter—two boxes, a single earring in one box for graduation, its mate in the other box for birthday? Dunaway's fear that Joan Crawford would be turned into a scapegoat may be the answer to the film's bizarre evenhandedness. So instead of telling God to get along without her, Joan tells the board of directors at Pepsi-Cola they can't get along without her, in a scene clearly designed to correspond to revisionist feminist readings of Crawford's career. Dunaway's fears that Joan would come across as a monster have, nonetheless, been fulfilled. But democratically: both Crawfords, victim and victimizer, have been trashed in *Mommie Dearest*. This is theoretically a modern horror movie about mother love, but it is actually one of the funniest movies about how *not* to make a movie ever made. The moral? Craig Russell reports Joan Crawford sent a message to all movie stars from beyond the grave: "Don't die: people'll dish ya." *(1981)*

Montenegro

Dusan Makavejev's satirical romp *Montenegro* is too much fun to be legal: it's robustly inventive but readily accessible, bracingly healthy but outlandishly Rabelaisian. And it has something to say. Set in Stockholm, the picture opens with a parable. "A little girl questioned a monkey in the zoo," the titles read: " 'Why do you live here? Isn't it nicer where you came from?' " Cut to a pier. On it, a woman. A mysterious, unhappy woman, in a fur coat. On the soundtrack, Marianne Faithfull sings "The Ballad of Lucy Jordan," the sad song of a thirty-seven-year-old unfulfilled female who realizes she'll never "ride through Paris with warm wind in her hair."

The thirty-seven-year-old female on the pier is Marilyn Jordan (Susan Anspach), a beautiful American married to a successful Swede. She has long legs and good teeth. She has two splendid children. She has several strings of pretty pearls. But she has no warm wind in her hair. In common with every other character in *Montenegro*, from the monkey on up, she is in exile. And in prison. Marilyn's particular exile is from herself, and her cage is a cushy, upper-middle-class nest of her own design. When she tries to take wing, she does so crazily and self-destructively. She devours the family's dinner. She sets fire to the bed. She feeds the dog poison. She reads Gay Talese. This section of *Montenegro* combines the upper-middle-class milieu used in American films such as *Kramer vs. Kramer*, *Diary of a Mad Housewife*, and *Blume in Love* with the upper-middle-class milieu used in films by Ingmar Bergman. The difference is that Makavejev, a Yugoslav filmmaker with the anarchistic temperament of the true infidel, can't take cant—bourgeois, Euro-American, psychiatric—seriously; what for Bergman is tragedy and what for Paul Mazursky is melodrama, is for Makavejev farce.

The casting is inspired—and deliberately fiendish in its overtones. Anspach is famous for her gelid portraits of unsatisfied women (*Blume in Love*, *Five Easy Pieces*) and the actor playing her husband, Erland Josephson, is equally famous for a well-nigh endless list of ice-king credits in Bergman movies. Makavejev is never cruel—Anspach is softer and more affecting than she has ever been—but he's not about to equate Marilyn Jordan's inchoate angst and well-upholstered boredom with Poland or El Salvador.

When Marilyn decides to follow her husband on his twenty-fourth business trip of the year, leaving behind the kids and a father-in-law who believes himself to be Buffalo Bill (and who is advertising in the newspaper for a wife who can shimmy to ABBA records), *Montenegro* changes tone. At the airport, Marilyn falls in with Tirke (Patricia Gelin), a Yugoslav immigrant in the process of attempting to smuggle a suckling pig into Stockholm. ("You are not allowed to bring meat in this city," the customs officer says snippily, "There's enough meat in this city.") Tirke introduces Marilyn to Alex (Bora Todorovic), who owns a Yugoslav nightspot, the ZanziBar, and Alex introduces her to Montenegro (Svetozar), a young, darkly handsome Yugoslav, Makavejev's symbol for the purity of paganism.

The Yugoslavs are also exiles and in prison. But in a series of broadly comic, almost slapstick sequences, Makavejev contrasts sharply the open sexuality and hedonism of their existence with the covert sexuality and intrusive "good taste" of Marilyn's culture. Marilyn finally all but joins the group and as "Suzi Nashville" sings "Gimme a Little Kiss" for the ZanziBar patrons (the song was to have been Randy Newman's acrid "Sail Away," about Negro slaves; the rights were not obtained in time). Her affair with Montenegro, staged by Makavejev at his most erotic, would seem to cinch her new-found freedom. But this pampered and pathetic woman ultimately proves unable to relinquish her past, and a dark cloud scuttles quickly across the movie's sunny sky. Makavejev does not condemn Marilyn for her failure; he merely records it as an example of the futility of the search for perfection.

If those shots of the monkey in the cage at the beginning of *Montenegro* were funny, they were not a joke. The contemporary condition, Makavejev is maintaining, is exactly congruent to the condition of that primate behind bars, with his dim memories of a better life (Eden?) from which he has been exiled. The message is depressing, but the movie is exhilarating. *Montenegro* is the pagan's *Paradise Lost*.   (*1981*)

Mrs. Soffel &
Paris, Texas

Crazy loves, deranged heroes, abandoned children, corroded hopes, and bludgeoned dreams: *Mrs. Soffel*, directed by Australia's Gillian Armstrong, and *Paris, Texas*, directed by West Germany's Wim Wenders, bear witness (as does *Witness*, directed by another Australian, Peter Weir) to the endless infatuation that American movie myths hold for moviemakers everywhere—both pictures were made in and about the United States by outsiders trying to come to terms with famous film fantasies. The movies lurking behind *Mrs. Soffel*, a story too crazy not to be true, are *Bonnie and Clyde* and *McCabe and Mrs. Miller*; the long shadow over *Paris, Texas*, a story at first too true not to be crazy, is the sentimentality of *The Searchers*.

An "insane infatuation," the turn-of-the-century newspapers shrieked when Mrs. Kate Soffel (Diane Keaton), wife of the warden of a Pittsburgh prison, helped the notorious Biddle brothers, Ed (Mel Gibson) and Jack (Matthew Modine), escape mere months before they were to be executed. (They were convicted of killing a grocer during a burglary.) But that's not all that Mrs. Soffel, a God-fearing middle-aged woman who once read to prisoners from the Good Book, did for the Biddles: *she went with them*, and she left behind a husband and four children without so much as a fare-thee-well. The only thing she asked of Ed Biddle, whom she loved more than life, was that he guarantee *not* to let the law bring her back alive.

Travis (Harry Dean Stanton), the equally cuckoo hero of *Paris, Texas*, initially wanted the same thing—to be left for dead. As the stately film begins (there's little vigor in Wim) and Ry Cooder's guitar gently weeps, Travis trudges across Monument Valley, site of *The Searchers*, going Lord knows where, coming from God knows what. When he faints and is taken to a clinic in Terlingua, Texas, his brother Walt (Dean Stockwell) is located in Los Angeles and flies at once to his crazy brother's silent side—Travis, it transpires, has stopped talking, and won't tell Walt what he's been up to, lo, these many years. Playwright Sam Shepard's script eventually clues us in: Travis is estranged from his wife Jane (Nastassja Kinski) and has abandoned his eight-year-old child (Hunter Carson, son of actress Karen Black) to the care of Walt and Mrs. Walt, a French-woman named Anne (Aurore Clément). It all happened four years ago—we see the once-happy families in a wonderfully edited, touching sequence of home movies—but then it all came apart, and Travis went on the road, and he's been a searcher ever since.

When *Mrs. Soffel* (filmed in Pittsburgh and Toronto) begins, Kate Soffel has already abandoned her life, but only in her head; when Ed Biddle is put in prison, he gives her the excuse her heart needs. Partly as the result of the work of cinematographer Russell Boyd (the Australian films of Peter Weir, *A Soldier's Story* and *Tender Mercies*), who has shot the period movie with the furry depth of a master mezzotint (an aerial view of a doomed sleigh racing across snow has the look of a drop of black blood spattered against white fur), the world of *Mrs. Soffel* is slow, sinuous, and off-center in its Arctic lyricism, not unlike the world of *McCabe and Mrs. Miller*. The color becomes a character—thick, heavy, unyielding, almost chocolatey in its smoothness, like the bars that confine the Biddles, like the society that confines *Mrs. Soffel*. Sexual sparks are struck between the convict and the warden's wife when Mrs. Soffel reads to Ed from the Bible and says to him, "God means to test our love for Him," and he says to her, "By torturing us?" And in seeing that there *is* no justice; and in thinking that Ed *might* be "innocent as snow," as he claims to be; and in feeling a heat she has never felt before—she madly but euphorically seals her fate. Keaton, who has rarely been better, makes Mrs. Soffel's transition from repressed society lady to fugitive tramp insanely logical, and Gibson, who has never been better, makes Ed Biddle's fall from dry self-sufficiency into sticky infatuation seem inevitable. (As the other Biddle, Matthew Modine is a startlingly effective paradox, a considerate cretin.) Director Armstrong (*Starstruck*, *My Brilliant Career*) takes her time, but she needs to: the credibility that gives the conclusion its whallop demands scrupulous preparation.

Wim Wenders takes his time, too, but *Paris, Texas*, a movie whose magnificent images of the modern American west (the cinematographer is Robby Müller) rival the best of the realist painters, peters out; the sentimentality toward the end becomes grotesque—it's existential sentimentality—and the attempt to get the audience to cheer for two fabulously unfit parents backfires. Travis and Jane shamelessly use the child for the gratification of their own egos. Fair enough. But Wenders doesn't appear to notice. Travis discovers Jane working in an incongruous Houston whorehouse, a voyeur brothel (everything happens with phones and two-way mirrors) that only a German director could invent—any Texan on a toot, on a lowdown Saturday-night drunk, would put a lizard-skin cowboy boot through those silly mirrors, beggin' your pardon, ma'am. When the whore turns out to be Kinski, looking like Bardot with black eyes and blonde hair and a pout protruberant enough to support oil derricks, the goodwill built up by *Paris, Texas* evaporates faster than spit on a short-order griddle. And when Travis remembers in a long theatrical monologue how he tied Jane to the bed and then roped a cowbell to her legs so he'd always know where she was (she stuffed a sock up it, and took her love to town), you can see what Shepard and Wenders are getting at—the cruelty of crazy love—but it's hard not to laugh. A sock up a cowbell is not the most inspired of metaphors. The resolution is rickety in its dippy romanticism, but even it might have scraped by if the Kinski role had gone to, say, Jessica Lange. In *Mrs. Soffel*, Diane Keaton is demented enough to embrace the improbable and chase the impossible; Lange has that same kinky, mercurial quality; and while it's true that Kinski can play kinky and mercurial, she can't play American—not yet—and she doesn't have the resources needed to depict the soul of a beautiful young woman who would (1) marry a man who looks like a piece of beef jerky; (2) leave the child he sires; and (3) go off blithely to work as a prostitute in a surreal whorehouse. In snowy *Mrs. Soffel* Gillian Amstrong finds meaning in frigidity; in dusty *Paris, Texas* Wim Wenders loses it in aridity.   (*1985*)

Muddy River

Muddy River is a beautifully realized remembrance of a childhood lived along the Aji River in Osaka in 1956. Making his debut as a director, Koehi Oguri, who was born the year the Pacific war ended, has received the kind of acclaim heretofore reserved for Kurosawa, Ozu, or Mizoguchi, the triumvirate of the golden age of Japanese cinema. *Muddy River* suggests the golden age may not yet be over.

Photographed modestly but effectively in black and white, with images of remarkable clarity, *Muddy River* is as spare—and as deceptively simple—as a haiku. The nine-year-old hero, the pudgy, naive Nobuo (Nobutaka Asahara), lives with his giddy young mother (Yumiko Fujita) and his much older father (Takahiro Tamura), a veteran of the Second World War, in the back of the restaurant both parents operate. Their lives are compelling, but not in any histrionic, obvious way: the big events consist of the death of an old man, the arrival of a houseboat with an elusive female occupant, and, most of all, Nobuo's friendship with nine-year-old Kiichi (Minoru Sakurai) and eleven-year-old Ginko (Makiko Shibata), son and daughter, respectively, of the mystery woman on the boat.

The era is post-war but pre-recovery; Hondas, Sonys, blue jeans, fast foods, and other accoutrements of the economic miracle are just around the corner. Nobuo's father, bitter because the government "has renounced war" and is now "getting rich on America's war in Korea," is not getting rich. The nostalgic old warrior belongs to a generation that has become an embarrassment to the Japan of the fifties, a generation that believed, and believes, in the rectitude of the Japanese cause. Nobuo sympathizes with his father's anguish but does not pretend to understand its origin. The first shot of the film, a light bulb floating in the turbid water, indicates the metaphorical use to which the river—Nobuo's front yard—will be put. Oguri has stated his aim exactly: "At the spring, the water is pure, but as it descends to the sea, it becomes more and more muddy. Yet, this mud is the essence of the river—a river is made of water and of mud. In the same way, a child may be as pure as spring water; it is experience—living, knowing, happiness and sorrow—that nurtures him. This is the mud of humanity and it is this which I wanted to celebrate in this film."

Oguri's statement recalls the goals of the Italian neo-realists (Visconti, Rossellini, Vergano, Lattuada, Zavattini, and De Sica) who flourished briefly after the Second World War, but *Muddy River* does not share the fiery passion of neo-realist politics. That is not, in this context, a criticism: because Oguri is far more philosophical (Eastern, if you will) than the Italians who inspired his style, his sentimentality is also less overt, his characters less idealized. Kiichi, Nobuo's young friend from the houseboat, has a pugnacity that is going to become a pain in a few years (Oguri lets us see, once the mystery of the mother is revealed, why he must become a fighter). Nobuo's father defies convenient categorization and Nobuo's mother reveals unexpected strengths and weaknesses.

Most of the movie is spent with the kids, and Oguri catches his children seconds before the attitudinizing of adolescence sets in. There is a wonderful scene when Nobuo's friends deride him for associating with the impoverished and illiterate Kiichi. Nobuo tells them he will not watch TV with them unless Kiichi can come along. When they refuse and leave, Kiichi suddenly turns a somersault at Nobuo's feet. A minor moment is made into something memorable and nearly miraculous. *Muddy River* puts a multitude of those moments together and comes up with a memoir that *is* miraculous.   (*1983*)

The Natural

The Natural, a sentimental and sanctimonious melodrama with Robert Redford, is the kind of movie that is usually built around a female star playing a singer making a comeback—*The Natural* is the kind of movie that is usually a musical, and the music usually makes up for the psychological primitivism and narcissism of the heroine's self-aggrandizement.

No such luck here. That *The Natural* is about an aging baseball player making a comeback doesn't stop it from looking like *Oklahoma!* and sounding like a locker-room parody of *Funny Girl*, and it doesn't stop director Barry Levinson from cranking up the mythic volume so high it could give Zeus a headache. In this film, when the hero hits the ball, the heavens part and lightning strikes. Literally.

A prologue introduces us to Roy Hobbs (Redford) as a child and young adult. "You got a gift, Roy, but it's not enough, you gotta develop it for yourself," Roy's dad tells him. "Rely too much on your own gift and you fail." (Roy does develop his gift, notably by making his own baseball bat from the wood of a tree struck by lightning.) The young Roy is treated as a modern Odysseus, and Homer is indeed mentioned in the script, adapted from a Mount Olympus fantasy novel by Bernard Malamud; there are many allusions to Arthurian legend, as well. The mythic, poetic, lyrical, epic treatment of baseball is no accident, in other words, but what works on the page—admirers of the Malamud novel are a vociferous lot—does not necessarily work well on screen. Malamud's conceit might have made a wonderful silent film, with Lillian Gish and Douglas Fairbanks, but paced sluggishly and glazed in the sheen of high art, this picture is both tedious and overpoweringly silly.

Like all American heroes, regardless of their epic pedigrees, ordinary Roy is not about to let himself get highfalutin. "The only Homer I know has four bases in it," he grins, displaying vintage Redford ivory. Like Rocky, Roy is a go-fer-it kinda guy, and he lets his Penelope, Iris (Glenn Close), know he's going to "reach for the best within me." But then disaster (best left unspecified, since it's the only surprise in the movie) strikes. Cut sixteen years into the future. Roy joins up with a failing team, the Knights, coached by two old geezers (Wilford Brimley and Richard Farnsworth, who make a great comedy team) under the thumbs of two crooks, one a porcine judge with chipmunk cheeks (Robert Prosky) and the other a creep with a glass eye (Darren McGavin). Roy wants to play ball but he's not about to play ball—he is not going to be party to corruption. He's a straight shooter, true blue, a Boy Scout basted in Coppertone. The bad guys use big words ("What's a canard?" ordinary Roy asks the slime-king judge) and, when things get tough, they try to sully ordinary Roy's virtue with an orchidaceous gal (Kim Basinger) as sickly as she is sweet.

Not to worry. Just when it looks as if ordinary Roy may turn out to be human after all, his saving grace, reliable Iris, on hold for sixteen years, arrives. Roy's career has slumped, but one afternoon he glances into the stands and there arises Iris, hat backlit by cinematographer Caleb Deschanel (*The Right Stuff*, *The Black Stallion*) to look like a Giotto halo, and Roy hits the kind of homer with four bases in it. Later, at a soda fountain—they both order lemonade—Roy asks the radiant Iris what's up. "I'm not married," she says. How could she be? She probably comes to earth only during the week and on weekends returns home to heaven. The film's treatment of women is thoroughly Victorian—moms and whores, with Close's plaster saint offset by two evil tramps, Basinger's blonde bitch, who drains Roy's vital juices, and Barbara Hershey's vengeful black widow spider.

Why is Redford, who has more power in Hollywood than any other actor with the exception of Clint Eastwood using that power as he did in *Brubaker*, to create an art-house answer to *Rocky*? (The cleverest aspect of the film is the plotting that allows a man of his age to play a kid on the make.) Redford has surrounded himself with the finest talent his fame can attract and his money can buy, but neither fame nor funds can do anything about the fact that he remains a bland and boring actor whose fortune is in a face that is not as charismatic as it once was. Mel Gibson, to whom Redford has been compared, has already surpassed him. It is inconceivable that Redford would take the sort of risk Gibson takes in *The Bounty* when Fletcher Christian has a nervous breakdown—Redford indicates especially overpowering emotion by squinting.

With Redford, less is not more, less is nigh on to nothing. He's natural in *The Natural*, but he's artless: it has been years since he played the politician in *The Candidate*, but he's still running for office on screen. The gig he wants is God, and that's what he gets to play in *The Natural*, a Greek deity with an arm made of home runs and a halo made of Sun-In. (*1984*)

Never Cry Wolf

Never Cry Wolf, director Carroll Ballard's rhapsodic follow-up to *The Black Stallion*, is a Walt Disney production, but it's a Disney movie like Beethoven's "Ode to Joy" is a tune: the description is accurate as far as it goes, but it leaves the art out, and *Never Cry Wolf* is a spectacular work of movie art.

Both the movie and its hero get off to a shaky start. Farley Mowat's memoir of life among the *Lupus* begins when the young Mowat—called Tyler in the movie, and played by Charles Martin Smith—is assigned to go north to study the habits of wolves. He is specifically assigned to garner evidence that wolves are devastating caribou herds, so the government can proceed in clear conscience with a plan to all but exterminate the species. The opening titles and the narration, written by C.M. Smith, Sam Hamm, and Richard Kletter, get all this across in indigestible lumps of prose, and the low comedy between Tyler and the pilot (Brian Dennehy) who will take him north is about what would be expected of a Disney picture—cute as a puppy. But once the plane has dropped Tyler into the middle of a vast, frozen lake, a lake smack in the middle of Lawren Harris's forbidding yet ravishing Arctic, Ballard assumes full control and *Never Cry Wolf* finds a hypnotic rhythm that it never loses.

Tyler's first order of business is to set up a base camp, which he does with great effort and a good deal of assistance from Ootek (Zachary Ittimangnaq), an aged Inuit conveniently passing by. Because the primary virtues of *Never Cry Wolf* are visual, descriptions of Tyler's activities are misleadingly mundane. One of the movie's exciting early sequences occurs when Tyler falls through the ice, swims back to the armored surface—he can't find the hole he fell through—and pokes an escape hatch through the thawing crust with his rifle. Ballard and his cinematographer, Hiro Narita, shoot the sequence from above; fall through the hole with Tyler; simulate his point of view by aiming the camera upward at the ice; and then suddenly cut to the top of the lake, to a frozen and silent expanse, to record the tip of the rifle exploding through the powdery, unbroken emptiness. Editing is the grammar of movie-making: this movie makes grammar sing.

Spring. Tyler jots down the temperature: it has "soared" to 41 degrees Fahrenheit. His days and a large portion of his nights are devoted to observing the activities of two whitish, none-too-impressive wolves (the animals mate for life, the narration tells us) and their cubs. Tyler's springtime Arctic has mellowed—it's softer and less stylized, more Ansel Adams or Ron Bolt than Lawren Harris. As the landscape changes, Tyler himself is transformed; his hair becomes a mane, and his mediocre looks give way, with the advent of his beard, to an odd combination of the intellectual and the erotic. The Arctic is turning Tyler into a sexy troll, and he is finding to his glee that the "animal" he had hoped to find hidden within himself—the animal he hoped would be reawakened by his sojourn in the Arctic—is a friendly, fuzzy critter with an immense capacity for ecstasy. Ootek and a younger, partially acculturated Inuit, Mike (Samson Jorah), pay a visit. Mike smiles a big toothless smile. "That's what happens when a meat-eater becomes a sugar-eater," he says. He also says: "To me, wolves mean money. One wolf pelt is about $350." Ballard adroitly and subtly contrasts four views of nature: Tyler's essentially romantic, ecologically pristine outlook (hands off at any cost); the pilot's capitalistically motivated opportunism (use it and abuse it, the long-range consequences be damned); Ootek's mystical, aboriginal beliefs (impossible to define, but communicated in the film by his strong, stoic presence); and Mike's cross-cultural contradictory grab-bag of all three attitudes, alternately religious ("The spirit of the wolf is in him," he says of Ootek) and Darwinian ("It's survival of the fittest").

The movie takes no sides, except to array itself against the pilot and the ecological ignorance his ultimately self-destructive willingness to exploit the Arctic represents. In lieu of argument, the picture presents a strange and wondrous reality where the howl of a female wolf wishing her mate well as he leaves on a hunt carries with it the majesty and resonance of the grandest of grand opera. Everything, *Never Cry Wolf* seems to say, came from nature, and this is what nature—the part of it you may have forgotten; the part of it you may never have known—looks like, and sounds like, and feels like, and smells like. Lamenting the loss of an animal friend and preparing to leave the land he has come to love, Tyler writes in his diary: "I can't really feel sad because it's here that I've begun to feel wonder again, just like when I was a kid, and this makes me deeply happy. I wish I could say thank you, directly into the universe." Carroll Ballard creates that same wonder, that same feeling of being a kid again, and that same deep happiness. Thank you.   (*1983*)

The Night of the Shooting Stars

Early evening, the night of August 10. A bedroom window. A woman's voice, hushed by the telling of a tale. Tonight, the woman says, is the night of San Lorenzo. Tonight is a night of special, magic meaning. Tonight is the night of the shooting stars—wishes are granted, dreams come true. Tonight the woman's thoughts turn to perhaps the most important night of her life, to the night of San Lorenzo in the troubled year of 1944, when she was six and her country was at war.

So begins, in the form of a prologue, Vittorio and Paolo Taviani's *The Night of the Shooting Stars*, one of the gentlest and yet most powerful anti-war films ever made. As the unseen narrator prepares the audience for her reminiscences—reminiscences transformed, as the directors have commented, "by forty years of storytelling, with all the exaggerations and gaps in memory, with all the artlessness and epic and fantastic leaps with which the collective imagination manages to heighten meaning"—the camera remains perched in front of the bedroom window. The bedroom is realistic (there is a TV set with a red plastic cabinet on a bureau), but the landscape beyond is fabulist, stylized, unreal, a landscape that could offer hospitality to Peter Pan. The contrast between the mundane and the magical is the raison d'être of *The Night of the Shooting Stars*, which takes place in and near the tiny Tuscan town of San Martino. Italy has been at war for what must seem like centuries. Families are divided by fascism—a boy is a black-shirted follower of Mussolini, his brother a member of the resistance. The Americans are coming. The peasants of San Martino ache for liberation. One night a group led by a village elder, Galvano (Omero Antonutti), sets out in search of the Yankees; another group stays behind, hidden in the village cathedral. There is no other plot: the movie is an adventure in which the old become young, the young become old, and life is lived at the extremes.

Everything happens, but nothing follows logically from anything else —the movie has the exhilarating, disorienting, maddening, and saddening unpredictability of life itself. A priest tells his parishioners it is their responsibility to survive, and then is a horrified witness to unspeakable carnage; young boys masturbate communally, watching a young woman urinate; an old man and an old woman bathe, fully clothed, in a stream, and give new dimension to the erotic; a battle in a wheatfield veers from the slapstick to the tragic—an old woman who croaks, "Who's winning?" is shot at point-blank range.

The Taviani brothers, winners in 1977 of a Golden Palm at the Cannes Film Festival for *Padre Padrone*, are not overly concerned with differentiating between the people to whom these events occur; as in a folk tale, it is the tale that takes precedence. Still, the personalities of the exceptional actors chosen by the directors manifest themselves, and the burgeoning relationship between the old man Galvano and his "superior," the regal widow Concetta (Margarita Lozano, who has appeared in movies for Buñuel, Sergio Leone, and Pasolini), is at the heart of the film's affirmative, spiritual sensibility. The Tavianis may not set out to persuade the audience to care for their characters by drawing psychological profiles or proffering "revealing" traits—their method of characterization is almost Chaucerian in its flat, ribald simplicity—but by the end of this unexpectedly moving film, the people in it are engraved as deeply on the memory as any of the people in any of the yarns spun by any of those travelers on their way to Canterbury five hundred years ago.   (*1983*)

Nineteen Eighty-Four

Sinister, decaying, but darkly beautiful—the new film version of *Nineteen Eighty-Four* is a rare exception to the law that great books cannot become good movies. As written and directed by Michael Radford, George Orwell's 1949 classic—reportedly the most-read novel in the Western world—has been reordered in a fashion flabbergasting in its ingenuity. Without substantially deviating from Orwell, Radford has magically converted a narrative, linear, garrulous novel into a non-narrative, not entirely linear, energetically visual experience, a movie dream-like in its logic and nightmarish in its cumulative power. Radford and his production designer, Allen Cameron, have resisted the temptation to incorporate recent technological developments (technology was never the point anyway) and have adhered to the Orwellian vision: as the film imagines it, the future is a grimy, bomb-blasted universe of post-Second-World-War paranoia and pain. The Everyman hero, Winston Smith (John Hurt), spends his days altering the past by doctoring newspaper articles at the Ministry of Truth, a junky building where High Tech means outdated pneumatic tubes and where surveillance means intrusive TV cameras bearing the visage of Big Brother. At night, Winston returns to his scummy flat and succumbs to dreams and nightmares—to dreams of a "golden country" where pleasure is possible, to nightmares of a childhood maimed by war. The dreams, which segue into hallucinations, are structural devices that supplement the narrative with a visual text more expressively suited to film than Orwell's literary melodrama. In order to define on screen what Orwell defined in words—the mind of Winston Smith — Radford stages portions of the drama in ochre dreamscapes, in scenes that are flashbacks, flashforwards, and even flashforwards-within-flashbacks. The strategy gives the film the suppleness and texture of memory itself. "From a dead man, greetings," Winston writes in the journal he secretes behind a loose brick in his flat. With his round glasses and his gaunt features, Winston is an icon for every dissident writer who ever took dangerous pen to perishable paper in search of a second of psychic freedom. He recounts visiting a prostitute, a forbidden activity, and we see the diseased harpy to whom he made love, a woman he describes as having had "a young face." "Standing there with the scent of dead insects and cheap perfume," he continues, with horror and pathos and pride, "I went ahead and did it just the same." At a Big Brother rally, shot to resemble Nazi gatherings in Leni Riefenstahl's *Triumph of the Will*, Smith meets Julia (Suzanna Hamilton). Young and foolhardy in her bravery, she shares Winston's rebelliousness and understands what he means when he whispers, "I hate purity, I hate goodness, I want everyone corrupt." The Newspeak Dictionary is in full force; when goodness has become guilt, love has become hate, freedom has become slavery, to communicate at all ("A beautiful thing, the destruction of language," intones a colleague), verbal subversion is imperative. Winston means the opposite of what he says. Because love for Big Brother is the only permissible love, the love between Julia and Winston is forbidden. Few images in the film are sadder than the sight of the lovely but pale Julia radiant in an ancient, illegal dress and maladroitly applied makeup, standing expectantly in the room she and Winston use for their trysts. "Do you like me, Winston?" she asks. He loves her, he says, and their lives are touched by grace.

As Winston, John Hurt performs with his flesh—his skin tones, whether chalky, grey or green, are keys to his anguish—and as Julia, Suzanna Hamilton acts with a nakedness figurative and (in her romantic interludes with Winston) literal. As O'Brien, the bureaucratic bigwig who "breaks" Winston, the late Richard Burton's character cascades through his voice, an instrument that mellifluously pronounces the obscenities of power as if devouring the food of the gods. Captured and tortured, Winston is reduced to a meaty smear of open-mouthed agony that might have been painted by Francis Bacon. His captor and torturer, O'Brien, looks on lovingly. "You're melting away," he purrs, as he casually pulls a loose tooth from Winston's mouth.

Earlier shots of Winston furtively scribbling in his journal evoked the international fraternity of idealistic prison writers; the torture chamber operated by O'Brien evokes another fraternity, that of the professional sadists who accompany totalitarian regimes. But although they have practiced their dark arts in the recent past in Chile, Argentina, and Greece, they already seem remote, primitive, naive. The only quibble with *Nineteen Eighty-Four*, and it is a quibble with Orwell, not the film, is the infamous torture chamber, Room 101, where so much time and so much pain are required to bend the minds of men. By now, having been schooled by so many tutors in so many nations, we know more than Orwell did about the horror beyond *Nineteen Eighty-Four*: we know that bending the minds of men can sometimes be accomplished in the thirty seconds it takes to watch a television commercial. The one thing Orwell reckoned without was the immense capacity of capitalism to co-opt its enemies; he could not predict a world in which control could be achieved through pleasure. Behaviorism teaches that the most efficient control is the result of administering or withholding rewards; punishment is messy and unpredictable. Capitalism understands behaviorism as totalitarianism does not. In totalitarian countries, there are coups and revolutions and liberation movements. In capitalist countries, there are sales.   (*1985*)

Oblomov

Retired St. Petersburg civil servant and landowner Ilya Oblomov would rather sleep than live—he spends each day in bed nursing torpor, using lethargy as a barrier to keep the world at bay. Brought to life in Ivan Goncharov's delightful 1856 novel, Oblomov (accent on the second syllable) was soon awarded immortality: *Oblomov* became so popular that "Oblomovism" entered the Russian vocabulary as an identifiable syndrome. During the revolution, the condition was said to be a dark Czarist germ that would vanish in the antiseptic Bolshevik dawn.

It didn't, of course, but the Communists never read the novel properly; if they had, the volume might have been proscribed—which is why the Soviet Union's release now of a superb film adaptation is doubly surprising. In Goncharov's fable, and in Nikita Mikhalkov's film of it, Oblomov's conundrum is treated comically, mythically, and mystically. Neither book nor film condemns Oblomov; both try to understand him and both come to share his nostalgia for the past as well as his respect for the immutability of the future. The Soviets have made a picture that satirizes but then elegizes the Czarist era, and that photographs the surviving architectural artifacts of the period with a love that borders on worship.

But the man and his self-defensive retreat are universal. Oblomov's aversion to what he sees as the triviality of modern life makes him a Romantic hero, while his attraction to lassitude as a solution is peculiarly modern. (He's the first downer freak.) Caught between the past and the present, he is also caught between West and East: his search for happiness in the oblivion of sleep is not substantially different from the search of the *sadhu* for oblivion in nirvana. Oblomov's rejection of the world has about it the scent of the saintly.

In the long and effortlessly accomplished first section of the film, Oblomov, portrayed impeccably by Oleg Tabakov, lies abed, harangues his valet (a stock figure from the Russian stage), and resists the efforts of a childhood friend to "civilize" him. Lyrical flashbacks to Oblomov's childhood reveal the reasons for his resistance: he was instructed in the fine arts of laziness and self-gratification by loving parents and indulgent peers. He lived in paradise ("I've never known hunger and cold, never earned my living,'' he whines) and he wants to stay there, even if paradise exists only in memory, even if he can live only in dreams. Pushed finally by his friend into attending balls, card parties, and salons, he is unimpressed. ''Are they asleep at cards all their lives?'' he asks. The question is Chekhovian.

In the second half (the movie is two hours and twenty minutes long), the love of a young woman awakens the sleeper in a way the ministrations of the friend could not. To appear proficient at the art of love, Oblomov engages in the business of the world, up to and including paying attention to the news. As in the first part, director Mikhalkov confidently balances the cinematic and literary and there are times when the film recalls Sergei Paradjanov (the flashbacks have been patterned after the lush peasant sequences in *Shadows of Our Forgotten Ancestors*). Filming a masterpiece, Mikhalkov avoids lugubrious stateliness. What could have been a deadly film about a living death is a vital film about a slumbering soul whose predicament—''To sleep: perchance to dream''—goes to the heart of what it means to be human.   (*1981*)

Ordinary People

Judith Guest's 1976 novel *Ordinary People*, in which an affluent WASP high-school student named Conrad Jarrett attempted to take his life (razors and wrists), was spare and lean and vigorously unsentimental. In the film adaptation, written by Alvin Sargent and directed by Robert Redford, what was spare seems stingy, what was lean seems thin, and what was unsentimental has franchised a Kleenex concession: *Ordinary People* has all the earmarks of an earnest hit, *Kramer vs. Kramer* division. The only thing that could keep it from box-office bingo is the fact that it is earnestly boring.

The setting is Lake Forest, Illinois, where the luggage is suede, the cars overpowered, the lipstick pale, the swimming pools aquamarine, and the autumns auburn. These are not Ordinary People: they are Ordinary Rich People, and John Cheever, worse luck, is nowhere in view. Into their careful yet paradoxically carefree existence (wealthy WASPs in Hollywood movies have earned the right to be carefree because they have been careful) comes Conrad (Timothy Hutton) with his dripping wrists. The blood oozes all over mommy's carpets (Mommy is played, and played very well, by Mary Tyler Moore) and it burns like acid through plastic poppa's facade (Poppa is played, equally well, by Donald Sutherland).

Mom, a snooty soul with a large circle of golfing friends, discovers that she cannot forgive Conrad for having bled on her carpets and she's not too happy about his failing to save the life of her favorite son, either (a boating accident). Pop, on the other hand, wants to get to know his boy: he wants to be rid of masks, to be Real, to Understand. Naturally, knowing how to be Real and how to Understand do not come easy in Lake Forest—which Redford records with the same libellously slick condescension Mike Nichols brought to the "plastics" party scene in *The Graduate*—and Pop sends Conrad to Dr. Berger, a godlike if not godfearing shrink (Judd Hirsch, in the Robert Redford role). Dr. Berger is the one character in the film who really does have all the answers, including the big one: there ain't any. He is the one character who does not want to be in control of his surroundings ("I'm not big on control," he says). He is the one character who believes emotions should be expressed. He is the one character whose environment—his office—is a mess. He is the one character who is wise beyond his income and profound beyond his syntax. (He is the one character who sounds like Jack Webb on "Dragnet" —after est.) And he is the one character who is Jewish. This final fact is absolutely essential to exposing the myths by which *Ordinary People* operates: its WASPs are as colorless as the WASPs in Woody Allen's *Interiors* (Moore's Mom is no more than a younger version of Geraldine Page) but its Jew is a brand-new stereotype: to Dr. Berger goes the Sidney Poitier Pristine Pedestal Award.

In his debut as a director, Redford has treated his cast lovingly. Within the boundaries of their wizened roles, his actors perform competently, although Timothy Hutton's Conrad can be caught calculating his effects, and his big *Night Must Fall* tour de force, when he regresses psychologically to the scene of his suicide trauma, is a psychiatric and esthetic embarrassment. If the problem is neither in the acting nor in Redford's direction (workmanlike), where is it? The filmmakers have said repeatedly that they have been "true" to Guest's novel, which is not entirely accurate. Where, for instance, is the Epilogue, in which she graciously acknowledged the essential banality and ephemerality of her tale? That other manipulative domestic tearjerker, *Kramer vs. Kramer*, was also based on a novel of merit, but when the story reached the screen it had shifted tone and altered allegiance; it had been reconceived for the movies. The problems of adapting *Ordinary People* are greater—its predominant virtue cannot be transferred to the screen. How do you pictorialize an author's analysis of the psychic states of people notable for refusing to articulate their thoughts, or even to feel their feelings? How do you communicate in images an omniscient psychological dissection? Redford and

Sargent sidestep the conundrum and settle for blindly reproducing Guest's dialogue. Unfortunately, out of Guest's precisely composed context, the words are archly literary: *Ordinary People*'s people are ordinary TV people in an ordinary, overwritten, overprocessed TV drama. The most this sincere little movie expects of you is tears; it would be modestly pleased if its mirror reflects a little glimmer of your life; it does not want to shock you, provoke you, frighten you, intellectually stimulate you, or even teach you anything you do not already know. If the hero of "Leave it to Beaver" had grown up, gone to high school, and taken it into his head to off himself, the made-for-TV-movie that could have ensued— *Leave It to Beaver Tries to Leave It*—might have been a lot like *Ordinary People*. (*1980*)

A Passage to India

"I rather like mysteries but I do dislike a muddle," declares the character played by Peggy Ashcroft in David Lean's film of E.M. Forster's 1924 novel *A Passage to India*. Chances are she'd rather dislike this long-awaited (and long: two hours and forty-three minutes) calendar-art picture that serves to wrap an enigma in a mystery. *A Passage to India*, a labor of love for the seventy-six-year-old Lean, is a beautifully wrapped enigma and a gorgeously packaged mystery, to be sure—there are sequences set in moonlit mosques, in the Himalayas at high noon, and on glistening midnight oceans that are as painterly as any ever put on screen—but the movie is a muddle, nonetheless. "Assuredly, the novel dates," Forster wrote in his preface to the 1957 edition; assuredly, portions of it do, and one of the most dated aspects of the story is the Victorian mustiness of the metaphor revolving around the question of what happened in those caves visited by the young British woman in the twilight of the British raj: was she assaulted by an Indian man, as she maintains, or was she merely hysterical? Lean doesn't get close enough to the woman to make the answer matter. Despite the efforts of a large and talented cast, *A Passage to India* is a victim of its own bombastic splendiferousness. Major effort has been lavished on landscapes in which the people figure as . . . figures. This is nothing new for Lean, but whereas *Lawrence of Arabia* revealed no more about T.E. Lawrence than a reader might learn from the dust jacket of *Seven Pillars of Wisdom*, and rather less than he might learn from the contents, the cast led by Peter

O'Toole and the script written by Robert Bolt compensated for Lean's obsession with eye-filling vistas. And in *A Passage to India*, the grandly authoritative Australian actress Judy Davis, familiar from *My Brilliant Career*, performs a near-miracle in the pivotal role of Adela Quested, the young woman wronged. Davis is admirable not because she is able to make the actions of Miss Quested believable, but because she is able to retain the audience's interest in, and sympathy for, the character. Somewhat resembling the young Julie Christie—the same sensual mouth—she has about her an air of sanity and intelligence that paradoxically works against the character. Thank God. Had the role been assigned to an actress actually expert at hysteria—to the British equivalent of Sandy Dennis, say—the film might have been sexist and offensive (not to mention intolerable), as well as soporific and dated.

Davis is ably supported (and then some) by a scene-stealing Ashcroft, who delivers Forsterisms such as "I suppose like many old people I sometimes think we are merely passing figures in a godless universe" with priceless panache, and by James Fox as another of his blustery Brits, a good-guy colonialist. But a couple of performances are hopeless. As Dr. Aziz, the Indian accused of raping Miss Quested, Victor Banerjee is ruined by what may well be the director's patronizing attitude toward what it means to be Indian. (Indians do not carry on like this in the films of Satyajit Ray or Mrinal Sen, but they do in the films of Richard Attenborough.) During the first part of the picture, Aziz is an eager-to-please sycophant of mindless and inexplicable innocence; accused of assault, he is photographed adoringly in the prisoner's dock with so many close-ups of brimming wet eyes, you may begin to think Lean is remaking Joan of Arc with a man. Innocence destroyed, he becomes a cold and vengeful creature. There is an authentic psychological and political progression in the Dr. Aziz of the novel, but Lean loses it on screen by requiring Banerjee to express each emotion singly and hugely—the actor laboriously connects the dots.

About Alec Guinness's ghastly portrayal of a comic guru: in a film that purports to examine British colonialism in India, the presence of an actor drenched in dark makeup, an actor who jumps about as if auditioning for Monty Python's parody of *A Passage to India*, is scandalous. Actors of one race should not be barred from playing characters of another, but casting Guinness as an Indian and painting him in sticky burnt umber down to his toenails—he looks like a Tootsie Roll in a diaper—proves that, while the sun may have set on British colonialism in fact, it has yet to go down on it in theory.   (*1984*)

Pauline at the Beach

Pauline at the Beach is a light-hearted but never light-headed look at an old friend who somehow never ages: love, true and otherwise. Like *Le Beau Mariage*, its predecessor in French director Eric Rohmer's Comedies and Proverbs series, *Pauline at the Beach* opens with an epigram from Chrétien de Troyes ("A wagging tongue bites itself") that acts as a witty moral for the amoral confusion to come.

Six people interact on a beach photographed by the great Nestor Almendros as a white-hot, erotic sandbox. Marion (Arielle Dombasle, as talented as she is beautiful) is a shallow, theatrical blonde given to posing and emitting statements on the order of, "I'm just waiting for that unpredictable thing called love." Marion is wooed, against her wishes, by Pierre (Pascal Greggory), blandly handsome and so pushy that Marion pulls briskly away. She is in turn enthralled by the much older Henri (Féodor Atkine), an ethnologist to whom love means physical release—unbeknownst to Marion, he is having a simultaneous fling with a mad candy-seller on the beach (Rosette). Marion meanwhile suggests that Pierre take a powder and take up instead with Marion's young cousin, Pauline (Amanda Langlet). Young is the operative word: Pauline is fifteen, and Pierre is properly horrified. But in Rohmer's gently cockeyed ironic view, Pauline is the oldest and wisest of the participants in this whirligig talkathon (the movie is basically ninety minutes of chatter) because she has not yet learned to lie, either to herself or to others. And she is effervescent in her candor. Asked by Henri if she has dreams, she quips, "At my age, I'd be dumb not to." She is responsible for introducing to the film the sixth and final character, a teenaged boy (Simon de la Brosse) whom she sees as a nice kid when she's cool and collected, and as an adolescent Adonis when she's charged up.

The director manages to invest what could have been nothing more than another Gallic sex farce with a style so understated as to be invisible and a wry worldliness. Because Rohmer has chosen to allow his characters to hold on to their illusions, more or less, and because he ends the picture with a sweet joke that recognizes the tenaciousness of ego-protecting strategies, *Pauline at the Beach* lacks the depth of *Le Beau Mariage*, which engineered confrontations that stripped the defenses of its characters away. *Pauline at the Beach* is far more sanguine: it argues that we do learn a little from the endlessly fresh, endlessly banal emotional gymnastics of love, though not much. Next summer, Pauline will be back on the beach.   (*1983*)

Personal Best

Advance publicity for *Personal Best*, writer-director Robert Towne's study of four years in the life of a young, Olympic-calibre pentathlete involved sexually with one of her team members, has predictably focused on the fact that the film is the most graphic ever released by a major Hollywood studio on the subject of lesbianism; what advance publicity has been powerless to suggest is that *Personal Best* is an exceptionally well-crafted, thoroughly accurate, emotionally galvanizing piece of filmmaking, easily one of the most intelligent explorations of competition on cinematic record. What's best about *Personal Best* is a lot more than just personal. Towne has cannily employed the initiation of Chris Cahill (Mariel Hemingway) into the obsessive, high-powered world of Olympic competition as a metaphor for the conflict between judging achievement by one's own abilities (hence the title) or against the abilities of others. When Cahill meets an older runner, Tory Skinner (ex-Olympic hurdler Patrice Donnelly in her acting debut, and what a debut it is), and falls in love with her, the metaphor expands exponentially: persons of any sexual persuasion should be able to find in the problems of these two women a reflection of their own struggles.

The love Towne feels for the sporting events and for the women who make them possible is palpable; his slow-motion celebrations of the beauties of physical effort render the races in *Chariots of Fire* sputtering funeral pyres. Certainly the techniques Towne calls into play—rapt music, fast cutting, sweeping camera movements—are familiar, but seldom before, except in portions of Leni Riefenstahl's work and in a few sections of Olympic compilation films, has the sheer erotic power of exertion been so fully expressed. The hottest sex scenes in *Personal Best* are not the sex scenes.

Chris Cahill's relationship with Tory Skinner eventually gives way to yet another experiment, this item with Denny Stites, a male water-polo player (yet another acting debut, this time from *Sports Illustrated* senior editor Kenny Moore). The move from female to male is made virtually without comment—*Personal Best* is not an ideologically militant picture. What it communicates effortlessly is the complexity and multiplicity of sexual interaction, and the futility of attempting to judge such action. It sees the ordering of occupation and affection, of friendliness and friction, as far more important than the physical configuration of those doing the ordering. And because Chris Cahill's relationship with her trainer (*Urban Cowboy* heavy Scott Glenn) is at least as complicated as any of her love affairs, it sees all human congress as problematic. (Anxious that Chris succeed—for his greater glory, of course—the trainer offers her Pepsi, Dr. Pepper, a joint, Haagen-Dasz ice cream, and, finally, himself: he is the compleat coach.)

Hemingway, who aged from seventeen to twenty (nearly the age-range covered by her character) as the film was being shot, is quietly effective in outlining Chris's evolution. The young Chris is upbraided by her father for allegedly lacking "the killer instinct" in competition, but she finds it through her relationship with Tory (love has always been a reliable catalyst for bringing out the killer) and through the relationship's demise she learns the instinct can be manipulated and, when necessary, sublimated. So much for the alleged exclusivity of men in groups.   (*1982*)

Places in the Heart

Sally Field was one of the actresses seated at the head table with Lillian Gish at the American Film Institute's tribute to the silent-film star not long ago, and it looks as if something rubbed off: there's much of the indomitable Gish—the original Miz Lillian—in Field's gritty, no-nonsense portrayal of Texas widow Edna Spalding, the heroine of writer-director Robert Benton's *Places in the Heart*, a nostalgic and soft-hearted memoir of life in the Depression. And there's plenty of D.W. Griffith, the director most often associated with Gish, in Robert Benton, but it's Griffith toughened up: *Places in the Heart* is sweet and relatively simple, a classic episodic melodrama of unabashed tenderness and unapologetic warmth, but its offhanded explication of racism in rural Texas in 1935 is integrated so seamlessly with its dramatization of the widow Spalding's crusade to keep her farm, that the dark undercurrents of the film are easy to overlook. Benton is loving, but he's not mindless, and he's far from uncritical.

Edna Spalding, presentable but by no means beautiful—her curls are tight and red, like a terrier's pelt, and her face is flat and stubborn, like a bulldog's puss—is initially stupefied by the sudden death of her husband. "Royce paid all the bills. I never even knew how much salary he made. What's gonna happen to us?" she wonders. What happens is this: she hires an itinerant black man, Moses (Danny Glover); takes in a blind boarder, Mr. Will (John Malkovich); and enlists the aid of her beautician sister, Margaret (Lindsay Crouse), and her philandering husband, Wayne (Ed Harris), in harvesting a cotton crop that is her only means of keeping the wolf from the door. There is also a tornado to contend with, a natural disaster presented with a startling ferocity that allows a long look at the human reality behind "events" normally reduced to two minutes of spectacular footage on the evening news.

There is no vanity in Field's performance—cinematographer Nestor Almendros has photographed her pitilessly in the clear light he uses throughout the picture, a light he has dubbed "Protestant"—and there is almost no sex. (It's hard to remember that this is the same actress who made Norma Rae such a hot number.) But there is generosity. The support Field receives from Glover's Moses, "a smart nigger and a real credit to his race," one of the townsfolk says, and from Malkovich's hostile and dignified blind man, would have swamped a lesser actress. As it is, the cast forms an ensemble devoted to a single vision. The most courageous aspect of the picture is not Field's willingness to act a less than glamorous woman, but Benton's readiness to embrace cliché if cliché is grounded in truth; there are no false notes in *Places in the Heart*, but there are a lot of familiar ones. The temptation to embroider a plain, unsophisticated story with cinematic flourishes and plotting curlicues must have been intense, but in true Protestant fashion Benton has eschewed ornamentation and has created a work of rough-hewn integrity, a film not afraid to let its supposedly iron-strong heroine collapse in the cotton fields (she is the least experienced as a picker), a film that allows her to return until her bloody hands (they ooze like fresh meat) move automatically to already empty plants, and a film that concludes with a surreal coda, the most daring sequence of its kind since Jean Pierre Lefebvre ended *The Last Betrothal* with the arrival of a pair of angels. *Places in the Heart* is a populist work that celebrates in common people an uncommon will to survive.   (*1984*)

The Pope of Greenwich Village

Mickey Rourke is only twenty-nine years old and has had significant roles in a scant three films—the arsonist in *Body Heat*, the Motorcycle Boy in *Rumble Fish*, the hairdresser in *Diner*—but in *The Pope of Greenwich Village*, everything he does reeks of déjà vue. His specialty is alienated catatonia, and while it may seem difficult to overact by doing nothing, he makes the difficult look easy. As Charlie, a flashy Little Italy hood, Rourke is so far into the character's private fantasy world that he refuses to emerge for the audience. The only thing we know for sure about Charlie is that he has a temper and a complexion with the pallor of an upturned fish belly.

Eric Roberts is twenty-seven years old and has also had significant roles in only three films—the kid who would be king in *King of the Gypsies*, the loving sailor in *Raggedy Man*, the homicidal Paul Snider in *Star 80*. But as Charlie's cousin and best friend in *The Pope of Greenwich Village*, a comedy-drama about male bonding among Italian crooks (call it *Butch Corleone and the Sundance Bambino*), everything he does is brand new, and some of what he does is so bizarre—especially what he does with his big mushy mouth and graceful wrists—that he appears to have invented a new form of female impersonation. His Paulie suggests Geraldine Page as a teenaged boy.

Geraldine Page happens to be in *The Pope of Greenwich Village*, and the movie is worth seeing for the single scene in which she demonstrates for all the amateurs in this misbegotten mess what *real* overacting is all about. Every muscle in her face moving at once, her voice cascading through more registers than Cleo Laine's, she picks the camera up and shakes it like a piddling puppy—Geraldine Page could eat Bette Davis for breakfast.

None of this thespian excess is dictated by the ostensible goal of *The Pope of Greenwich Village*, adapted from the novel of the same name by its author, Vincent Patrick, which is to lyricize and sentimentalize male bonding. With its close attention to the Little Italy milieu and its farcical treatment of a safe-cracking, the picture is designed to turn Martin Scorsese's scathing *Mean Streets* into a sitcom. It could be done, and done well, in the right hands, but those hands do not belong to the callused paws of the pugilistically inclined director Stuart Rosenberg, whose past punching bags have included *Cool Hand Luke* and *Brubaker*, not to mention the unforgettable *Amityville Horror* and the forgotten *Voyage of the Damned*. Rosenberg's fists are unerring: when the picture is supposed to be serious, he lands a punch on the funny bone, followed by an uppercut to the emotions when he's going for a laugh.

Two other stars are worth mentioning. Burt Young, most famous as Rocky Balboa's brother-in-law, is magnificent here as a piggy godfather —he's eating the same plate of pasta he was snarfing down in *Once Upon A Time in America*, where he rehearsed the role. Daryl Hannah, the famed fish of *Splash*, is exploited shamelessly for her looks (who's going to mind?) by a script that orders her to exercise aerobically and then to doff and don articles of apparel too teeny to clothe a titmouse. She's not much of an actress, but they said that about Marilyn Monroe, too, with whom Hannah shares a certain dewy ingenuousness spiked with the slightest taste of sleaze. She gives great airhead.   (*1984*)

The Postman Always Rings Twice

"Then I saw her. She had been out back, in the kitchen, but she came in to gather up my dishes. Except for the shape, she really wasn't any raving beauty, but she had a sulky look to her, and her lips stuck out in a way that made me want to mash them in for her." Thus is Cora Papadakis, the wife of a Greek gas-station owner, described by Frank Chambers, the narrator of James M. Cain's tight, tough, sexy 1934 novel *The Postman Always Rings Twice*. (The book was banned in Canada and Boston. It was filmed by Visconti in 1942 as *Ossessione*, filmed in 1946 with John Garfield and Lana Turner, and was said by Camus to be his inspiration for *The Stranger*.) Frank has arrived at the Papadakis place during the Depression. He stays because he has no reason to go. He stays because "from the filling station I could just get a good view of the kitchen." From the first scene of playwright David Mamet's screen adaptation for director Bob Rafelson, the tone is set—existential foreboding. More frightening than most horror movies, more erotic than most pornography, *The Postman Always Rings Twice* is a sour slice of bona fide Americana, a relentlessly pessimistic melodrama that conjures memories of *They Shoot Horses, Don't They?*, *Bonnie and Clyde*, *The Godfather*, and *Chinatown*. It is not conceived in homage to film noir: it *is* film noir, but in color, in an Edward Hopper palette that Ingmar Bergman's cinematographer Sven Nykvist correctly considers the finest work of his distinguished career.

Noted for elliptical, unstructured films—*Stay Hungry*, *Five Easy Pieces*—Rafelson is not always interested in reproducing the simplicity and clarity of the novel's plot: what builds in the book to a climax drifts along in the movie from catastrophe to catastrophe. The sexual, violent, and sadomasochistic interludes are brutally paced and edited—they become arias of hysteria—but the film feels as if it could end several times before it does, and several plot points are fuzzy. In addition, because the novel's ending has been altered, the metaphoric title has lost its resonance. ("Postman" is slang for the hanging judge: in the book, Frank ends his days on death row, paying for a crime he did not commit—ironic retribution for having earlier gotten away with a crime he did commit.)

Oddly, none of this detracts inordinately from Rafelson's achievement, which is immense. The episodic nature of the film may even be its own reward—the novel has been inadvertently modernized. As Frank Chambers, Jack Nicholson gives his most controlled performance since *One Flew Over The Cuckoo's Nest*, and it is possible that he has never been better than he is here, scanning the world through suspicious (but not suspicious enough) eyes, controlling his impulses toward destruction (but not controlling them enough) and sizing up the limited possibilities available to him (but not sizing them up cleverly enough).

Jessica Lange, best known for the black I. Magnin dress she was barely wearing when she was discovered in the remake of *King Kong*, holds her sultry, aggressive own against Nicholson. Her Cora is a hot, lewd, snarling tramp trapped by the era's prejudice against women and by the era's economics, which have forced her to live with an aged Greek husband (Canada's John Colicos, in a portrayal so natural it seems a found object) who might as well be her old-country grandfather, so little can she relate to him. When she cries, "I can't have his baby," you can feel her skin crawl. When she says, "I'm tired of what's right and wrong, Frank," you can feel *your* skin crawl. Cora's relationship with Frank is volatile— tempestuous in its tenderness, sizzling in its sensuality, terrifying in the ease with which it moves from the erotically consuming to the maliciously devouring. If it seems remarkable and strange, it is only because it is contained in a commercial American film, and because the lovers' lack of intelligence allows them to be viewed as pure id, a primal Adam and Eve re-enacting the acquisition of original sin. The movie's argument, dramatized forthrightly, is that sexual excitement is allergic to the settled— when Cora and Frank murder the Greek, their first act is to make love, but when they have lived comfortably together for months, they grow restive. To sustain their attraction, they whirl, biting and scratching and spitting, on each other.

In the end, the villain (no wonder Camus was fascinated by Cain) is the randomness and the absurdity of existence, an existence in which insurance companies can decree that murderers will go free and in which an accident can rule that a loved one will die. God Himself is a hanging judge, and He determines the identity of the dead by shooting craps. "She wanted something, and she tried to get it," Frank said of Cora in the novel. "She tried all the wrong ways, but she tried." Like the book, the movie admires effort: in their shared universe, effort is all there is.   (*1981*)

Pourquoi pas!

Once upon a time, there was a French film as light as Tom Thumb's left glove. It was named *Cousin, Cousine*. It was about heterosexual fornication. Once upon a time there was a French director named Coline Serreau with a talent as delicate as, and no more odoriferous than, a droplet of fresh sweat on the forehead of a cupid. She had never made a feature film before, but she must have seen *Cousin, Cousine*, and she must have decided to remake it with an airy twist. So she made *Pourquoi pas!* and what she made was a bisexual, trisexual, polysexual *Cousin, Cousine*, as light as the sparkles on Tinker Bell's diaphanous wings. Why not?

Pourquoi pas! is the sort of movie that praise can damage—it should be discovered without help, but it is precisely the sort of movie that is not likely to be discovered without help. It is precious, but not sentimental; witty, but not outlandishly funny; cute, but not cutesy. It's pretty, and tasty, but poke it as one would poke cotton candy and it will vanish, with the sighing, sweet sound made by air that has been held happy captive in a spun-sugar cage.

Alex, who is a woman, lives with Fernand and Louis, who are men, in a suburb of Paris. Fernand (Sami Frey) is the most masculine of the three, but he is the housewife, and he rages at his housemates for their slovenliness. Alex (Christine Murillo) reads the same novel over and over to an old woman who seems to be dying, and finally does. Louis (Mario Gonzales) has no mechanical aptitude and is constantly crossed up by a recalcitrant vacuum cleaner. An agreeably disoriented inspector (Michel Aumont, in a finely farcical performance) keeps showing up to look for something, but he doesn't know what it is—the influence of the French comic director Jacques Tati is very strong here.

The film begins with Louis and Fernand making love, and in time all three make love singly and en masse, to each other and to a new enlistee, Sylvie (Nicole Jamet), who is as recalcitrant as the vacuum cleaner: she hasn't read Norman O. Brown, presumably, and doesn't know about polymorphous perversity. But this is not a sex movie, or even a sexual movie: it is a love movie that affirms life by turning it into a tall tale. There are jealousies, there are problems, but they are mainly whimsical problems, solvable jealousies: *Pourquoi pas!* takes us back to the communes of the sixties, when all you needed was love and a little consideration. It could also have been called *The Ménage Made in Eden*.   (*1978*)

Providence

Providence, French director Alain Resnais's first film in English, commences with a long visual quote from the opening of *Citizen Kane*—the camera leads us slowly through a tangled, Lovecraftian forest surrounding an ancient, unkempt estate, then cuts to hand that drops a glass of wine, and we hear a voice saying "Damn, damn, damn." The voice belongs to John Gielgud. Of that you can be sure, at this juncture, but of little else. Like Resnais's *Last Year at Marienbad* and, to lesser extent, *Hiroshima Mon Amour*, *Providence* immediately begins to play mind games by playing time games. There are shots of a lycanthropic old man in the woods (what woods? doesn't matter). He asks David Warner to kill him. Warner obliges, and is tried in a fantastical court (located where? doesn't matter). The prosecutor is Dirk Bogarde, who is married to Ellen Burstyn, who sits in the audience. Meanwhile, back at the manse, Gielgud consumes more wine, complaints of rectal pain, talks of dying. Resnais cross-cuts to a cadaver being eviscerated. Elaine Stritch, Bogarde's mistress, arrives (whence to where? doesn't matter). She is dying. Wait. She is not Bogarde's mistress: she is his mother . Gielgud's wife. Warner is his bastard son. The werewolf in the woods is John Gielgud.

Slowly, the method in the seemingly mad but actually lucid screenplay by David Mercer begins to dawn: this is a long night's journey into day. Gielgud is a seventy-eight-year-old writer putting together his last novel. Bogarde is his son, Burstyn is his daughter-in-law, Stritch was his wife (she's now dead, a suicide, but remains alive in Gielgud's mind, where most of *Providence* takes place), Warner is his bastard son. The final novel Gielgud is writing, which is being played out for us, is an attempt to summarize a complex life in complex terms, which defines the *Citizen Kane* allusion in the beginning as irony—Kane summarized a complex life in simple terms, claiming that a sled made him do it. As Gielgud boozes and rants and takes notes, his life is rearranged to correspond to the demands of fiction. Identities change, wives become mistresses and mistresses wives. At one point, Warner enters a hotel room and a Gielgud voice-over says of the character (his own son), "He's intractable. I'll never get the hang of him. Out, out." And Warner leaves the room.

Not until the end of the film do we leave Gielgud's mind and enter objective reality, when the family arrives the next morning to celebrate the seventy-eighth birthday. It is then that the deliberate confusions and apparent false starts earlier in the movie fall into place with a click: this movie about dying is also about the creative process, and is also about the misty windows of perception. Gielgud's family is not at all as he has imagined it; not at all as he will immortalize it in his novel. *Providence* tells us that we live our lives without ever seeing each other as we really are, and that in the mind (this was the theme of *Marienbad*, too) time is an illusion: all yesterdays are today. Imagine the twilight-time juggling of memories that Samuel Beckett used in *Krapp's Last Tape*, combined with the stream-of-alcoholic consciousness and pressure-cooker language that Malcolm Lowry used in *Under the Volcano*, and you have an excellent idea of the feeling and form of *Providence*, which comes as close to being a masterpiece as damn is to swearing.

And an exceptionally humorous masterpiece. Gielgud's novel, as we see it enacted, does not in the last analysis look as though it's going to be a very good novel. "Do you approve of violence, Miss Boone?" Bogarde asks a travel agent. When she replies, "Certainly not," Bogarde's rejoinder is, "Neither do I. It reeks of spontaneity." To Warner, he says: "I know that you have inner peace. That usually implies no powers of rational thinking. Whatsoever." Gielgud's book, in other words, may turn out to be second-rate Pinter with a lot of joyless but sniggering sex. On the screen, it becomes a parody of any number of atrocious European movies, with motiveless actions, splendiferous photography, and phony backdrops.

In any movie this ambitious, there are going to be scenes and performances that don't work. The lycanthropy theme, for example, seems to symbolize several things in general (the right to end one's life when life is no longer worth living; the fact that death is nature's way of telling us that we're animals after all) but nothing in particular. And although the performances are, in the main, extraordinary, with Gielgud incandescent and Bogarde (as seen by Gielgud) doing Gore Vidal, Burstyn is out of her depth. It's not a question of her ability, but she hasn't the rarefied (quintessentially British) technical facility to make the *sounds* of words fascinating. Part of the point of *Providence* is that Gielgud's creations are paper people, with lots of style but no more substance than a limerick, and Burstyn is incapable of acting a concept instead of a character. In the end, when she's allowed to be a person, she is predictably convincing, but the role should have gone to Maggie Smith. Quibbling. *Providence* is, as *Variety* said, "a fascinating puzzle" (which probably means that *Variety* didn't know what the hell was going on), but it's a puzzle in which almost all of the pieces fit. Resnais and Mercer have earned the right to begin with *Citizen Kane*: what looked like hubris is healthy pride.   (*1978*)

The Purple Rose of Cairo

Bad enough it's the Depression. Worse still it's New Jersey. Bad enough the poor girl (Mia Farrow) is a waitress. Worse still her husband (Danny Aiello) is a heel. Bad enough she has to say to him, "All you do is drink and place dice; I wind up getting smacked." Worse still he feels he has the right to say to her, "I hit ya when ya get outta line." Bad enough she has to do what she always does when he stamps on her like a gob of chewing gum: she goes to the movies. Worse still the movies aren't what they used to be: they don't stay on the the screen.

The frail girl with the porcelain face settles into her silvery world of make-believe ready to lose herself in the current attraction. It's a Noël Cowardish drawing-room adventure in glistening black and white called *The Purple Rose of Cairo*, which is also the title of the film about the waitress and the heel, Woody Allen's newest comedy. His *Purple Rose of Cairo*, the film that plays host to the film-within-a-film, is in the sentimental, bittersweet mode of *Broadway Danny Rose*, only more so—it's an odd combination of realism, pathos, and intellect, as if Allen had collaborated with Walt Disney and Pirandello.

As the waitress sits in the dark, Tom Baxter (Jeff Daniels), the male ingenue in the black-and-white *Purple Rose*, begins to cruise her from the screen. "How many times," he asks her, after he's stepped into the theater and commenced his courtship, "is a man so taken with a woman, he walks off the screen to get her?" Tom Baxter wants to live like a real person, wants "to be free," wants to know what it means to have character instead of be one. The waitress is not so sure that's a good idea. Real life, she points out, is not so hot in a depression. But she loves being loved. "I just met a wonderful man," she tells herself. "He's fictional, but you can't have everything." Maybe she can. Before long, Gil Shepherd (Daniels again), the Hollywood actor who played Tom Baxter, finds out that his creation is running loose; the producers order him to find the guy and have him get back on screen. "The real ones," someone notes, stating the theme, "want their lives fictional and the fictional ones want their lives real."

Allen and his cinematographer, Gordon Willis, technically exploit the premise for all it's worth, and then some. The black-and-white *Purple Rose of Cairo*, which features Zoë Caldwell as a Tallulah Bankhead type, Annie Joe Edwards as a maid, Milo O'Shea as a priest, and Karen Akers as a night-club singer, along with Deborah Rush, Ed Herrmann, and Van Johnson, is a flawless re-creation of films of the thirties. And the Depression envisioned in the other *Purple Rose of Cairo* is an equally detailed facsimile—an Edward Hopper painting magically set in motion. Daniels is charmingly innocent as Baxter the movie hero, a kind of celluloid Candide, and is properly callow as Shepherd the actor, a man who's forever the guest on his own talk show. As the waitress, the most victimized woman since the little match girl, Farrow does indeed have the "magical glow" the script ascribes to her. She's endearing enough to allow Allen to sneak by an ending so flagrantly Chaplinesque you expect his heroine to produce a hat, a cane, and a waddle.   (*1985*)

Raging Bull

As Jake La Motta, a world-champion welterweight prizefighter whose career collapsed in the mid-fifties, Robert De Niro brings to Martin Scorsese's *Raging Bull* one of the most astonishing metamorphoses in the history of movies: he ages by more than twenty years and balloons by more than forty pounds—real pounds—in the space of two harrowing hours. When we first see La Motta under the credits (*Raging Bull* is in glorious black and white, save a few home-movie sequences in faded color), he is warming up in the ring in 1941 and De Niro is clearly in the best shape he has been in his life. A title (New York City, 1964) appears and Scorsese cuts to a dressing room in an unidentified theater where a paunchy, gross-featured figure with a battered face that has the texture of potato skin is reciting doggerel in front of a mirror: "So give a stage/Where this bull here can rage." As the camera glides toward the face, recognition comes slowly: poked into the monstrous flab are two porcine eyes that could belong to Brando or James Caan. De Niro flashes his goofy, moronic grin, and one accepts the incredible.

The story of Jake La Motta, rags to riches to rags, is an actor's dream, but both De Niro and Scorsese have been careful not to make their palooka into a conventional (or even an unconventional) hero. Violent, vindictive, volatile, childish, and psychotically jealous of his beautiful second wife, a succulent blonde named Vickie (Cathy Moriarity), La Motta is portrayed in a melodramatic format—a homage to Warner Brothers of the thirties—that deliberately suggests tabloid newspapers and newsreels. Scorsese achieves his remarkable effects through surprisingly modest means. Period music ("Big Noise from Winnetka," Monroe singing "Bye Bye Baby") is used sparingly; the original score is MGM pastoral (the lyric theme recalls "Over the Rainbow" in both melody and orchestration). There are simple but stunning visual contrasts between De Niro's café au lait skin tones and the creamy vanilla of Moriarity's cheeks. La Motta's slippery grasp of reality is signalled by scenes of Vickie seen through La Motta's eyes, photographed in slow motion—very fast slow motion, a nearly imperceptible shift of speed. Where *Rocky* and *Rocky II* saw boxing as a groaning waltz of dinosaurs (Rocky Balboa was a heavy-weight), the battles in *Raging Bull* are jitterbugs of death danced by stinging insects—quick, vicious, blistering exchanges of venom. Over all, *Raging Bull* is so tough (it is, however, restrained in comparison to Scorsese's most expressionist exercises, *Taxi Driver* and *Mean Streets*) and so intransigently anti-romantic that some viewers are certain to wonder why it was made at all. Where's the moral? Twice married, La Motta beats both wives and throttles Joey (Joey Pesci), his long-suffering brother, when he paranoiacally decides Joey has been fornicating with Vickie. La Motta is not a nice guy; *Raging Bull* is not, and does not want to be, a nice movie—Scorsese is after verisimilitude, not myth.

(Sexual possessiveness and its inevitable vitriol, the strong subtext of *Raging Bull*, has always been a major motif in Scorsese's work. The most illuminating example is perhaps *Taxi Driver*, where Scorsese himself plays one of Robert De Niro's fares. He orders De Niro to park outside a high-rise, points to two figures silhouetted in a window and calmly informs De Niro the figures belong to his wife and her black lover. He is going to kill both of them, he says. Jake's attitude toward Vickie in *Raging Bull* is neither as concentrated nor quite as pathological: in all other respects, it is identical, and it is that attitude, more than the boxing, that gives *Raging Bull* its edge.)

Miraculously, La Motta's relationship with his wife survives the beatings—for the time being—though the relationship with his brother does not. Retirement provides a nightclub in Miami (called Jake La Motta's, of course) and it seems likely the old pro will settle into a reasonably profit-able and pleasantly easy dotage. Except that the old pro, who has turned his free-floating hostility toward his patrons and does a stand-up comedy routine—he's an unfunny Don Rickles precursor—is allergic to the profit-able, the pleasant, the easy, and the reasonable. The boxer who gratu-itously smeared an opponent's nose "from one side of his face to another" because Vickie found the opponent "good-looking" is not about to stay out of trouble. In the scene that climaxes De Niro's performance, La Motta has been thrown into the Dade County Jail. For the first time, the fighter sees the brick wall—the prison of his own personality—he has been shadow-boxing all his life, and he bangs his head and his hands into the concrete blocks lining his cell over and over again, screaming, ''Why?! Why?!'' The intensity of the film verges on the intolerable.

Hemingway would hate *Raging Bull*—it's about the life of boxing, not the art—and many of the men in the audience who had come for a true-life Rocky and who had originally egged La Motta on regardless of his activities (a tantrumy up-ending of the dinner table set by the first wife was greeted with cheers and applause) were finally bludgeoned into silence as their hero became aged and corpulent and unmistakably cruel. La Motta lost them, but De Niro didn't; one may lose empathy for the bruiser, but one never loses sympathy for the human being. ''I wanted this film to be real,'' Scorsese has said, and in his smoky primal world, heroes are something taking up space on TV sets in the background. When La Motta, in the neatest, sickest joke of the movie, appears at a benefit and reads the ''I coulda been a contender'' speech from *On the Waterfront*, *Raging Bull* comes full circle: Jake La Motta was champion of the world, but he's one of the world's champion losers. And he's still raging.   (*1980*)

Reds

Rumors that *Reds* was the Bolshevik *Heaven's Gate* can be laid readily to rest: Warren Beatty's $33.5-million biography of journalist John Reed, one of the founders of what was to become the American Communist Party, is a respectable movie. (And then some: it is three hours and forty-five minutes long, including intermission.) Rumors that *Reds* was the Bolshevik *Godfather* can also be laid readily to rest: the reach of this sprawling, ambitious epic often exceeds its grasp. It has something in common with its hero.

The idea of a sympathetic study of Reed (author of *Ten Days That Shook The World*, participant in the Russian Revolution and free-love advocate) arriving in Ronald Reagan's America is delicious, and for the first couple of hours Beatty, who not only stars as Reed but also produced and collaborated with British playwright Trevor Griffiths (*Comedians*) on the screenplay, piles on the goodies. We are introduced to Reed and Louise Bryant (Diane Keaton), his wife-to-be, in Oregon in 1915, where Bryant, currently wed to ''the finest dentist in all of Portland,'' takes a shine to the luminous journalist and opines as to how, ''I'd like to see you with your pants off, Mr. Reed.'' Presumably impressed with what she sees and, more importantly, anxious to make a career for herself, Bryant leaves the dentist and journeys to New York to live with but not, for a time, to marry Reed. As one of the narrators tells us, "Marriage was not important in Greenwich Village." (Isn't it nice that some things never change?) Bryant is forthwith introduced to Reed's friends, foremost among them a tormented playwright, "Gene" O'Neill (Jack Nicholson), and a feminist-anarchist, Emma Goldman (Maureen Stapleton). Both characters are fascinating, both performers electrifying. Stapleton's "E.G." is a no-nonsense, self-assured dynamo not afraid to jump a sinking ship—years later, exiled to Moscow but disillusioned with the revolution, she quips, "The dream may be dying in Russia, but I'm not." Nicholson's O'Neill, sloshed in whiskey and masochism, is a man wriggling painfully but creatively on the point of self-contempt, a victim of his own unrelieved insight. These two characters represent the antipodes (romantic artist/pragmatic politician) between which the more modulated and middle–class Reed and Bryant lie.

As their story unfolds, Beatty cuts constantly to his narrators, whom the credits call "witnesses." In researching Reed's life, Beatty interviewed dozens of "witnesses" and saved the results, among them interviews with aged luminaries such as Henry Miller, Rebecca West, Will Durant, and George Jessel. Their recollections, alternately senile and self-serving, or illuminating and self-revealing, form the matrix within which *Reds* is set. The use of the "witnesses," of talking documentary heads in a big-budget feature film, is Beatty's single formal innovation, and it works wonderfully well.

Unfortunately, very little in the second half of the picture works well at all. The boyish, macho naiveté Beatty has always projected is as effective for John Reed as it was, with different contours, for Clyde Barrow in *Bonnie and Clyde* or for George the hairdresser in *Shampoo*, and Keaton is acceptable, if anachronistic, when engaging with Beatty in volatile domestic psychodrama. (Reed and Bryant behave as adults in love are wont to do: as children.) But the movie runs out of momentum the instant Reed returns to Russia to serve as a cog in the Party's propaganda mills. To be sure, novelist Jerszy Kosinski, making his movie debut as a Party bureaucrat, is an intriguing foreman, and Vittorio Storaro's cinematography is consistently exquisite, but the film is unconscionably burdened by discussion and incongruously lightened by the employment of romantic clichés more at home with Scarlett O'Hara and Rhett Butler than with John Reed and Louise Bryant. Beatty's method of getting his message across is to sell the film as a love story, as a Commie *Gone With The Wind*. It's easy to imagine him ingenuously telling his backers that all that "political stuff" is merely requisite historical backdrop for one of the world's great love stories. At its best, *Reds* does indeed resemble the high romance of *Gone With The Wind*; at its best, it even resembles the insouciant subversiveness of *Man of Iron*. For those moments, you can almost—but not quite—forgive it what it resembles at its worst: a co-production, by *Ms.* and *Mother Jones*, of *Dr. Zhivago*. (*1981*)

The Return of Martin Guerre

How many men were born to wear a codpiece? And how many modern men who *were* born to wear that article of archaic clothing ever get the chance? Gérard Depardieu, the stocky actor whose potbellied sex appeal has made him the most adored actor in France, is probably the only movie star in the world who could pop into a painting by Breughel unnoticed, and that's exactly what happens in *The Return of Martin Guerre*, a sixteenth-century courtroom drama. Peasant togs do for Depardieu what tuxes did for David Niven: coverings reveal the essence of the beast.

This is the time of Copernicus, Rabelais, Calvin, and Ronsard. During the years covered by the film—1541 to 1560, with a coda in 1572— Michelangelo completes his *Last Judgment*, the third book of *Gargantua* is published, Martin Luther dies, peasants revolt in Guyenne against the salt tax, and Charles II becomes king. But in the village of Artigat a teenaged boy, Martin Guerre (Stéphane Penn), marries a young women, Bertrande (Sylvie Meda), and then leaves her, ungallantly, for nine years. Returning as a man (Depardieu), he is warmly embraced by his now mature wife (Nathalie Baye)—not one to hold a grudge—and, after some hesitation, by his son, Sanxi (Adrien Duquesne). All is well.

Or seems to be. Director Daniel Vigne is initially content to stage loving but lively tableaux of sixteenth-century life, and for a time the camera is content to act as a historical voyeur: watching a "cure" for impotence, performed by a blind crone who lustily orders the "blessed flesh" to life, really is like looking at animated Breughel. But this is no documentary; when interest in the ethnographic might be expected to subside, the plot arrives in force. Inspired by an actual report published in 1561 by the presiding judge, Jean de Coras of Toulouse, the film tells the story of a judicial investigation into charges by villagers that the man claiming to be Martin Guerre was an imposter. The picture that began as a folkloric celebration of peasant life rapidly segues into a compelling consideration of the laws and morals that alternately bind and tear apart human society. The consideration becomes so complicated—a metaphysical "To Tell The Truth"—that the viewer is placed in the position of choosing between morality and legality. That's not all: another choice is proposed between truths that harm and lies that heal. One of the movie's themes is that the law can be an ass. Another is that truth can be a pig.

Vigne and his co-scenarist, Jean-Claude Carrière, who collaborated on many of Buñuel's scripts as well as on Godard's *Every Man For Himself*, Volker Schlöndorff's *Circle of Deceit*, and Andrzej Wajda's *Danton*, net nearly everything in the sea; despite the daunting complexity of the project, the film is thoughtful, graceful, gorgeously detailed, witty and effortlessly entertaining. The only fish that gets away is that silvery minnow Nathalie Baye, who wears her peasant turbans (perched above plucked eyebrows) as if they were cotton tiaras and who manages to invest the rest of her apparel with the esthetic of Chanel. Rising above one's station by sheer haughtiness may be an advantage for a model, but it doesn't do much for an actress hired to play a peasant. Baye's repertoire of smiles and sniffles is always effective but not always appropriate; in this instance, she is undeniably fetching but she is also jarringly contemporary, in league with the Elizabeth Taylor of *Ivanhoe*. You expect the judge, having disposed of the first case, to turn his attentions to the women of the village and inquire: "Now, will the real Mrs. Martin Guerre please stand up?"   (*1983*)

The Revolt of Job

When the Hungarian film *The Revolt of Job* was screened in Budapest for a number of foreign journalists in February 1983, the heads of the state-controlled movie production company, which had cooperated with *Job's* directors during the actual filming, claimed no knowledge of the picture. "I don't know what you will be seeing," a bureaucrat said, as writers from New York's *Village Voice*, a leftist London daily, and other newspapers and magazines climbed into taxis one cold, snowy night. "I haven't seen it."

It was inconceivable that an event of this magnitude, a world premiere of a major movie, could take place in an East European country without state knowledge and approval, but the illusion never let up. As far as the Hungarians were concerned, *The Revolt of Job* was basically a German film, even though the cast and crew were Hungarian, even though the picture was shot entirely in Hungary, even though a Hungarian television appeal for child actors brought forth four thousand candidates. Nonetheless, as officials defensively pointed out, the filmmakers live part of each year in Munich and work for German television and were able to secure some German financing.

Why this peculiar form of shadow-boxing, when it would have been easy enough to ban *Job* outright? And what, in any case, could be considered censorable in a picture dealing with the adoption of a Christian child by two elderly Jews in 1943? The answer is complicated. In raising the issue of Hungarian anti-Semitism, the film broaches a topic that is taboo even in Budapest intellectual circles. Historically, the Communist Party and the film industry have harbored large numbers of Jewish intellectuals. They are people of unenviably divided loyalties. As Communists they are members of the establishment, but as Jews they are potential pariahs. They are also, as Jews, in natural opposition to the anti-Semitism of the Soviet Union, but as Communists they must recognize the latter as the mother of their own communism. On the other hand, as Hungarians they must despise the lordly Russians as the bane of true Hungarian independence. One Hungarian Jewish Communist summed it up this way: "Our saving grace is that Hungarians are even more anti-Soviet than they are anti-Semitic."

The Budapest screening had been organized in self-defense by co-directors Imre Gyöngyössy and Barna Kabay. After it was over, at a party in the large home the two men share with a female scriptwriter, Katalin Petenyi, their associates explained they were afaid that, had the film not been seen by at least a few non-Hungarian writers, it might have been allowed to "vanish." Months later, *The Revolt of Job* was allowed to open in Hungary, but without benefit of advertising and, as the filmmakers had feared, there were efforts to block distribution to other countries. But the efforts failed: *Job* went to Cannes and was nominated for the best foreign-film Oscar (it lost to *Fanny and Alexander*). Jewish Hungarians were disturbed by the film because they were loath to raise the hackles of non-Jewish Hungarians with what might appear to be special pleading. Non-Jewish Hungarians were disturbed by the truth, a truth that had been kept out of popular entertainment. Hungarians are proud they resisted Hitler as long and as vociferously as they did. But they tend to forget that, when they finally did give in near the end of the war, many of them gave in with a vengenace and carried out orders to transport Jews to Auschwitz and other death centers with alacrity. As the film notes, of six hundred thousand Jews sent out of Hungary between May and October 1944, half a million never returned.

The Revolt of Job approaches the facts without manipulation or exploitation, and is all the more shattering for its exceptional purity. The picture opens in an orphanage bathhouse (the Hungarians are bathing fanatics) full of squealing, pink-skinned children. Job (Ferenc Zenthe) and Roza (Hedi Temessy) have been unable to "proliferate" and have decided to buy a child for "two fine calves." When Job picks out an active little blond brat, Lacko (Gabor Feher), of whom Roza complains, "He bites like a rabid fox," there is a discussion as to what else they might have offered. Roza thinks they might have got away with "the old cow," but Job is disgusted by her parsimony.

The remainder of the film, much of it shot with a hand-held camera by Gabor Szabo in a style that would be characterized a kinetic tour de force were it not so subtle, is a series of Isaac Singer and Sholem Aleichem vignettes that combine the spiritual and the earthy. The scenes show how the child, brought to life by Feher in an explosively straightforward performance, overcomes his hatred of his abductors and learns to love them, even as he is entranced by and imitates their strange religious rituals. Lacko is entranced by other things as well. Job is a shepherd; his Christian assistant, Jani (Peter Rudolf), falls in love with a young woman servant, Ilka (Leticia Caro), and before long Lacko is carting pails of cold water to toss on the copulating pair (one of the great joys of Hungarian films is their unself-conscious bawdiness). "Why do they keep doing it?" the boy wants to know. "The bull and the stallion do it once and that's it." A silent movie comes to town and the whole family goes. The picture is called *The Frozen Child*. "How stupid," the assistant shepherd grouses. "They make people cry and they charge for it."

This idyllic, lovingly evoked existence is shadowed by Job's conviction that the days of his people are numbered. He has revolted in two ways, by adopting a child in the face of a fate that has decreed he shall have none of his own, and by arranging to save the child in the face of society that has declared Jews non-persons. Job has adopted a Christian so that he can legally leave his wealth and his spiritual legacy when he is taken to the camps. He advises Lacko to tell the truth if he should be asked where he lives, "but you must always add, 'But I am not a Jew.'" (Yet Lacko *is* a Jew by the end of the film.) Roza, initially cool to the idea of procuring a child, stages her own rebellion. "I won't give you up," she whispers defiantly to Lacko. "Neither God nor man has the right."

Not the right, but the might. And when, God having turned his back, man is given permission by omission to exercise his evil and Lacko's parents are taken away, *The Revolt of Job* pares its soundtrack of all music and its images of all excess, and focuses—simply, beautifully, unforgetably—on one tiny tow-headed child lost in an ocean of lost causes.

But the child is alive, and has a memory, and is named Gyöngyössy, and is one of the directors of this film, and did live in wartime Hungary with a Jewish couple, Mr. and Mrs. Emmanuel Kohn, who disappeared. But before they did, they told him to "run after the Messiah, after eternal liberation," and he has been doing that ever since "in all my films," and that is why he says, "We are at one with Job's belief in tomorrow." *(1984)*

Rich and Famous

Mommie Dearest has been in national release only three weeks, and already it is time to bestow the Mommie Dearest Memorial Award for Mega-Trash to *Rich and Famous*, eighty-two-year-old director George Cukor's new comedy with Jacqueline Bisset as a writer who gets famous and Candice Bergen as a writer who gets rich *and* famous. *Rich and Famous* is a remake of *Old Acquaintance* (1943, with Bette Davis and Miriam Hopkins) and it's almost as entertaining as its progenitor: how many films are there these days daring enough to offer a teddy-bear motif? The teddy bear is a gift from Merry Noël Blake (Candice Bergen), a Texan, to Liz Hamilton (Jacqueline Bisset), a Brit, when the two are students at Smith College in 1959 (Bergen wears the plaids she wore for the college sequences in *Carnal Knowledge*; Bisset wears an intense expression intended to convey youthful, idealistic passion). "Have a wonderful life," Liz tells Merry Noël as Merry Noël boards a train west with hubby "Doug Bug" Blake (David Selby). Snow that looks like shredded Styrofoam obscures the teary tableau.

Cut to Malibu, 1969. Liz has published her first novel and has been called "a master of irony" by *The New York Review of Books*. Merry Noël has given birth to her first child and her first novel. The child is a pretty little girl and the novel is a great big dreck epic all about Merry Noël's rich and famous neighbors—Merry Noël is Jackie Susann crossed with Annie Oakley (though Bergen, outfitted in outlandish but expensive Theoni V. Aldredge gowns, often resembles a Beverly Hills Minnie Pearl). For no reason at all, a reunion between Liz and Merry Noël degenerates into a catfight (homage to *The Turning Point*) when Merry Noël reads her novel to Liz. Liz allows as how the book is trash and quotes her literary agent, who believes the only audience for serious work is composed of Jews and homosexuals. "Don't you want to write major art and knock 'em dead at the local gay Hadassah?" Liz enquires rhetorically and bitterly, believing herself to be deserving of the fame and wealth that she fears—quite rightly—will come Merry Noël's way.

Cut to 1975. Merry Noël, dressed like a West Coast Barbara Cartland, is on Cavett and Griffin, but there is trouble at home. Merry Noël derides her unemployed husband, then apologizes. "Sometimes words just slide outta my mouth," she sighs "Like a snake out of its hole," the uncharitable Doug Bug responds. Meanwhile, in New York, Liz, who has a weakness for making love in the toilets of 747s, listens to Bessie Smith records.

Cut to 1981. And to a new movie. The old *Rich and Famous* had been about the rocky relationship between two women. The new one is about their rotten relationships with men. While walking one day near the Algonquin Hotel, Liz is accosted by an eighteen-year-old stranger (Matt Lattanzi, a less masculine Robby Benson look-alike). She takes him back to the hotel and makes love to him. (We see him nude, but we do not see Bisset. Does Cukor believe the literary agent's theory of the audience for high art?) Later, she makes love to an interviewer (Hart Bochner) from *Rolling Stone*. Merry Noël is not given to such Erica Jong-ing but she, too, has her problems with males. The movie's theme seems to be that while all relationships are a mess, relationships between women last longer than relationships between men and women. A subsidiary theme is that neither wealth nor fame is enough for the liberated dame.

One of the pleasures of *Old Acquaintance* was watching two fanged pros chew scenery. One of the pleasures of *Rich and Famous* is watching two toothless amateurs gum everything in sight, including each other (the penultimate confrontation, when the teddy bear, symbol of the friendship, is ripped into stuffing, is outrageously funny). Bisset, who has been allotted far more screen time than Bergen, has fleeting moments when a character seems on the verge of creation, but Bergen, whose acting is as bad as ever except that it is far more enthusiastic than in the past, is a figure of incompetent fun; she offers one of the great bad performances of our time, a performance that must be giving Ali MacGraw fits of envy. Cukor's direction is adequate—no, perfect—for the task of allowing the film to run stylishly amok. In a cameo role as the literary agent, Steven Hill is responsible for the one seamless, professional performance, and for an exchange that summarizes *Rich and Famous*. Liz has brought Merry Noël's novel to Levi. "What's it about?" he asks. "Feelings," Liz replies with mild distaste. "What kind of feelings?" Liz grimaces: "The kinds of feelings they have in Malibu." *Rich and Famous* is about the kinds of feelings they have a little farther inland, in Hollywood. Doug Bug has the last word: "You put together enough trash, you get some major garbage."   (*1981*)

Sheena

In the depths of darkest Africa, two American scientist-explorers killed in a cave-in leave behind a little blonde girl in underpants. "A golden god child!" cries the local wise woman, who goes by the handle of Shaman, and who informs her incredulous tribesfolk that the orphaned tyke is going to grow up and save them from evil outsiders. Prophecy, says Shaman, says so. It come to pass that the little blonde one grows straight and strong and bosomy on the African veldt and comes to be called Sheena, Queen of the Jungle, and comes to be played by Tanya Roberts, the last angel begat by Charlie unto the tube. From Shaman, Sheena learns all things African—how to greet and call the pink flamingo, how to converse with (and wonder about) the lion, the elephant, and the rhinoceros, and last but certainly not least, how to apply makeup to look like the greatest of all golden god children, Marilyn of Monroe. It is only fitting that Sheena should learn all manner of beauty aids and aerobic skills and sartorial tips from Shaman, for Shaman is played by Princess Elizabeth of Toro, once a lawyer, once a model, once Minister of Foreign Affairs for Idi Amin. "Her diplomatic career ended, however," saith the *Sheena* press kit, "when she refused Uganda President Amin's proposal of marriage and she took exile in Kenya." A wise woman, indeed.

As Sheena grows in amplitude and pulchritude, there are evil machinations in the cities to the South. The tribe to which Sheena is attached roams across valuable land, the dust of which is miraculous even unto the curing of cancer, and the evil men of the South would seek to conquer that land and retain the dust of that good earth. One of the evil men is in fact an evil woman, an evil black woman, wife of the evil black King Jabalani (Clifton Jones), who is brother to the even more evil Prince Otwani (Trevor Jones), a sports hero who would be king now that his career in professional football is kaput. The evil black woman, Princess Zanda (France Zobda), teams up with the evil Prince Otwani to kill the less evil and therefore more reprehensible King Jabalani, the better to conquer and market the magic dust of the North. "I am the most wicked woman in Tigora," exults Princess Zanda, clicking her false fingernails together, and giving even the legendary Joan of Collins a run for her rhinestones as Wickedest Bitch on This or Any Other Earth. In the meantime, two American journalists, a thin and sexy one, Vic Casey (Ted Wass), and a fat and funny one, Fletcher (Donovan Scott), catch a glimpse of Sheena swinging her T & A through the trees. "Back when we played doctor, *that's* what we called a *girl*! A blonde!" So says fat 'n' funny, but it is thin 'n' sexy who later smooches up Sheena, Q. of the J., from her callused toes to the tips of her burnt-umber eyeliner, and causes her to sigh wonderingly as she rubs her raspberry Elizabeth of Toro lip gloss: "Mouths we were given to eat with, why did you touch yours to mine?" Forsooth she finds out forthwith and becomes Sheena, Siren of the Jungle, Slutress of the Bush, and in her sexualized euphoria is able to save her people merely by putting hand to head and ordering about three-and-a-half-million flamingos, a dozen rhinos, a scattering of elephants, and a collection of chattering chimpanzees to attack the minions of wickedness that up from the South come, in uniforms, driving Land Rovers, throwing hand grenades and bad acting hither and thither. But she is not able, magnificent creature that she is, rustic and wild centerfold though she may be, to summon all the king's horses and all the king's men to put her movie together again.   (*1984*)

A Soldier's Story

It is foggy in the fields near Fort Neal, Louisiana, the night Master Sergeant Vernon C. Waters (Adolph Caesar) is shot to death. The gray vapor that instantly shrouds the deed in mystery is more than a simple physical fact: throughout *A Soldier's Story*, the featurelessness of fog, its ability to obscure sharp colors and to soften rigid definitions, is used as a metaphor for the complicated, stormy reality of relationships between the races in the United States—and for the equally complicated and even stormier reality of relationships *within* the races.

Directed by Norman Jewison (*Best Friends*) utilizing a script adapted by Charles Fuller from his Pulitzer Prize-winning play, *A Soldier's Story* brings to the screen for the first time in a major Hollywood film a particularized black milieu, and a new point of view. There have been black Hollywood films that purported to dramatize everyday life (*A Raisin in the Sun*) and there have been black musicals (*Porgy and Bess*, *Carmen Jones*) and there have been dozens of black exploitation films and a few comedies, but not until *A Soldier's Story*, set in 1944 and featuring the men of the fictitious 221st Smoke Generating Unit's "C" Company, has there been a black movie that examines seriously and without sentimentality the effect of prejudice not only on blacks, but among blacks. Jewison's powerful picture is a look at blacks who would be blacker, at blacks who would be gray, at blacks who would be white.

Sgt. Walker, theatrically played by Caesar with a hissing James Cagney malevolence that hides an abyss of insecurity and self-hatred, despises "geechees," by which he means the kind of Southern "niggers"—his word—without which he feels "white folks wouldn't think we was all fools." Walker would like to be liked by whites, and he is determined to expunge all traces of "yassur" from his vocabulary and all traces of Uncle Tom from his life. But Sgt. Walker is not a simple man. He also hates whites: the fellow soldier who says of him, "Any man who ain't sure where he belongs gotta be in a whole lotta pain," says volumes. In an unconscious, eerie echo of Hitlerian racism, the thing he is supposed to be going to war to fight, Walker rejoices when "geechees" come to a bad end. "One less fool for the race to be ashamed of," he crows. But he paradoxically experiences soul-destroying fury when confronted by white racists. Drunk, weaving through the fog in those fields near Fort Neal seconds before his death, he moans, "I ain't doin' nuthin' white folks say to . . . look what it's done to me . . . I hate myself . . . " In the fullest sense of the term the eminently dislikable but oddly empathetic Walker is a tragic figure.

His death is investigated by Captain Richard Davenport (*Ragtime* star Howard E. Rollins, Jr.), a Howard University-trained military attorney, also black, who is the first "colored" officer ever glimpsed by most of the whites or blacks in the godforsaken Louisiana outpost. Rollins does his best with a remote role that requires him to function primarily as a sounding board for the men he investigates. It is those men—black men as variegated, for once, as any group of white men—who give *A Soldier's Story* its depth and, sorry to say, its novelty. That it should be novel to see blacks interact on screen is close to criminal, but you may find watching the film that you suddenly become transfixed by the way dark skin looks in stylized light, or by the cadences of speech overheard on street corners but never in movie theaters. A whole population on this continent is as alien to its most popular art form as any of the aliens that take up so much of that art form's time and resources.

Actors who demand compliments include Art Evans, David Alan Grier, David Harris, Dennis Lipscomb, William Allen Young, Denzel Washington, Robert Townsend, and, above all, Larry Riley, whose portrait of C.J. Memphis, a happy-go-lucky "backwoods nigger," is virtually an anthropological essay. Congratulations are also due Herbie Hancock, whose score is brassy and bluesy and unabashedly vulgar; cinematographer Russell Boyd, who has transformed atmosphere into character; and to Jewison and his co-producers, Ronald L. Schwary and Patrick Palmer, for undertaking what must have seemed an unrealizable project. There are flaws—the flashback structure creaks with theatricality, and the camera is not always as fluid as one might wish—but they are minor in comparison to the film's virtues. Fuller has altered the play's ending by removing a notation that the company was killed in Europe, a change that has been seen by some writers as a sop to the audience, an attempt by Jewison to "commercialize" the piece. Well, the only way to commercialize the script of *A Soldier's Story* would be to give it to Eddie Murphy and tell him to eat it on camera. We don't need to be told what happened to the men in this movie: their fates are worn on their faces. We know how the Second World War came out. And we know what it meant on an individual basis, which is what *A Soldier's Story* is about—individuals. In the end, the soldiers' stories were all the same. Everybody who didn't live lost.   (*1984*)

Sophie's Choice

Entertainers have risen to fame and fortune on the strength of their voices, their shapes, their talent, and even their lack of same (remember Mrs. Miller?), but Meryl Streep may be the only performer in history to achieve notoriety on the basis of her skin: she is the first major movie artist to act with her complexion.

Sophie's Choice is the most exhaustive display yet of Streep's pores and pallor. As Sophie Zawistowska, the heroine of William Styron's best-selling novel, she is constantly on screen, usually in full close-up. Streep has made a career of acting under the magnifying glass, but the close-ups in *The French Lieutenant's Woman*, *Kramer vs. Kramer*, and *Still of the Night* are inadequate preparation for the extravaganza of microscopic scrutiny that represents writer-director Alan J. Pakula's modus operandi in transferring *Sophie's Choice* to the screen. Streep's acceptable performance, her best work since *Kramer*, has been hailed as a one-of-a-kind star turn, and it is, not because it is great (it is not), but because seldom in screen history, even in the probing work of Ingmar Bergman, has a camera fastened so tenaciously on a face. The mannerisms Streep has used so often—the darting and brimming eyes, the nervous pat of the hair, the sudden eruption of laughter, the quirky cock of the head to one side—are all in evidence, and there are moments when Sophie seems a peculiar composite of the least attractive elements of Greer Garson and Sandy Dennis. But the mannerisms mostly work for the character instead of against it; the artifice fits because Streep is playing a woman who is not what she seems. And her ear for language is faultless: the

Polish accent is at once comic and moving. This might seem a classic performance if its genesis in Streep's previous films were not a matter of cinematic record. At the movie's killer climax, however, the actress commits an egregious act bordering on sacrilege: her use of Helena Weigel's famous silent scream from Bertolt Brecht's *Mother Courage* is an unconscionable act of unearned emotional plagiarism.

Streep aside, Pakula's decision to film Styron's upwardly mobile potboiler in cameo would have resulted in disaster had it not been for the supporting cast. Peter MacNicol, as the writer Stingo (the young Styron), whom Sophie meets in a Brooklyn boardinghouse in 1947, and Kevin Kline, as the "utterly, fatally glamorous" Nathan, with whom she is having an affair, are exceptional artists, capable not only of holding their own with La Streep, but of stealing scenes from her. MacNicol is not asked to do much more than worship Sophie, but he projects adoration of such intensity the veneration nearly materializes in the air between the two characters. Kline, whose role is much smaller, combines the dark, almost effeminate good looks of Laurence Olivier, circa *Wuthering Heights* (Kline has Olivier's sly, satyr's sense of humor) with a macho dash of Errol Flynn—the revelation of Nathan's ultimate secret is exactly as surprising as it should be (not very).

Structurally, *Sophie's Choice* marries the Holocaust Movie to the How I Lost My Virginity Movie, a match made somewhat lower than heaven. The film is a respectable, claustrophobic, and slick piece of work, and cinematographer Nestor Almendros's color strategies—Rembrandt-like light at night, lemony tones during the day, desaturated sepia at Auschwitz —are arty to a fault. Without any obvious vulgarity, the Final Solution is transformed into the stuff of a romantic weepie; the heroine of what is essentially a Harlequin Romance by way of psychoanalysis has been given the most sordid and mysterious past of all—the concentration camp. In the novel, Sophie, a gentile who tried everything to save herself (she was incarcerated for a misdemeanor, smuggling a ham), suffered chronic survivor guilt that was exploited viciously and pathologically by Nathan, a Jew. Nathan's key sadomasochistic confrontation with Sophie —she is abused and all but glories in it—has been removed from the film, imparting to the bitter story a sweeter taste. The film is both better than the book (those endless digressions into the horniness of the narrator are gone) and worse—readers of the novel did not emerge with sentimental nostalgia for a psychosexually sophisticated Romeo and Juliet, which is precisely what Pakula has made of the pair. No disrespect is intended here, and Pakula and his cast are without doubt sincere, but the stately, textbook tearjerking of this film is a bit much: Abnormal Psychology 305 goes to Auschwitz.   (*1982*)

A Star is Born

With much immodest backslapping and horn-blowing on the part of the studio that cut it in the first place, the new, improved, "reconstructed" *A Star is Born* returns with twenty-seven extra minutes, and although it's not quite *Napoleon*, it is nice to see that director George Cukor's immortal Hollywood soap opera has stood the test of time superlatively.

The twenty-seven minutes encompass two restored musical numbers that are not necessarily aural revelations—they have been heard on the soundtrack recording for years. But the new footage does allow the viewer to see that the point of one of them, "Lose That Long Face," was to give Judy Garland one of the most flamboyantly romantic and moving moments of her career, and that *is* a revelation. It occurs at the end of the number, near the end of the three-hour film. Singer Esther Blodgett (Garland), discovered by drunken matinee idol Norman Maine (James Mason), has married her benefactor and become a major star in her own right. But Maine has taken to drink again, and Esther, now known by her movie-star name, Vicki Lester, is distraught. She films "Lose That Long Face," a lively little tune featuring tap-dancing, pickaninnies, and watermelons, and then goes to her dressing room to deliver a long monologue regarding her tangled feelings for her husband. She is asked to return to the set. Controlling hysteria, she reapplies her freckles, steps in front of the camera, spreads her arms, and is—suddenly, in a second—transformed into the bluebird of happiness. It's the quintessential Garland myth: tired of living and scared of dying, but singing like a cotton-candy angel.

There are other new "jolts of pleasure," in Norman Maine's words, to be found in the first half. Missing entirely from the earlier version was a digressive interlude (it need not have been cut, but you can see why it was) during which Maine goes on location and Esther waits for him to return (she becomes a carhop, among other things). Only scattered seconds of footage could be found in the archives, so Ronald Haver, responsible for the archeology and assembly, has simulated the experience via the artful use of a dialogue tape and still photographs (a comment overheard by a friend at intermission: "That must have been a very avant-garde technique for 1954!"). The effect is distancing and gives the film the feel of a documentary, which, in a profound sense, it may be—a documentary of Hollywood's masochistic fantasies about itself. The other restored musical number, a five-minute sequence in which Esther sings and then turns down Maine's proposal of marriage, is a delightful, surprisingly comic addition. The performances by Garland and Mason remain perfection; always underrated as an actress, Garland is here at her peak, and the dimensions Mason imparts to the tortured Norman Maine are tragic. This is one time when the atheist and the agnostic can join the believer in cheering the born-again.   (*1983*)

The Stunt Man

The Stunt Man, which is scary and sorrowful and stirring and sexy —everything a big Hollywood popcorn-cruncher of a movie should be—is the best movie about making a movie ever made. The achievement merely begins there: this is the Hollywood dream movie, the flick every producer thinks he wants to make, the perfect marriage between art and commerce, the picture that should pack 'em in for blistering action while critics are off in corners constructing spidery exegeses of debts to Luigi Pirandello and Jean-Luc Godard. This is also the movie Hollywood wouldn't touch: not only did every studio reject the script (financing was raised privately, and the picture was shot in San Diego in 1978), but every studio rejected the film—Twentieth Century-Fox agreed to distribute it only after Richard Rush, the director, opened it in Seattle himself and demonstrated that it had an audience.

In superficial specifics, *The Stunt Man* is simple: Eli Cross (Peter O'Toole), a director reminiscent of Patrick Dennis's outlandish Leander Starr in the novel *Genius*, is making an anti-war First World War movie with Nina Franklin (Barbara Hershey), a semi-competent actress and completely competent bitch, when his set is invaded by Cameron (Steve Railsback), an apparently paranoiac Vietnam veteran running from the police. Eli decides to use Cameron as a replacement for a dead stunt man. Asked if he has stunt experience, the nutsy Cameron replies, ''I got outta 'Nam in one piece; that's a helluva stunt.'' The rest of the movie is about making of the rest of the movie.

How can a picture in which a stunt man falls in love with his leading lady and maintains an ambivalent relationship with his director operate on virtually every level open to a work of movie art? In that opening sequence, bound to become famous, Cameron runs smack into a scene being played out on Eli's movie set. But we don't know that a movie is being made. When at last we get our bearings, something else has thrown us off kilter, has put the sky where the sea should be. Nothing is what it seems. There are no red herrings, but we are constantly provided visual information from which we draw erroneous conclusions. *The Stunt Man*'s message is in its method. ("My own tastes," Rush has said, "are for Proust and Batman.")

I am being nebulous intentionally because I don't want to spoil the fun. For all its depth, or maybe because of its depth, *The Stunt Man* is as much fun as any great movie extant; imagine a comedy an eight-year-old and Wittgenstein could love with equal fervor. The entire picture is a shimmering mirage, as dizzyingly complex, unpredictable, and original in tone as any American movie since *Bonnie and Clyde*, and as justifiably self-celebratory as Robert Altman's *Nashville*.

Like the anti-war movie Eli is directing (the film within the film), *The Stunt Man* is concerned with heroism and mortality. "We're afraid we're going to die of nothing more important than wrinkles," Eli observes. His stunt men risk death to prove they are alive; his audiences risk involvement with the characters portrayed by the stunt men for the same reason—movies let them hang from cliffs, face speeding locomotives, and battle entire garrisons. By proxy. "If God could do the tricks that we can do, He'd be a happy man," Eli smirks. Once upon a time, God could. But *The Stunt Man* argues that movie (or television) magic—media magic—has replaced the magic of yore, when little boxes holding bones of saints were worshipped and the appearance of the face of the Virgin on a dishcloth was a decade's marvel. "Everybody wants something to believe in—even policemen," Eli says. "Without something to believe in, life is meaningless." So Eli plays God: he gives the masses movies. Stars. Stories. Something to care about. Something to make the pain go away.

There's a catch. Eli, who's seen life from both sides now, knows he's not God. (As played by O'Toole, in his finest performance since *The Ruling Class*, he is a variation on the half-mad Lawrence of Arabia. Except that this world-weary, effete figure in Dr. Zhivago shirts is Larry of Araby—a deity who shops on Rodeo Drive.) He knows the only time his stunt men feel alive, the only time their problems cease to be petty, is when they have faced and vanquished danger; that's the only time Eli himself feels alive. His movies, at their best, reproduce for the audience some of the excitement that went into making them. Eli is a purveyor of a very modern religion: Vicarious Living. But he is a leader with no place to take his followers, and he would like to make a movie about that, about the impotence of his art in the yawning maw of death; but to come right out and say that nothing makes sense, you would have to "sneak it in," he suspects. Toss it to the audience between the laughs, the tears, and the sex-cum-violence turn-on. Eli is talking about *The Stunt Man*'s own modus operandi: the phenomenological sophistication of this movie is extraordinary. The irony is that an incredibly self-conscious, analytical film can make you care deeply about its characters: when one of them is placed in great danger during the climax, you may find yourself clawing your arm rests.

Side by side with the originality, any number of movie clichés are recycled, as they must be—one of the tasks *The Stunt Man* has set itself is to illustrate how the dynamics of the filmmaking process have been reflected, historically, in the movies themselves. In the eyes of Eli and his leading lady, for example, the tattooed, blue-collar Cameron is an object of romanticized respect (because he has lived), fear (because he is volatile), condescension (because he has no social graces), and erotic attraction (for all those reasons). Cameron is the most obvious example, but every character in *The Stunt Man* has been molded by the movies. The actress comports herself as she thinks a hip leading lady should; her notions of how to orchestrate her love affair with Cameron are all movie-oriented. Truth and illusion collide in Cameron: part of *The Stunt Man*'s mystery involves the kind of person he really is, as opposed to the kind of person Eli and the actress (and a wonderful cast of supporting characters) think he is. On this level, too, we are toyed with: personality is just one more special effect. Cameron is convinced that Eli is out to get him, that the actress may not love him, that nobody is what he seems. Is Cameron paranoid—or aware? Crazy or sane? Do people care or could they care less? Cameron can be seen as Everyman on the lam: his message is that we are all stunt men. We are all forced to find authenticity by threatening life itself (in big ways or small), to support values that the next move of the camera may reveal to be false fronts. What knowledge of the nature of life is possible, finally? *The Stunt Man*'s answer comes from Cameron, in a description of a Vietnam booby trap. If a man stepped on this trap, nothing happened; if he removed his foot, it exploded. "So all he could do was just stand there."   (*1980*)

Three Brothers

In an Italian farmhouse, an aged woman dies. Her husband Donato (Charles Vanel) sends telegrams to his three sons. The eldest, Raffaele (Philippe Noiret), is an idealistic judge; the middle child, Rocco (Vittorio Mezzogiorno), is an idealistic teacher of delinquent children; and the youngest, Nicola (Michele Placido), is a worker whose idealism takes two forms: he believes in the cause of the working man and he believes that a reconciliation with his estranged wife is possible. In Francesco Rosi's beautiful new film *Three Brothers*, the sons respond to the telegrams by coming home to attend their mother's funeral. That is all this movie is about —that, and everything else.

Rosi, director of *Eboli* and *The Mattei Affair*, is sixty. There is a theory in psychology to the effect that the last stage of development is "self-actualization," reached, if at all, in the later years, when the achievements of a lifetime are thought to be enough and when the personality turns inward to take warmth from itself. It is a comforting theory, positing as it does a kind of unsentimental heaven on earth, and it may be the source of *Three Brothers'* rigorous formality and austere compassion; this is a film it would have been impossible for a young—or even a younger—man to make.

As the three brothers arrive at the sun-bleached stone home, we share their memories and dreams. Raffaele has nightmares: he has decided to preside over the trial of terrorists charged with murdering one of his colleagues, and his sleep is filled with images of assassination. Rocco dreams of rats in slums, but he also dreams of a world swept clean by his kids. Nicola, the attractive hedonist, dreams of an erotic reconciliation with his wife. Donato, the widower, dreams of the dead, and remembers a day on the beach, a day when nothing much happened—when nothing much happened, and when everything happened.

Three Brothers opens to the sound of a heartbeat, an indication that this is a movie concerned with the elemental, a movie that will attempt to place its hand on the heart of existence. The background and foreground flutter together—a black dog in a courtyard becomes an ancillary character, and the soft sighs of pigeon wings are as moving as the cries of the bereaved. The tale has purposely been stripped to the sharp, stark lines of a classical perspective: this is a picture framed for posterity.   (*1982*)

Under the Volcano

Malcolm Lowry's mad and maddening 1947 novel *Under the Volcano*, which takes place on the final day (November 1, 1938) in the life of Geoffrey Firmin, ex-British Consul stationed in Cuernavaca, Mexico, is said by its proponents, of whom there are many, to be the apotheosis of alcoholism in literature, a statement of the transcendence to be found in addiction. The fascinating film version, directed by the legendary John

Huston, means to reproduce that apotheosis, but it fails; and in failing to convince us that Firmin is, in the words of one of the subsidiary characters, "a great soul," it succeeds at something else, at something neither Lowry nor Huston could have predicted (or would have wanted)—instead of ennobling its alcoholic hero, *Under the Volcano* straps him to the rack of psychological realism.

With its clotted prose and hallucinatory digressions—reading it is exactly like trying to follow the bouts of mania and depression, of insight and incoherence, that any reasonably intelligent drunk is heir to in any random half hour—the Lowry novel has been considered "unfilmable" for many years, and while Huston and his admirable screenwriter Guy Gallo have been faithful to the book's events, its subtext has eluded them: how do you photograph and render persuasive an aria of alcoholic rationalization? When *Under the Volcano* was previewed at the Cannes Film Festival, Huston was at pains to point out that for him Firmin's drunkenness was the result of his ability to see things too clearly, that Firmin required liquid anesthetic to dull the agony of existence, and that Firmin's perceptions, and his refusal to lie to himself regarding them, were the cornerstones of his greatness. Huston was following the line of critic Stephen Spender, the book's most indefatigable champion: "It is no more *about* drinking than *King Lear* is *about* senility."

On screen, *Under the Volcano* is "about" drinking, and Firmin's compressed literary monologues—speeches having to do with the forthcoming "Age of the Dead" ("We'll learn to laugh at the sight of stinking cadavers," he predicts) and a *cri de coeur* in which he says, "Hell is my natural habitat"—come across as excuses to get to the next shot of tequila, as bombast and bilge. (This is not a man to ask people in Alcoholics Anonymous to see as "a great soul.") Spectacularly photographed in the tropical cartoon colors of the Mexican painter Jose Clemente Orozco by cinematographer Gabriel Figueroa, the picture is a detailed, clinical account of a mouthily self-destructive drunk; thanks to Albert Finney's amusingly grandiloquent performance, he's far better company than he has any right to be.

Introduced in black tie and black sunglasses, prowling a graveyard, Firmin is in mourning for his life, like the woman in *The Seagull*. Firmin's wife, Yvonne (Jacqueline Bisset), has left him, and his only close English-speaking companion, his half-brother Hugh (Anthony Andrews), a politicized twit who cuckolded him with Yvonne, is a tedious esthete, a British rhinestone cowboy in jeans and a silver Navajo belt with *conchas* the size of hubcaps. Firmin wants Yvonne to return to Mexico from

New York, despite the "dust in my heart," and in one of the movie's most touching moments he delivers a whispered plea in a deserted church: "I'm dying without you . . . come back to me. . . ." She does, in the photogenic person of Bisset, whose brows stay knitted and whose face stays otherwise immobile—the motivations of Yvonne's character are apparently as inscrutable to Bisset as they are to the audience.

Bisset is the salient failing, along with a badly staged scene in a bordello that has Fellini written all over it, but Huston is otherwise confident —the stylistic simplicity of *Under the Volcano* is hard won, but seems newborn, pristine. Following the formula with which he brought Flannery O'Connor's novella *Wise Blood* so memorably to the screen, Huston relies on dense set decoration and dialogue rather than camera motion to create his milieu, and perhaps because the milieu in this case is also his home (he lives on the west coast of Mexico), he is able to fill the theater with the fruity stench of indolent Central American decay as no one else (not even Luis Buñuel) has: Mexico is as immediate in its sunny rot in *Under the Volcano* as Peru was in its slithering menace in Werner Herzog's *Aguirre, The Wrath of God*.

Commenting on the delicate art of alcoholic intake, Firmin says, "Surely you appreciate the fine balance I must strike between the shakes of too little and the abyss of too much." In bringing this hugely difficult novel to the movies, Huston has found the same balance, the state of grace God sometimes provides to drunks and to those who attempt the impossible—to those who film the unfilmable.   (*1984*)

The Verdict

As Paul Newman has aged, his art has gone through a process of refinement —his characterizations have become clearer, sharper, and more effortless. Frank Galvin, the alcoholic attorney he plays in *The Verdict*, is an exception: it's as if Newman had finally taken to heart the reviews he received in *Fort Apache, The Bronx* and *Absence of Malice* and had decided that he might be a great actor after all. This time, you can see him out there working for those awards.

Galvin, a Boston ambulance-chaser who's had only four cases in three years, is a dream role for an actor. Too dreamy. He has the shakes so bad he has to suck the first drink of the day out of a jigger that stays on the table. He haunts mortuaries, dispensing his business card to the bereaved with an offer to be of help should the need arise. Screenwriter David Mamet and director Sidney Lumet appear at first to be fabricating a gritty character study, a judicially oriented companion to Lumet's *Prince of the City* that will give Newman the chance to etch another unforgettable, middle-aged, run-of-the-mill guy onto the audience's admiring eye. At first. That's before *The Verdict* turns into a Western and Paul Newman settles into the business of being Paul Newman, white hat.

None of this is Newman's fault; a split personality is built right into the movie. The first half, photographed in the dingy but glowing green of an illuminated but uncleaned aquarium, is a sequel to *Prince of the City*, a critique of the justice system. A desperate Galvin, in it for the money, takes on a malpractice case and suddenly, improbably, rejects a $210,000 out-of-court settlement, having developed high ideals he intends to pursue at the expense of his clients, if need be. "If I take the money, I'm lost," he declares. "I'll be a rich ambulance-chaser." This attack of integrity has complex causes, few readily available to the viewer. But if motives are obscure, *The Verdict* does at least hold out the promise of facing difficult issues without simplification. The promise is discarded in the second half, a courtroom melodrama that lets Newman grandstand heroically in the manner audiences have come to expect of Robert Redford, the Gentleman's Own Jesus. Skin pulled translucently taut across the bones, gray hair long and lush, sapphire eyes a-sparkle, Newman is in fine physical form, and the restive audience settles in at last for some satisfying cheerleading when he drops his transparently phony pose as a boozy loser and gets down to the nitty gritty of saving the day. Lumet, Mamet, and Newman engender so much sympathy for Galvin that, when the attorney slugs a woman, and slugs her *hard*, applause breaks out. At that juncture, *The Verdict* loses its last claim to verisimilitude and becomes a manipulative, rabble-rousing, liberal crowd-pleaser.

As always in Lumet's films, the casting of the supporting roles is faultless; James Mason, an elegant Boston Brahmin, and Jack Warden, a rumpled Back Bay untouchable, are especially memorable. Charlotte Rampling, whose character seems to have hitchhiked in from film noir, is also admirable, despite *The Verdict*'s craven use of her hooded eroticism. But the movie stands or falls with Newman, and it does neither: it coasts. His acting in the second half is safe and self-assured, while his acting in the first—watch for his announcement of his erupting integrity—is not only shy of good, it's downright bad. It would be ironic but predictable if he were to win an Oscar for his weakest performance in years. Justice, as this movie contends, is a good guy, but a good guy hard to find.   (*1982*)

The Wars

Marinated in melancholy and steeped in psychological and political skepticism, the immensely intelligent Robin Phillips film of Timothy Findley's novel *The Wars* begins what should be a long, exciting process of reclaiming the Canadian past. Set in 1914, this is one of the few movies to present the nation's forebears as something other than tuque-bearing, plaid-coated, maple-sugared hams, and it may be the only major feature film to have examined in depth the Rosedale ruling class. What is shocking about *The Wars* is that it wasn't made sooner. In terms of style and unapologetic self-absorption, it's the first Australian–Canadian film, arriving nearly a decade after the Aussies resolved to please and educate and enlighten themselves rather than cater to the phantom ciphers of the "international market."

Findley's cinematic transcription of his novel has inevitably lost texture —where the book was a kaleidoscope of complexity, the film is an inventory of incident. But what incident! In recounting the short and none too happy life of the hero, Robert Ross, the filmmakers are able to survey a panorama of colonial Canadian activity, ranging from the dark drawing rooms of the new world to the pretentious estates of the British gentry to the urine-drenched trenches of the frontlines. The survey is conducted with a moody reserve and an esthetic precision that sometimes suggests an Ingmar Bergman remake of *All Quiet on the Western Front*. That's a compliment.

The domestic sojourns in Toronto introduce Robert (Brent Carver), a soft and aimless boy—a nascent homosexual, in all likelihood, who might have reached happiness had he reached a life beyond confusion; Robert's sister Roweena (Ann-Marie MacDonald), physically maimed beyond repair; Robert's grande-dame mother (Martha Henry), alcoholically sodden beyond salvation; Robert's father (William Hutt), spiritually absent beyond reach; and the family's governess, Miss Davenport (Jackie Burroughs), a retainer whose eyes, black and sweet as fine chocolate truffles, have viewed endless upper-class conflicts beyond her ken. Each is a victim of the genteel repression *The Wars* defines as a national characteristic of the English Canadian upper class.

There are great scenes showcasing great acting, and the greatest is Mrs. Ross's visit with her son in the family's arena-sized green bathroom. "A mother's prerogative, to visit the wounded," she says, the voluptuous exhalation of her cigarette smoke the last vestige of sensuality she permits herself. The interlude follows a death in the family; Mrs. Ross is irrationally incensed with her son, but she is also disturbed by their estrangement. And we can see, as she casts an agonized but appreciative eye over his body, that she is attracted to him on levels of which she is thoroughly ignorant. When the attraction threatens to reach consciousness, her defensive alter ago, the ice queen, intervenes. "We're all cut off with a knife at birth and left to the mercy of strangers," she hisses. Almost as memorable is a scene in which Mrs. Ross furiously exits a church one Sunday morning, the feathers of her black hat tall and stiff and imperious, like the smokestacks of a battleship. Trailed by Miss Davenport, bouncing a comically stuffed bird on her uncomprehending head, Mrs. Ross is disconsolate: "What does it mean to kill your children and then go in there and sing about it?" To numb the pain, she fingers a discreet flask. Meanwhile, a world away, her son is writing letters that express, but barely, his own increasing disillusion with the meaning of manhood.

Phillips is an awesomely gifted director of actors (these actors are awesomely gifted) but he does not have enough experience behind the camera to impart to sequences taking place far from the human face the *cinematic* three-dimensionality that comes naturally to, say, Steven Spielberg. More often than not, the spatial strategies in *The Wars* are static or lateral, and even intricate camera movements result in an oddly flattened mise-en-scène (the cinematography is competent—just). What we see of the actual war is neither plastic nor kinetic; it resembles a mural, or a diorama, and if the effect is intentional, it evokes little.

This sort of thing is minor, a shortcoming easily rectified with experience, but it does take its toll in the second half of the picture, when the audience should be overwhelmed by the affront to the senses that war represents. Instead, the knowledge is reached vicariously, through Brent Carver's finely shaded performance (a performance lacking only the indefinable magic that transforms actors into stars—the camera likes Carver, but it doesn't love him) and through the soundtrack's dextrous mix of martial songs, choral arrangements, and the piano of the late Glenn Gould. An inordinate amount of expectation has been attached to this film, and it is a pleasure to be able to report that it carries most of it without strain. Flaws aside, *The Wars* is a historically important event and, like so many important historical events of late, it bruises the heart.   (*1983*)

Winter Kills

Let us now praise melodrama. In the United States, which has virtually no tradition of overtly political filmmaking, melodrama has always carried the burden of social consciousness, and has sometimes carried it with surprising ease and subversive sophistication. Film noir gave us, in the forties, a rat's-eye-view of modern times in which the desire for the dollar had reduced Americans to the status of laboratory animals; in the fifties, Douglas Sirk utilized melodramatic soap opera (as in *Imitation of Life*) to sneak in some rather radical statements to the effect that human relationships were hemorrhaging casualties of the cut-throat economic system. Director William Richert's film of Richard Condon's novel *Winter Kills*—which posits an outrageously improbable conspiracy theory of the Kennedy assassination—brings Sirk's sudsy social criticism to film noir by way of a plot that owes a little to *Hamlet* and a lot to Richard Nixon. Nick Kegan (Jeff Bridges) is the son of an entrepreneur (John Huston) patterned on Joseph P. Kennedy and the Old Testament God. Nick is also the late brother of the late President of the United States, shot by an assassin on February 22, 1960, in Philadelphia—although Nick should not be confused with Ted Kennedy. (This is a work of fiction—sort of.) If the first son, the President, was the apple of Pa's eye, the second son, Nick, is the lemon. "Do you get laid?" the old man asks, expecting a negative reply. "You know how many times your brother got laid when he was in office? One thousand and seventy-two. With his schedule. The man was a giant."

In the first few seconds of *Winter Kills*, the naive Nick meets a man with inside knowledge of the assassination, and his testimony—coupled with a spectacularly filmed multiple murder—leads Nick to the inner sanctums of the elite. No one is further inside, no one is more sanctified, no one more elite than Nick's own father: "The CIA?" snorts Pa when Nick suggests calling on the acronym for assistance. "They smuggle my cigars from Havana." The plot of *Winter Kills* is recondite in the extreme—having to list who killed whom and for what reason would be more difficult that naming the ancillary characters in a half-dozen novels by Dickens—but plot is not at issue here, and it is not what gives the film its distinction. There are performances to treasure from people such as Richard Boone, Dorothy Malone (at her Sirkian best in a psychotic monologue), Anthony Perkins, Sterling Hayden, Eli Wallach, and, in an uncredited and speechless cameo (she silently mouths one epithet), Miss Elizabeth Taylor, playing the President's personal procuress and wearing a red Edith Head thing on her head. Jeff Bridges, of the loose limbs and winning smile, is never less than likable, and when the carcinoma of power has covered the globe (and when Huston is giving a political lecture while hanging from what is said to be the largest American flag ever made), he emerges as a tragic hero: the Hamlet of the Baby Boom. Huston's performance is a full-scale, three-dimensional reprise of Noah, the land-grabber in *Chinatown*: he imparts to this paranoid potboiler the icy magnetism of the North Pole, on the one hand, and the lusciously decadent aroma of fermenting tropical fruit, on the other. He's Tennessee Williams's Big Daddy updated for the eighties.

Condon's novels have usually worked well in movies (think of *The Manchurian Candidate*) and Richert's hyper-realist pop sensibility keeps logical objections at bay. How can you question the balance or objectivity of a film in which a bisexual woman, the girl of Nick's dreams, tells him to content himself with calls to her answering machine because it only goes one way? Or in which the major villain is quite literally a vampire who repairs to the hospital twice a year to have his aged hemoglobin exchanged for fresh platelets from Amherst College students? There's even a Samoyed kept as a pet at a Death Valley resort: the dog's name is Shogun. There is something deliciously sinful about the lurid overstatement in *Winter Kills*, something that takes us back to *The Little Foxes*, but *The Little Foxes* as Costa-Gavras might have filmed it. There is method in this madness: the film's attitude toward the way business is conducted in the United States is identical to Francis Ford Coppola's in the two *Godfathers*, but the right-wingers who objected to Coppola's use of the Mafia as a metaphor for capitalism may not object to the anti-American, anti-corporate politics of *Winter Kills* because they'll be having too good a time.   (*1979*)

Wise Blood

In 1962, when Flannery O'Connor's novel *Wise Blood*—a comic Gothic parable about the sickness of sainthood and the sainthood of sickness —was ten years old, she added a brief introduction to a new edition. "The book was written with zest and, if possible, it should be read that way," advised the dark mistress of southern literature. "This is a comic novel about a Christian *malgré lui* (in spite of himself), and as such, very serious, for all comic novels that are any good must be about life and death."

Hazel Motes, *Wise Blood*'s hero, a backwoods son of a preacher man with "eyes the color of pecan shells," blows into the southern town of Taulkinham (played in the John Huston film by Macon, Georgia) to preach the Church of Truth Without Jesus Christ, a church of his own invention —"Jesus," Hazel has decided, "is a trick on niggers." While ministering, Hazel (Brad Dourif) meets a phony blind evangelical named Asa Hawks (Harry Dean Stanton) and his raunchy daughter, Sabbath Lily (Amy Wright); he rents a room from a sad, lonely woman who will fall in love with him (Mary Nell Santacroce); and he makes the acquaintance of an idiot named Enoch (Daniel Shor) who will steal a mummy from a museum to serve as "the new jesus" when he learns Hazel has not been able to find the old one. ("Enoch," O'Connor wrote in a passage that cannot be translated into the language of images and is therefore missing from the movie, "couldn't get over the expectation that the new jesus was going to do something for him in return for his services. This was the virtue of Hope, which was made up, in Enoch, of two parts suspicion and one part lust.") *Wise Blood*—the movie—is an adaptation so faithful to O'Connor's style, mores, and wit it may confound viewers not familiar with her unique (uniquely Catholic, uniquely crazed) universe, a universe that makes the south of Tennessee Williams appear tame, even timorous. The movie is amusing, but it is humor of a blackly specific brand—not for lovers of farce, but for lovers of the comedy inherent in anguish. (Which is not to imply that it is sadistic: O'Connor is, her God knows, a humanist.) When Hazel is accused by a cab driver of being a preacher, he defends himself with, "I don't believe in anything." The cabbie shoots back, "That's the trouble with you preachers. You've all got too damned good to believe in anything." The novelist means for that to be hilarious, and Huston means for it to be hilarious— gruesomely hilarious—when we see Sabbath Lily in a Virgin Mary mantilla, cradling the mummy in a blasphemous Pietà. O'Connor again: "Everything funny I have written is more terrible than it is funny, or only funny because it is terrible, or only terrible because it is funny."

The south is the North American locus of what the movie calls "the religion business," as O'Connor was very much aware. Hazel confuses the secularization of religion with religion itself and reacts against it, but for O'Connor his baroque pilgrimage is actually *toward* the ideals of Christianity. "My gravest concern," she said, "is always the conflict between an attraction for the Holy and the disbelief in it we breathe with the air of the times." If there are saints today, Hazel is one of them, but because he has devised an idea of the holy on his own while denying his spiritual needs, his quest is the stuff of pathos.

Huston was forced by his budget to update *Wise Blood*, but the contemporary locales are not as disturbing as one might have thought. Jim Bakker and his Praise the Lord Club are but a state distant: the revival of fundamentalism has rendered the parable far more relevant than it would have seemed a decade ago, although certain vignettes are admittedly damaged by the modernity of the backdrops. A man in a gorilla suit, for example, comes into town and causes a sensation at a theater: pre-TV, maybe; post-*Star Wars*, never. Huston has said that filming *Wise Blood*—the title refers to the possession of extrasensory perception—was "an absolute labor of love." Watching the film unreel—zestily, as prescribed—you cannot doubt it. To the tune of "The Tennessee Waltz," Huston and his sterling cast (many untrained locals) take us deep into O'Connor's mystical garden of bizarre delights. In her 1962 introduction, she pointed out that Hazel's integrity lay not, as critics had said, in what he could do (refuse Christ), but in what he could not do (escape Him). "Free will does not mean one will, but many wills conflicting in one man," she explained. "Freedom cannot be conceived simply. It is a mystery and one which a novel, even a comic novel, can only be asked to deepen." Huston has respected and maintained that depth.   (*1980*)

Witness

Australian director Peter Weir's first American film, *Witness*, begins with a visual joke. Across a *National Geographic* landscape of undulating wheat fields and clear blue skies, dour men and women dressed in the plain black clothing of nineteenth-century farmers travel in horse-drawn carriages. Idyllic music plays. A title appears at the bottom of the screen: "Pennsylvania 1984." Welcome to Amish country, home of the cultural time warp.

Despite its playful opening, *Witness* is not a comedy, though it's full of humor; and it's not exactly a thriller, though it's full of thrills; and it's certainly not a sex film, though it's full of steamily suggestive sexuality; it's not a documentary, but there is a raft of ethnographic insight; it's anything but a musical, but its exultant respect for rural American values harvests the corn of *Oklahoma!*; and while it may prove to be as commercial as Michael Jackson's glide, it is designed as an art film—it occasionally puts its plot on hold and wanders casually through the Vermeer environment it has painstakingly constructed. *Witness* is satisfying on so many levels it stands near *Cabaret* and *The Godfather II* as an example of how a director in love with his medium can redeem its mainstream clichés. That it should come from the director of *Picnic at Hanging Rock*, *The Last Wave*, and *The Year of Living Dangerously* is not altogether unexpected —Weir is a wizard with the camera, a magician at summoning hallucinatory cinematic power—but there is nothing in his previous work to rival the lucidity of *Witness*. The opposite, in fact: his weakness has always been an attraction to the pretentiously ambiguous, the metaphysically pompous. In *The Last Wave* and *The Year of Living Dangerously*, flimsy melodrama was freighted with a cargo it couldn't carry—*The Last Wave* promised aboriginal enlightenment and wound up a disaster picture, *The Year of Living Dangerously* posed as a demanding trek into the heart of Indonesian darkness and emerged with a remake of *Casablanca*. The *Witness* script by Earl W. Wallace and William Kelley has no such pretenses; it has an absorbing story to tell, it tells it, and that's that. Because the premise (in witnessing a murder, an eight-year-old Amish boy places himself and the cop who questions him in danger) is straightforward and strong, Weir has the latitude to wobble artily without irritating the audience, and he uses the periodic intermissions from the story to impart to the picture the multiplicity of life itself.

Take the scene where the boy, Samuel (Lukas Haas, Jane Alexander's youngest child in *Testament*), shuffles through a Philadelphia police station, the camera perched on his shoulder. Samuel's adventure results in a plot payoff, but what the sojourn is mostly about is how strange the people in the cop-shop appear to an isolated Amish child for whom a drinking fountain is an exotic experience. Or take the scene in an Amish barn when the cop, John Book (Harrison Ford), dances with an Amish woman, Rachel (Kelly McGillis), to a crackly car-radio rendition of the Sam Cooke tune "(What a) Wonderful World." Amish taboos against premarital sex afford Weir the opportunity to return the yearning to sex without becoming ridiculous or coy—as he shoots the smoldering looks of longing that pass between Rachel and John Book, he electrifies the screen with the erotic charge. Finally, take the scene in which the Amish community erects a barn for a recently married couple—Weir transforms the event into a rhapsodic depiction of communal effort that carries the unabashed sentiment (and the cinematic expertise) of the farmers digging the irrigation ditch in King Vidor's 1934 *Our Daily Bread*.

The Amish are treated with respect in *Witness*, and the impossible love that develops between the mildly rebellious widow and the wildly profane cop is irresistible, as impossible loves usually are. In fiercely difficult roles, Ford and McGillis are unimpeachable. Other actors assigned the daunting task of portraying living relics include opera singer Jan Rubes, as Rachel's stern father, and expatriate Russian ballet dancer Alexander Godunov, as her would-be beau; both skirt caricature in favor of characterization and both are convincing. Back in heathen Philadelphia, Danny Glover, the reliable black handyman Moze in *Places in the Heart*, is unrecognizable as an evil cop, and Patti LuPone, Broadway's treacherous Evita, has a memorable minute or two as John Book's sister. They round out the ensemble of a film that never exploits the community it explores—a community that ironically cares less about the quality of *Witness* than the fleeting appearance of a single white cloud in an otherwise sunny sky.   (*1985*)

The Woman in Red

Twenty questions to ask while watching *The Woman in Red* (written by, directed by, and starring Gene Wilder), a comedy that is much less painful than a walk in the summer heat, but not quite as pleasant as a swim in a cool pool:

1. Why is Gene Wilder, who plays a philandering husband living in San Francisco, wearing so much eyeliner?

2. Why is Stevie Wonder singing mushy love duets with Dionne Warwick on the soundtrack, when the movie is full of middle-aged guys cheating on their wives?

3. Why is Stevie Wonder turning into Neil Diamond?

4. Why has Dionne Warwick turned into Dusty Springfield?

5. Why has Judith Ivey, who gets such good reviews on Broadway and who plays Wilder's wife, been wasted by Hollywood?

6. Why has Gilda Radner, who's the funniest thing in *The Woman in Red*, been made to look like a particularly unattractive Nancy Walker (Rhoda's mommy)?

7. Why has Gilda Radner been given a role smaller than a chickpea?

8. Why does the discovery that one of the guys is gay—the movie is about four buddies played by Wilder, Joseph Bologna, Charles Grodin, and Michael Huddleston—elicit virtually no comment?

9. Is San Francisco really this blasé?

10. Can you really tear apart a bar in San Francisco, as Charles Grodin does, and not go to jail or get a fine?

11. Does everyone in San Francisco live in mansions and drink all day?

12. Is San Francisco really this rich? This clean?

13. What time is the next flight to San Francisco?

14. Why do homely middle-aged comedy directors think there is nothing funnier than adultery?

15. Why do homely middle-aged comedy directors all want to be Woody Allen?

16. Why do homely middle-aged comedy directors always let themselves get the girl?

17. Why does the girl they get—her name is Kelly Le Brock in this case—always look like a goddess?

18. Where can I meet a goddess like this?

19. Why do sex farces make adultery look great and then say: no, no, stay home, stay married, stay faithful?

20. And why—*The Woman in Red* is a rewrite of the French sex farce *Pardon mon affaire*—do the wrong kinds of movies travel?   (*1984*)

Index